Rivals for Power

Presidential–Congressional Relations

Rivals for Power

Presidential–Congressional Relations

Second Edition

Edited by
James A. Thurber

ROWMAN & LITTLEFIELD PUBLISHERS, INC.
Lanham • Boulder • New York • Oxford

ROWMAN & LITTLEFIELD PUBLISHERS, INC.

Published in the United States of America
by Rowman & Littlefield Publishers, Inc.
4720 Boston Way, Lanham, Maryland 20706
www.rowmanlittlefield.com

12 Hid's Copse Road, Cumnor Hill, Oxford OX2 9JJ, England

British Library Cataloging in Publication Information Available

Library of Congress Cataloging-in-Publication Data

Rivals for power : presidential–congressional relations / edited by James A. Thurber.—2nd ed.
p. cm.
Includes bibliographical references and index.
ISBN 0-7425-0990-7 (alk. paper)—ISBN 0-7425-0991-5 (pbk. : alk paper)
1. Presidents—United States. 2. United States. Congress. 3. United States—Politics and government—20th century. I. Thurber, James A., 1943–
JK585 .R59 2001
320.973—dc21 2001031992

Printed in the United States of America

∞ ™ The paper used in this publication meets the minimum requirements of American National Standard for Information Sciences—Permanence of Paper for Printed Library Materials, ANSI/NISO Z39.48-1992.

For Claudia and Mark, Leonor, Kathryn, Greg,
Tristan, and Bryan

Contents

Preface

This book builds on the knowledge of a variety of scholars and practitioners from the White House and Capitol Hill and is designed to explain the political dynamic between the president and the U.S. Congress. The examination of the rivalry between the president and Congress uses a variety of approaches and perspectives. The title *Rivals for Power: Presidential–Congressional Relations* highlights the continued competition between the two branches, whether the White House and Congress are controlled by the same party or by different parties. The book focuses on the divisions in our democracy that create the rivalries between the president and Congress. It explores the structural, political, and behavioral factors that establish incentives for cooperation between the two branches.

As director of the Center for Congressional and Presidential Studies (CCPS) at American University and a former congressional staff member, I have spent almost thirty years studying and teaching about the relationship between the White House and Congress. Much of my understanding of this complex rivalry comes from a combination of my independent research and knowledge from scholars, White House staff, members of Congress and staff, and the press. All of these are essential sources for this book. I have many people from the White House and the Hill to thank for sharing their knowledge and expertise—not the least is U.S. Senator Hubert H. Humphrey, for whom I worked. Many interviews with persons in Congress and the White House were helpful to me in preparing this book.

Rivals for Power is intended for students, scholars, public officials, the media, and the general public. Every chapter reports on original research on Congress and the relationship between the president and Congress from the unique viewpoints of the authors, often players from inside the policy-making process. Scholars, journalists, and political practitioners have contributed to this volume. Most of the scholars are experienced hands who have worked in Congress and the White House.

This book relies on the support of people from Rowman & Littlefield and

American University who contributed their expertise and dedication to assure its publication. I thank Rowman and Littlefield for its support of this work. Jennifer Knerr, executive editor, has been a friend for many years and has provided encouragement and support to me and to this project that have been invaluable. I particularly thank Elisabeth Graves, copyeditor, for her masterful editing. I also thank Brigitte Scott, assistant editor, for her careful assistance.

At American University, I first want to express my gratitude for the dedication and help from the staff of the CCPS, especially Dave Dulio, Sam Garrett, Leslie McNaugher, Lindsay Musser, and Erin O'Brien. Special thanks go to Mark Siegel for his comments and additions to the chapters in this work. His careful editing of them is appreciated. All of these center faculty and staff helped at each stage of this project.

I am especially thankful for the support of the center and this project from Walter Broadnax, dean of the School of Public Affairs. As chair of the Department of Government, Gregg Ivers has been a friend and strong supporter of the work of the center. My close friend and colleague, Neil Kerwin, provost of American University, has been an unfailing and enthusiastic proponent of my efforts to build the CCPS and to continue our scholarship about the president and Congress.

Sean Treglia of the Pew Charitable Trusts has supported our efforts to understand and improve election campaigns for the White House and the Hill. In so doing, the Pew Trusts and Sean have indirectly contributed to our understanding of the impact of campaigning on the quality of the relationship between the two institutions and on democratic governance itself.

Chris N. Huabert of the Panetta Institute for Public Policy and Jordan Tama of the Woodrow Wilson Center were of great assistance for the chapters submitted by the Honorable Leon Panetta and the Honorable Lee Hamilton. I thank them both.

I would also like to thank David S. Broder of the *Washington Post*, Nelson S. Polsby of the University of California at Berkeley, Tom C. Korologos of Timmons and Company, Burdette A. Loomis of the University of Kansas, and Jeffrey R. Biggs of the American Political Science Association Congressional Fellowship Program for their careful comments about these papers, which were presented on panels held at a CCPS conference.

This book is clearly a collective effort. I thank all the contributors who have contributed original and important scholarship to each chapter. As editor and author, I take full responsibility for any omissions or errors of fact and interpretation.

I dedicate this book to my family. Thank you, Claudia, Mark, Leonor, Kathryn, Greg, Tristan, and Bryan, for your gifts of love, ideas, support, and humor.

1

An Introduction to Presidential–Congressional Rivalry

James A. Thurber

In just about every respect, the 2000 election made history. It was essentially a tied election for the presidency (with its outcome uncertain for five weeks), for the U.S. Senate, and, effectively, for the U.S. House of Representatives. It marked only the fourth time in U.S. history—and the first time since 1888—that the winner of the electoral vote did not win the popular vote. George W. Bush's electoral college win over Al Gore—271 to 267 votes—was the second narrowest win ever. The popular vote totals for former vice president Al Gore (50,996,000) and newly elected president George W. Bush (50,456,000) were the second and third highest totals ever. Gore's edge of nearly 540,000 votes constituted the third smallest margin in the popular vote since 1900. Gore's margin in the popular vote was also the largest margin of any candidate not to ascend to the presidency. The result of the 2000 election was power sharing both in the Senate, with an equal split between Republicans and Democrats, fifty to fifty, and in the House, with the Republicans holding an exceedingly narrow margin over the Democrats, 222 to 211 with two independents. Republicans added another seat to their majority after winning a special election in Virginia in 2001. George W. Bush won the presidency without a majority of the popular vote, without any kind of mandate, and without a significant majority in the Senate or the House. Any hint of a mandate was further undermined by Bush's controversial win in the U.S. Supreme Court. Here a court normally devoted to federalism twice overruled, in a five-to-four vote, a state's highest court on the interpretation of state electoral law.

Fully 40 percent of all presidential elections since the early nineteenth century have produced "minority" winners, including Abraham Lincoln, Grover Cleveland (twice), Woodrow Wilson (twice), Harry S. Truman, John F. Kennedy, Richard M. Nixon, and Bill Clinton (twice). These sub–50 percent winners have often had at least one of the following three factors to help them govern: a clear-cut edge in the popular vote, a decisive advantage in the electoral college, or the backing of party allies firmly in command on Capitol Hill. President George W. Bush had none of these advantages at the beginning of his administration and faced a unique problem involving legitimacy considering the outcome of the five-week Florida recount and its resolution within the ultimate forum, the courts. Election results shape the context for presidential–congressional relations by setting the partisan majorities in Congress. This was especially true after the 2000 election.

There is little doubt that congressional Democrats lost ground politically during the first two years of the Clinton presidency, both in the Senate and in the House, but this did not guarantee a new Congress that would favor President George W. Bush. The 2000 congressional elections left the Democrats with forty-six fewer House seats and seven fewer Senate seats than when Clinton was first elected in 1992. Every two-term president in the twentieth century has lost seats in the House and the Senate (save Franklin D. Roosevelt, during whose eight-year presidency the Democrats picked up seven Senate seats), and Clinton was no exception to this trend.

The 1994 midterm congressional election reversed a generation of Democratic dominance in the House, brought back divided party control of government, and dramatically reshaped the rivalry between the president and Congress. The 1996 and 1998 elections, despite marginal Democratic gains, reinforced the dominance of the Republicans on Capitol Hill, and 2000 continued the trend, if just barely. The 1994 election not only brought an overwhelming victory for the Republican Party and major changes in the policy agenda and the structure of Congress; it also dramatically changed the balance of power between the president and Congress.[1] Having received an electoral mandate to implement their legislative program of cutbacks, devolution, and deregulation, Republicans in Congress boldly and unilaterally set about dictating the policy agenda. In contrast, President Clinton found that his negotiating power had been significantly diminished after the 1994 election. The Republicans centralized decision making in the House of Representatives and, in the process, limited the president's ability to influence Congress. These changes did not last long.

After the historic 1994 midterm election, President Clinton was compelled to reach out to the new Republican leadership in the House and the Senate. After Speaker Newt Gingrich (R-Ga.) received a boost in power from a highly unified House Republican Conference and the structural reforms that it imposed on the House, President Clinton's activist agenda during the 103d Congress was overshadowed by the "Contract with America" and the GOP–led drive to balance the budget and cut back the federal government.[2] Ultimately, however, neither President Clinton nor the new Republican leadership could govern effectively without the cooperation of the other. Elections can have an impact on presidential and congressional relations, as shown so clearly in the shift in political mood and policy from 1992 to 1994.

The 1992 presidential election brought a Democrat to the White House and unified party control of government for the first time in twelve years. At the heart of the 1992 presidential campaign was President Clinton's promise to fix the economy and to use the presidency to do so. He believed in an activist role for the federal government. The election produced the largest turnover of membership in the House of Representatives in more than forty years; 110 new members took office in January 1993. Although President Clinton had a majority of Democrats in the House and the Senate, unified party control of government, and many new members of Congress who wanted change, he discovered quickly that 43 percent support in the three-candidate election (all but four House members ran ahead of him in absolute votes) did not translate into a mandate or an easy coalition to push his activist agenda.[3] Although he was a "New" Democrat from the Democratic Leadership Council (DLC), Clinton sent strong signals to the Hill that he wanted to cooperate with a policy agenda along centrist lines. However, it was difficult for the president to find common ground for his centrist agenda with the Republicans and liberal or "Old" Democrats who were aligned with organized labor (opposing the DLC).

Unified party control of government did not bring an end to the presidential–congressional rivalry for President Clinton, nor has it for President George W. Bush. Within a few months of their inaugurations, bitter struggles had broken out pitting both of these presidents with their own parties and against opposition party leaders. Although Presidents George W. Bush and Bill Clinton presented themselves as moderates, pragmatists, and bipartisans, both veered off ideologically at the outset of their administrations, leaving serious problems building centrist coalitions to support their programs. Both had to work with the majority of their party members, whose centers of gravity had moved to the left on the political spectrum for the Democrats and to the right for the Republicans and who, as a result, frequently opposed the president's policies. For example, President Bush had major opposition within his party from key committee chairs to his first legislative initiatives: a $1.6 trillion tax cut proposal and major changes in education policy.

Although Clinton also had unified party government for his first two years in office, eleven Democratic House subcommittee chairs voted against President Clinton's economic package in May 1993, and the president's program barely survived. In a clear indication of the lack of discipline in the Democratic Party, some House members, especially newly elected members, subsequently demanded that the eleven chairs be stripped of their gavels, although the House leadership rejected this exhortation.[4] Clinton also had to build cross-party coalitions with more conservative Republican leaders to pass several major bills on his agenda, such as the North American Free Trade Agreement (NAFTA), the General Agreement on Tariffs and Trade (GATT), and normalized trade relations with the People's Republic of China. Many of President Clinton's initiatives were stopped or amended so thoroughly that they bear little resemblance to his original proposals. Unified government did not guarantee presidential dominance in Clinton's relationship with Congress.

In 1989, President George Bush had similar problems with Congress. Immediately after his inauguration, President Bush, in a gesture of goodwill like his son George W. Bush's, praised Congress: "To the Members of the Congress, to the institution of the House of Representatives and the Senate of the United States, may they flourish and may they prosper."[5] In response to President Bush's efforts to build better relations with Congress, Thomas S. Foley (D-Wash.), then House majority leader, said, "That's another example of President Bush reaching out. We're going to respond very positively to that."[6] Despite all this, President Bush went on to have one of the lowest records of support for his policy initiatives in Congress in the last fifty years. Presidents George H. W. Bush, Clinton, and George W. Bush had every good intention of working with broad, bipartisan, centrist coalitions in Congress, but whether they were working under unified or divided party control of government, it did not work out that way.[7]

Goodwill does not generally characterize the institutional relationship between Congress and the president. President Clinton earned some of the highest presidential support scores (the percentage of presidential proposals that are approved by Congress, calculated annually by *Congressional Quarterly Weekly Report*) in his first two years of office, but he never achieved an approval rating over 50 percent in national public opinion polls. He became known as a president who could not get his agenda through Congress—particularly his revolutionary proposals on health care reform.[8] He was impeached stemming from an affair with a White House intern. Personal scandal followed him from his political career in Arkansas, through his eight years in office, and into retirement. However, while in office he did continue to reduce the federal budget deficit, and he did build enough bipartisan support to effect passage of NAFTA and GATT, the family and medical leave law, normal trade relations with the People's Republic of China, and a variety of other programs.

In his first year in office, President George H. W. Bush fared worse than any other president elected in the postwar era, winning only 63 percent of the roll-call votes on which he took an unambiguous position.[9] Despite Bush's popularity with the American people during Desert Storm (when he achieved the highest approval rating for any postwar president at the end of his first year) and his sincere efforts to build bridges between the White House and Capitol Hill, executive–legislative relations during his presidency remained deeply confrontational and rooted in political and institutional divisions. These divisions did not evaporate for President Clinton with unified government in 1993–94, and they were clearly revealed in Clinton's relationship with Congress until he left office on 20 January 2001 (and even after, with respect to congressional reaction to his controversial pardons). President George W. Bush also called for bipartisanship, comity, and a more civil relationship with Congress in his 2000 campaign and during the first days of his administration. However, President Bush veered to the Right on many issues like the environment, Social Security, missile defense, and health care, leaving moderates such as Senator Jeffords with no political projection and with an incentive to leave the party. Bush inherited a deep-seated rivalry and difficulty in building coalitions around his policy initiatives, especially on the Right. Where does this conflict come from? What are the roots of the rivalry between the president and Congress?[10] In this introduction to *Rivals for Power,* several root causes of the rivalry between the president and Congress will be examined: the constitutional design with its formal presidential and congressional powers, different electoral constituencies for the president and Congress, varying terms of office, increased partisanship and polarization of Congress, the ongoing competition for power between Congress and the president, narrow majorities in both houses, congressional individualism, and the nature of American pluralism.

CONSTITUTIONAL DESIGN

The Framers of the Constitution bequeathed to us one of the most enduring rivalries in government, that between the president and Congress.[11] The Constitution separates the three branches of government (legislative, executive, and judicial) but combines their functions, creating conflict and shared powers.[12] As Richard Neustadt has observed, the Constitution created a government "of separated institutions sharing powers" that makes it difficult for presidents to bridge the constitutional gap even in the best of political circumstances.[13] The Constitution gives the president and the Congress different powers, and each is jealous of the other's constitutional prerogatives regardless of context.

The Constitution invests Congress with "all legislative Powers," but it also authorizes the president to recommend and to veto legislation. If the president vetoes a bill, "it shall be repassed by two-thirds of the Senate and the House of Representatives" (Article 1, section 7). Because it is so difficult for Congress to gain a two-thirds vote, presidential vetoes are usually sustained. Through 1998 presidents used the veto 2,540 times; 1,065 of these were "pocket vetoes" not subject to congressional override. Congress overrode slightly more than 7 percent of presidential vetoes (105) when it had the opportunity to vote on them.[14] Thus, the threat of a veto in the legislative process gives the president an important bargaining tool; however, President Clinton did not use this tool until 1995, when he vetoed a $16 billion rescission bill. Clinton went on to skillfully use the veto repeatedly in his confrontation with the Republican-led Congress over the cuts in Medicaid, Medicare, welfare, education, and federal environmental programs in the fiscal year 1996 federal budget (1 October–30 September). This showdown ultimately helped to shut down government and stop the drive of the Contract with America supporters in the House and the Senate. The greatest power of the president in divided government is often the power to say no, as President Clinton did in his last six years of office. Clinton embraced that notion in his historic budget battle in 1995 when he said, "This is one of those moments in history when I'm grateful for the wisdom of our Founding Fathers. The Congress gets to propose, but the president has to sign or veto, and that Constitution gave me that authority and one of the reasons for the veto is to prevent excess. They knew what they were doing and we're going to use the Constitution they gave us to stand up for what's right."[15] His confrontation with House Speaker Gingrich and the Republican-controlled Congress—and the public's assessment of responsibility on congressional leadership—was a defining moment in Clinton's reelection strategy.

Congress is given a broad list of powers in Article 1, section 8, of the Constitution, but the greatest power of Congress is its authority to pass laws directly binding on all citizens. Also of great importance is the power of the purse. Congress must authorize and appropriate funds for the president and executive branch agencies. Presidents may propose budgets for the federal government, but Congress has the final say on spending. This creates an automatic and quite deliberate rivalry between the two and conflict over spending priorities. Congress also has the power to levy and collect taxes, to borrow and coin money, and to regulate foreign and interstate commerce. A central element of the rivalry between the president and Congress has been battles over tax and trade policy. The powers to declare war, to provide for a militia, and to adopt laws concerning bankruptcy, naturalization, patents, and copyrights are also bestowed on Congress. The interpretation of presidential and congressional war power has changed over time and is another contemporary source of conflict. Congress has the authority to establish or eliminate executive branch agencies and departments and to oversee their operations. The Senate must approve Cabinet nominees, ambassadors, and Supreme Court and federal judicial appointees before they can take office. A president cannot enter into a binding treaty with a foreign government without a two-thirds vote of the Senate, nor can the president declare war, a power the Constitution purposely gives to Congress. All of these constitutional congressional and presidential powers force both institutions to confront each other in governance, which more often than not creates rivalry and conflict.

A dramatic but rarely employed check on the president is impeachment. President Clinton's impeachment was historic and yet rare. The president and executive branch officials can be impeached (formally accused) by a majority vote in the House, following which the impeachment charges are tried in the Senate. If two-thirds of the senators vote to convict, the official is removed from office. Only Presidents Andrew Johnson and Bill Clinton have been tried on impeachment charges. For Johnson the vote fell one short of the number required to convict, and for Clinton the Senate failed to convict by a significant majority—no less a two-thirds majority for the two articles of impeachment passed by the U.S. House of Representatives. The House Judiciary Committee recommended that Richard M. Nixon be impeached for transgressions in connection with the Watergate burglary involving the Democratic National Committee offices and the ensuing cover-up. Nixon, however, resigned the presidency before a full session of the House could vote on the impeachment charges. The threat of impeachment establishes an important check on the president and executive branch by limiting the power of the president.

The Framers of the Constitution deliberately fragmented power between the national government and the states and among the executive, legislative, and judicial branches.[16] They also divided legislative powers by creating two coequal houses—a bicameral Congress—which further magnifies rivalry and conflict. Although divided, Congress was designed to be independent and powerful, able to check the power of the executive and to be directly linked with the people through periodic popular elections. The Framers wanted an effective and powerful federal government, but they also wanted to limit its power in order to protect personal and property rights. Having experienced the abuses of English monarchs and their colonial governors, the Framers were wary of excessive executive authority. They also feared "elective despotism," or excessive legislative power, something the Articles of Confederation had given their own state legislatures.

Therefore, the Framers created three branches of government with none having a monopoly. This separation of powers restricts the power of any one branch, and it requires cooperation among the three in order for them to govern effectively. Today, as then, political action requires cooperation between the president and Congress. Yet in dividing power between the two branches—in creating a separated presidency and two equal legislative chambers—the Framers created an open invitation for conflict and guaranteed an ongoing rivalry between the president and Congress.[17]

DIFFERENT CONSTITUENCIES

The U.S. system of government, unlike parliamentary systems throughout the world, elects the executive and members of the legislature independently. The president is elected through coalitions that are vastly broader than those for electing representatives and senators, who have narrow constituencies in districts or states. Members of Congress, even those who belong to the president's party or who hail from a president's home state, represent specific interests that can conflict with the interests of the president, who represents the nation as a whole. James Madison well understood this dichotomy of interest as an important source of conflict between the president and Congress: "The members of the federal legislature will be likely to attach themselves too much to local objects. . . . Measures will too often be decided according to their probable effect, not on the national prosperity and happiness, but on the prejudices, interests, and pursuits of the governments and the people of the individual States."[18]

VARYING TERMS OF OFFICE

The interaction between Congress and the president is shaped not only by their different constituencies but also by their different terms in office. The constitutional structure of U.S. government, which separates the Congress and the president, sets different terms of office for representatives, senators, and the president and ensures that they will be chosen from different constituency bases. House members are elected every two years, and senators every six. Presidents have only four years, possibly eight, in which to establish their programs. They are expected to set the national policy agenda and usually move rapidly in the first year before the traditional decline in their popularity.[19] Presidents are not concerned about reelection after the first four years of office; establishing good public policy and an honored place in history is their first priority. For members of Congress, although other interests are certainly operative, reelection concerns are most important, even for new members who support term limits.[20] Legislators, then, are often reluctant to allow their workloads and policy agendas to be dictated by a president who has no electoral mandate to do so.

Congress moves more slowly than the president; it is deliberative and inefficient primarily because it represents a vast array of local interests. Congress passes new laws slowly and reviews old ones carefully. The House of Representatives of the 104th Congress had centralized power and was more efficient than the House of any other modern Congress, but this too caused conflict with President Clinton's agenda. The decision making paces of Congress and the president differ because of varying terms of office, electoral bases, and perceived constituency mandates. The result of these differences is rivalry, conflict, and often deadlock.

POLITICAL PARTIES

The federal system of state-based political parties contributes to the independence of members of Congress from the president. The president must work with weak, decentralized national political parties that exercise little discipline and even less leverage over members. Senators and representatives usually run their own races with their own financing. The way they respond to local conditions has little to do with national party platforms or presidential politics. Members freely pursue their own interests without fear of discipline from the president. Independence from political parties and the president allows legislators to seek benefits for their own constituents and to serve specialized interests. Thomas Mann argues further that

> the changes that swept through the political system during the 1960s and 1970s—the increase in split-ticket voting, the growing cost of campaigns and reliance on contributions from special interests, the rise of television, the expansion and growing political sophistication of interest groups in Washington, and the democratization and decentralization of Congress—may well have weakened the classic iron triangles, but they also heightened the sensitivity of politicians to all forms of outside pressure.[21]

For Republican members of the House, the 1994 election deviated from the normal individualistic election. The Contract with America, signed by 300 Republican candidates for the House, "nationalized" the campaign for most of those candidates. No incumbent Republican House member lost in the 1994 election. With the Democrats losing fifty-two seats in the House and eight seats in the Senate, the mandate of the new Republicans was to stay loyal to the contract, to the House Republican leadership, and to the reduction of individualism in the House. Party discipline came from the congressional party leaders, not from the grassroots party organizations throughout the United States. This was unique in modern congressional elections and created the basis of conflict with President Clinton.

PARTY CONTROL OF GOVERNMENT

Another electoral-base impediment to legislative–executive cooperation is divided government, as shown by the dramatic election of 1994, which left a Democrat in the White House working with Republican majorities in the House and the Senate.[22] There are two varieties of divided government (the condition that exists when the majority party in either or both houses of Congress differs from the party of the president): divided party control of Congress and split control of Congress and the White House. Opposing parties have controlled the presidency and one or both houses of Congress in twenty-six of the thirty-two years from 1969 through 2001 (81 percent of the time), with the Republicans mainly controlling the White House and the Democrats controlling Congress. From 1887 to 1954, divided party control of government occurred in only eight years (12 percent of the time), but from President Dwight D. Eisenhower's first year (1953) through President Bush's first year in office (2001), it occurred in thirty-three years (69 percent of the time) (see table 1.1). Therefore, divided party control of government at the federal level has been the norm in modern U.S. politics.

Presidents are more likely to be successful in their relationship with Congress under unified party government than under divided government. This has been especially true since the post-1980 resurgence of party line voting and party cohesion in Congress. *Congressional Quarterly* defines its measure of party line voting as the percentage of all votes when a majority of voting Democrats opposes a majority of voting Republicans. Overall, Ronald Reagan and George H. W. Bush had low presidential support scores in Congress because of divided party government. Clinton's victories on votes in Congress during his first two years in office (1993–94) averaged over 86 percent in the House and the Senate but dropped to 36 percent in 1995 when the

Table 1.1 Unified and Divided Party Control of Government, 1887–2003

Years	*President*	*Senate*	*House of Representatives*
1887–1889	D	R	D
1889–1891	R	R	R
1891–1893	R	R	D
1893–1895	D	D	D
1895–1897	D	R	R
1897–1899	R	R	R
1899–1901	R	R	R
1901–1903	R	R	R
1903–1905	R	R	R
1905–1907	R	R	R
1907–1909	R	R	R
1909–1911	R	R	R
1911–1913	R	R	D
1913–1915	D	D	D
1915–1917	D	D	D
1917–1919	D	D	D
1919–1921	D	R	R
1921–1923	R	R	R
1923–1925	R	R	R
1925–1927	R	R	R
1927–1929	R	R	R
1929–1931	R	R	R
1931–1933	R	R	D
1933–1935	D	D	D
1935–1937	D	D	D
1937–1939	D	D	D
1939–1941	D	D	D
1941–1943	D	D	D
1943–1945	D	D	D
1945–1947	D	D	D
1947–1949	D	R	R
1949–1951	D	D	D
1951–1953	D	D	D
1953–1955	R	R	R
1955–1957	R	D	D
1957–1959	R	D	D
1959–1961	R	D	D
1961–1963	D	D	D
1963–1965	D	D	D
1965–1967	D	D	D
1967–1969	D	D	D
1969–1971	R	D	D
1971–1973	R	D	D
1973–1975	R	D	D
1975–1977	R	D	D
1977–1979	D	D	D
1979–1981	D	D	D
1981–1983	R	R	D
1983–1985	R	R	D
1985–1987	R	R	D
1987–1989	R	D	D
1989–1991	R	D	D
1991–1993	R	D	D
1993–1995	D	D	D
1995–2001	D	R	R
2001–2003	R	R/D	R
Unified party control of government n = 62, % of total 60.8			
Divided party control of government n = 40, % of total 39.2			

Source: For 1887–1995, Lyn Ragsdale, *Vital Statistics on the Presidency: Washington to Clinton* (Washington, D.C.: Congressional Quarterly, 1996), table 8-1, 369; 1996–2003 compiled by the author.

Republicans captured the Congress. Although President George W. Bush has a unified Republican government for the first time since 1954, the closeness of the election and the tie in the Senate have created the foundation for conflict and, in effect, divided government.

The trend toward ticket splitting between presidential and congressional candidates further exacerbates already strained relations. Election returns for Congress have increasingly diverged from national presidential returns: "the range in the . . . variance, which measures the extent to which changes in local returns differ from the change in national returns, has more than doubled."[23] During the past thirty years, as the power of political parties has declined significantly, there has been a corresponding rise in individualistic candidacies for the presidency, the Senate, and the House. Fewer and fewer members of Congress ride into office on the electoral "coattails" of the president. This has led to the election of presidents who find it difficult to translate electoral support into governing support. The scarcity of presidential coattails for Bush in 1988 and Clinton in 1992 brings the conclusion that "the emperor has no coat."[24] George H. W. Bush was the first candidate since John F. Kennedy to win the presidency while his party lost seats in the House. Clinton ran behind all but four members of the House. With the decline of presidential coattails, strong-willed members of Congress are largely beyond the president's control. They are often more responsive to district and specialized interests than to the national agenda of the president.

Unified party control of government does not mean that the two branches will work closely together. Divided government does not always mean that the two branches will fight. David Mayhew has found that when it comes to passing major legislation or conducting investigations, it "does not seem to make all that much difference whether party control of the American government happens to be unified or divided."[25] However, we do know that it has generally been easier for presidents to govern during periods of unified government—such as the early days of the New Deal (1933–37), during World War II (1941–45), and during the Great Society (1964–65)—than during periods of divided government (especially since 1981, Reagan's first year in office).

The balance of power among and within the institutions of Congress and the presidency is dynamic and inevitably leads to conflict, another root cause of the rivalry between the president and Congress. The congressional institutions of a stable committee system, party leadership organizations, the seniority system, and behavioral norms such as reciprocity all have an impact on presidential–congressional relationships. The 1994 election brought the most centralized power structure to the House since the appointment of Republican Speaker Joseph G. "Czar" Cannon, who served from 1903 to

1911.[26] Just one year before, the 103d Congress, under Speaker Thomas Foley, was decentralized and fragmented. What the public expects from each institution varies over time, as is dramatically shown by the differences between the 103d and 104th Congresses.[27] For 200 years Congress has continued to represent local interests and to respond (some think too habitually) to political preferences and public pressures.[28] Nevertheless, the institution has changed dramatically. The reforms of the past two decades have made Congress even more representative and accountable and, in the 104th Congress, more centralized. The reforms of the last twenty years have changed the way it makes laws, passes budgets, oversees the executive branch, and confronts presidents. The degree of centralization or fragmentation of power among committees and members has major consequences for Congress's power vis-à-vis the president. It is difficult for the president to build predictable coalitions around a highly fragmented legislature, but committee decentralization can also play into the president's favor if divided party government exists.

As the congressional leadership is centralized and made more effective by one party, the power of a president of the opposition party is often diminished, as we saw in the 104th Congress. This creates more tension between the two branches, with a clash between the president's national policy agenda and the agenda of Congress. President Clinton's legislative successes during the 103d Congress (1993–94) were impressive, with a remarkable 86 percent win record on the votes on which he took a position. The 1994 election changed his success and the competitive environment with Congress; he was overshadowed by the Contract with America, the leadership of Speaker Newt Gingrich, and the Republican drive to balance the budget. Unified government and a decentralized Congress helped his legislative successes in 1993 and 1994; a massive loss in the midterm elections to the Republicans created conflict and a deadlock between the two branches. If the president is popular with the American public, he can bring into Congress on his electoral coattails many new members who are beholden to him, and if he has a well-organized and well-run White House and administration, he is more able to control the national policy agenda. An example of a president meeting these criteria is President Lyndon Johnson during his first two years of office, before the war in Vietnam undermined his influence in Congress and his popularity with the American people. His central core of authority in dealing with Congress reduced conflict between the two branches. Structural reforms within the presidency (for example, the establishment of the Bureau of the Budget and, later, the creation of the Office of Management and Budget [OMB] and the post–World War II expansion of the White House staff) and changes in Congress (for example, the centralization of power by the Republican Party congressional leadership and increased party unity in the 104th Congress) directly impact the ability of the president to dominate the legislative agenda and the ability of Congress to act independently from the president. Thus, cooperation and conflict between the two branches are the norm.

Pressure to check the power of the president through the War Powers Resolution of 1973 and the Budget and Impoundment Control Act of 1974 brought changes that helped Congress reclaim some of the power it had lost to the president during the previous decades. Many institutional reforms of the 1970s, however, resulted in decentralization, which made Congress more democratic but also less efficient. With the new openness came greater accountability and responsiveness—but at the price of efficiency and effectiveness as a lawmaking body. Modern presidents find Congress harder to influence than their predecessors in the White House did; its members are now more independent. And with the weakening of strict seniority rules wielded by strong parties, coordinating the legislative process was more difficult for congressional party leaders until House reforms of the 104th Congress centralized power with the Republican leadership.

Although Congress created new ways of checking presidential power in the 1970s, legislative–executive relationships ultimately are not zero-sum games. If one branch gains power, the other does not necessarily lose it. The expansion of the federal government since World War II has given vast new power to both branches. Events and public policy issues contribute to the policy making power of both the president and the Congress. The War on Drugs, environmental concerns, the savings and loan crisis, Desert Storm, and continuing budget deficits have led to new administrative (and legislative) powers expanding the scope of both branches. Even these crises, however, are not enough to reduce the rivalry between the two institutions.

The decentralization and fragmentation of power within Congress were dramatically altered for two years as a result of the 1994 election, which Speaker Newt Gingrich considered a mandate to implement the Republican Contract with America. The already significant power of the speaker, the only structural feature of the House dictated by the Constitution, was further expanded by Speaker Gingrich, who appointed the committee chairs and increased his influence over committee assignments, placing newly elected members on the Ways and Means, Appropriations, Rules, and Commerce Committees. For the eleven Republican openings on the Appropriations Committee, Speaker Gingrich appointed nine freshmen, thus ensuring cohesion and loyalty from the new Republicans in the House. Gingrich's control over committee assignments for freshmen and over the selection of chairs was a dramatic break from the decentralized and more democratic House of the previous twenty years. He abolished proxy voting in committees, thus limiting the power of committee chairs. He reduced committee staffing, abolished independent subcommittee staff, and placed six-year term limits on committee chairs, thus reducing the power of the chairs and increasing the power of the leadership. Gingrich, with the support of the Republican Conference, also limited committee assignments and restructured the committee system generally. All of these reforms helped to centralize power in the speakership. Under the reformed House of Representatives, Speaker Gingrich gained substantial power to control the policy agenda using key provisions in the GOP Contract with America. He was able to overshadow President Clinton (and the Senate) and pass far-reaching legislation that projected a balanced budget in seven years; cut taxes; cut back spending on Medicare, Medicaid, and welfare; and decentralized the federal government, sending more programs and money to the states. Republican Party dominance of the House and the Senate and internal changes in the House power structure fundamentally changed the relationship with the president in 1995.[29] However, after the shutdown of government resulting from a conflict over the budget in 1995, the committee chairs and members reasserted themselves in the House, and the normal decentralized system of policy making was reestablished. The power of the committee and subcommittee chairs became the locus of decision making, and President Clinton had to build coalitions in a highly fragmented, individualistic House for the last six years of his administration.

PLURALISM

Pluralism, or group-based politics, limits the power of the president and Congress to pursue their own agendas and thereby increases the competition between them. Policy making gridlock often comes from competition among organized interests in society, not from divided party control of government. As more people are organized, as the political process is opened to more groups and classes than ever before, and as the demands and needs of those competing interests are weighed and mediated in the political process, the power of the president and Congress to control the policy agenda is reduced. The constitutional First Amendment rights, especially freedom of speech, freedom of assembly, freedom of the press, and freedom to petition the government for grievances, are the foundation of pluralism in U.S. politics. The decay of political party organizations in the last thirty years in the United States has helped the growth of pluralism.[30] As political parties have lost power to recruit and elect candidates who are loyal to party leaders in government, interest groups have gained political power. The United States is experiencing "hyperpluralism" or extreme competition among groups that makes it almost impossible to define the public good in terms of anything other than the collection of narrow special interests. Hyperpluralism contributes fundamentally to the rivalry between the president and Congress and often leads to deadlock between the two branches of government (as with the fiscal year 1996 budget) by making it difficult to reach necessary compromises between the national interests of the president and the parochial interests of members of Congress.[31]

CONCLUSION AND OVERVIEW

Organization theorists suggest that conflict produces incentives for organizations to centralize decision-making power.[32] When an organization is threatened, a premium is placed on efficiency, effectiveness, and cohesiveness in setting strategy. After forty years of Democratic control and two years of conflict from the Clinton White House, the House Republicans centralized their decision-making power structure in unprecedented ways. The House Republican centralization of decision making in the 104th Congress reduced individualism and brought about a more efficient and cohesive institution in its battle with President Clinton. Threatened by a unified Republican House, President Clinton reorganized and centralized his White House staff through Leon Panetta, his chief of staff. He simplified his policy agenda and built a more tightly knit and more effective legislative affairs operation. Faced with a Democratic majority in the House in the 1980s, then–Minority Whip Newt Gingrich helped to build a cohesive, centralized, and efficient opposition that was eventually used as a majority party organization against President Clinton and the congressional Democrats in 1995.

Intense rivalry between the president and Congress is inevitable in an electoral system that can produce divided party control of the two branches. Cooperation may be more likely when both the president and the Congress are of the same party. Even so, because of the wide range of views within a party, unified government is no safeguard against conflict, as was shown with President Clinton and the congressional Democratic Party in 1993 and 1994 and the first six months of the Bush presidency in 2001. Partisanship may also serve to move legislation. For example, the 1986 tax reform law benefited from the battle between Democrats and Republicans because both sides saw political advantage in moving the bill or disadvantage in being seen as obstructionist. The conflict and then compromise over education and tax legislation in 2001 between Bush and Congress revealed a response to public demands to act in a bipartisan fashion. That was not the case with other policies early in the Bush administration. The give and take between national and local representation, deliberation and efficiency, openness and accountability, specific interests and the "public good" ensures a certain amount of confrontation between Congress and the president. As we have seen, their relations are shaped by an amalgam of factors: constitutional design, different constituencies, varying terms of office, weak political parties, divided party control of government, ongoing competition for power, and pluralism. Although the rivalry and conflict between Congress and the president are inherent in our system of government, presidents must find support in Congress, and members must seek assistance from the White House. To succeed in office, all presidents must surmount the constitutional and political obstacles to pass their legislative programs and establish working relationships with Congress.

Separation of powers and the division of political control between the president and Congress do not present insurmountable barriers to good public policy making. Presidents need to both lead public opinion and build a consensus among the policy communities in Congress to solve the problems that are so readily visible. Overcoming divided government, changing public opinion, building consensus, and establishing the nation's policy priorities call for leadership from the president and from inside Congress. Congress and the president must work together. Unified partisan control of both branches of government does not guarantee cooperation, as President George W. Bush has discovered early in his administration. Divided government does not guarantee conflict, but it does make governing more difficult, as Bush has seen with Senator Jeffords's shift from Republican to independent, thus creating a Democratic majority, and Democratic committee chairs with new policy agendas confronting the president. Governing calls for bargaining, accommodation, and compromise by Congress and the president—these are the basis of our "separated" and pluralistic system of government.[33]

The chapters in this book present original research organized around several themes and written from a variety of perspectives. Political scientists, legal scholars, historians, journalists, former White House and Capitol Hill staff, and former members of Congress all contribute. All of the authors bring unique experiences, methodologies, viewpoints, and theoretical backgrounds to the study of the relationship between Congress and the president.

In chapter 2, "The President and Congress at the Turn of the Century: Structural Sources of Conflict," James P. Pfiffner argues that relations between the president and Congress have recently become even more polarized and combative. Pfiffner describes the structural sources for the recent increase in polarization between Congress and the president, including the loss of the South as the undisputed territory of Democrats as well as the increased frequency of divided government. He further shows how contemporary presidents do not enjoy the ideological sympathies of some members of the opposing party. Political parties are more homogeneous—"Rockefeller Republicans" and "Boll-Weevils" are a thing of the past. As a result, presidents find it difficult to build and maintain the support of members from the opposing party for their legislative agendas. Filibusters have also increased, as have presidential threats to veto. Pfiffner argues that all these factors contribute to the contentious relationship between the president and Congress. He also documents a decline in civility in both chambers of Congress since the 1970s and shows how this affects presidential–congressional relations. These myriad sources of conflict leave presidents with no natural coalition partners in Congress. There are no permanent friends or enemies for the president on Capitol Hill. Presidents need to cobble together a fluid coalition of policy partners in Congress but cannot count on support from their own parties or on crossover support from members of the opposing party.

In chapter 3, "Presidential Leadership of Congress: A Functional and Institutional History," Stephen J. Wayne emphasizes the fact that the constitutional design set forth by the Framers assigns the president little role in legislating. Contemporary presidents maintain "public relations teams" and seemingly try to influence legislative activity at every turn. Wayne uncovers why this change occurred. He first provides a historical description of how and why presidents first began to enter the legislative arena. He argues that nineteenth-century presidents began to legislate through members of Congress. They also used their veto power, and threats of vetoes, to influence congressional activity. As the twentieth century progressed, presidents went even further into the legislative arena. They developed a two-track agenda for influencing legislation. Major policy decisions received presidential attention, while OMB and executive agencies handled more minor legislative activity. Wayne points out that the presidents since Reagan have most dramatically moved away from the Framers' intent. Presidential chiefs of staff now focus almost exclusively on the legislative agenda, policy directors have Cabinet-level status, and the press is regularly used by presidents and their operatives to influence legislative activity. Presidents seek to sway public opinion and define legislative issues through sophisticated, permanent public relations teams centered in the White House. These teams use polling, focus groups, and the press to strategically set priorities, cycle issues, and package proposals in ways most likely to ensure legislative success. This ongoing public relations campaign within the White House stands in contrast to the specified legislative role for the president. It also has major ramifications for presidential–congressional rivalry.

In chapter 4, "The Presidency and Congressional Leadership," Roger H. Davidson uses a historical perspective to trace the development and fluctuation of strong party leadership within the House and the Senate as well as the implications for relations between Congress and the president of according varying levels of power to party leaders. Within the House, strong party leadership emerged as a result of the chaos and lack of responsiveness that characterized the chamber during the Gilded Age. Davidson shows how strong party leadership saw its zenith in the late nineteenth and early twentieth centuries, eroded in the mid–twentieth century because of structural and partisan factors, and then gradually reemerged in the 1970s. On the Senate side, strong party leadership emerged roughly during the same period. Davidson argues that the increased prominence and power of party leaders, especially since the 1950s, can be traced directly to the need for Senate leaders to confer with activist presidents and help them manage their legislative agendas. He goes on to analyze four distinct periods of party leadership since the New Deal on Capitol Hill and shows how each period has been accompanied by more power for party leaders—but has yet to parallel the amount of power afforded House leaders since the early twentieth century. Davidson concludes his chapter with an in-depth discussion of the relative strength of party leaders in today's Congress, including the structural and partisan reasons for this resurgence, despite the individualist tendencies of most members, and some discussion of recent party leaders.

In chapter 5, "The Impact of Campaigns on Presidential–Congressional Relations," journalist Richard E. Cohen focuses on the skills needed to campaign effectively for the presidency. He argues that they are not the same skills that allow presidents to legislate effectively. Although this is well known, Cohen, a prominent writer for the *National Journal* who has followed many presidential candidates and covered several presidents in the White House, suggests that campaigns do have lasting effects on a president's legislative success. Candidate behavior and election results create the climate in Congress that governs the president's legislative possibilities. Using the experiences of the modern presidents, and particularly the events surrounding the 2000 election, Cohen argues that inclusive candidates with large election majorities experience the most success with Congress. Citing Lyndon Johnson and Ronald Reagan specifically, he maintains that new presidents are best positioned to gain acceptance for their legislative agendas when they enjoy clear mandates, demonstrate inclusion and agreement with a substantial number of members of Congress throughout the campaigns, and articulate clear legislative agendas throughout the campaign. When these presidents "hit the ground running" at the onset of the presidency, Congress is most likely to respond favorably. They are still likely to lose seats during midterm elections, but this loss is tempered by creating a lasting legislative package. Presidents who do not enjoy strong mandates, who run against Congress, and who do not articulate clear legislative agendas during their campaigns are not successful and fail when they adopt proactive legislative agendas, as shown with Presidents Carter and Clinton.

In chapter 6, "Presidential Influence on Congress: New Solutions to Old Problems," Nathan Dietz uses the logic of formal theory and innovations in quantitative empirical analysis to tackle the problem of effectively measuring presidential influence. The literature on measuring presidential success in Congress has been plagued by two factors: (1) presidential influence often takes place in relative seclusion (in committees, subcommittees, staff markups, leadership chambers, and elsewhere) and is inaccessible to scholars and (2) presidents often exert influence by doing nothing at all. (These points are also reinforced in chapter 7.) Taking into account nonaction when examining presidential influence over Congress is difficult at best. After outlining these problems, Dietz delineates the "basic gridlock model" of presidential influence over Congress. His model predicts when policy changes will occur, what changes will be acceptable to moderate members, what policies will be in the "gridlock range," and what conditions will prompt the president to veto a policy. While this approach has much predictive power, most derivations fail to consider how electoral conditions, divided government, constituents, party in government, and contextual factors affect the president's ability to influence Congress. Dietz uses existing empirical literature to take these factors into account and applies them to his formal model. He also accounts for the impact of presidential reputation and prestige and relaxing the "perfect information assumption," adding to the basic gridlock model. Dietz applies his predictions to the post–2000 election relationship between the president and Congress.

In chapter 7, "Successful Influence: Managing Legislative Affairs in the Twenty-first Century," political scientists Gary Andres (a Republican) and Patrick Griffin (a Democrat), both former senior-level White House aides, critique existing conceptualizations of presidential "success" and "influence" based on their many years of experience in the White House and on the Hill. They argue that most existing analyses of presidential success with Congress fail to realize the importance of four factors. First, the president alone cannot drive the legislative agenda—Congress influences presidential behavior just as the president influences congressional behavior. Second, the president is both an endogenous and an exogenous force in the legislative process. Third, contextual factors greatly affect the influence of the president, which fluctuates rather than remaining constant. Fourth, institutional considerations outside the president's control play an important role in governing the relationship between Congress and the president. Andres and Griffin note that most considerations of this relationship are outcome centered, such as analyzing roll-call votes or the president's ability to maintain and build legislative coalitions. These measures obscure the strategies that effective presidents can use to shape legislative outcomes. They are not often used in the White House. From their practical experience with hundreds of legislative battles between the White House and the Hill, Andres and Griffin highlight the factors most important to understanding presidential success in Congress.

In chapter 8, "Herding Cats: Presidential Coalition Building in the Senate," C. Lawrence Evans and Walter J. Oleszek use interviews and conversations with White House officials and congressional staff and leadership conducted during the 106th Congress to delineate three relatively unexplored mechanisms that contemporary presidents use to facilitate communication, policy coordination, and coalition building across the branches (especially in the Senate). First, over time, a number of important and routinized meetings have developed for the transmission of information between the White House and congressional leaders, primarily within the president's own party. Second, both national political parties now develop organized message agendas, which feature policy proposals and symbols that party leaders and activists believe will resonate for their party among voters. These message agendas help foster party unity within Congress and facilitate presidential coalition building—primarily within a president's own party. Third, the most significant formal prerogative that presidents use to influence the Senate (and the House) is the veto. Regarding the third mechanism, Evans and Oleszek show that within the interbranch bargaining game, threatened vetoes probably are more important than actual vetoes. They also show how presidents use formal Statements of Administration Policy to send carefully calibrated messages to the Senate and the House about their legislative preferences and the likelihood of a veto. These policy messages have become an important and institutionalized aspect of legislating in Congress, and they serve to enhance the role of the veto and the role of the president in the interbranch bargaining process. Evans and Oleszek go on to show that the modes and extent of presidential coalition building within the Senate are conditional and vary substantially from issue to issue. Based on an analysis of twenty-three major proposals considered by the full Senate during the 106th Congress, the level of direct presidential involvement in the Senate legislative process is not closely tied to the message status of an item.

In chapter 9, "Politics of the Federal Budget Process," the Honorable Leon E. Panetta, former White House chief of staff, director of the OMB, and chairman of the House Budget Committee, draws on his experiences and knowledge to explain the political relationship between the White House and Congress in the federal budgetary process. He analyzes the role of the executive and legislative branches in budgeting. He describes the time that each branch takes to act on budgetary issues and reveals their considerable differences in style when it comes to budgetary politics. The actions of executive branch offices and the White House are predictable, and the president is always the ultimate arbiter. Congress is different—there is no central authority, and each member tries to shepherd pet projects and influence the process. As a result, congressional action surrounding the budget is less detailed and more unpredictable. With these broad differences delineated, Panetta offers a temporal discussion of budget development and implementation, noting the relative strength of the president and the Congress at each stage. Panetta pays particular attention to how the budgetary process has been shaped by deficit politics over the last twenty years. He concludes with a discussion of budgetary politics in an era of surpluses. Panetta argues that the battle over budgets has become more contentious in this era and highlights a number of factors that contribute to this bitterness.

In chapter 10, "The Making of U.S. Foreign Policy: The Roles of the President and Congress over Four Decades," the Honorable Lee H. Hamilton, a member of Congress from 1965 to 1998, uses his own extensive experience in foreign and defense policy making on the Hill to show how the commonly accepted view that presidents and presidents alone make foreign policy decisions must be revised. Hamilton, former chair of both the House Select Committee on Intelligence and the Foreign Affairs Committee, argues that presidents are still the chief actors when it comes to foreign policy making, but that their dominance is no longer uncontested. Vietnam, Watergate, Iran–Contra, and the end of the Cold War fundamentally changed the relationship between Congress and the president in foreign policy. Vietnam and Watergate made the public less trustful of presidents, especially on matters of foreign policy. The end of the Cold War made international threats and objectives less clear cut, and this undermined the president's dominance over foreign policy. As the issues and international actors changed, members of Congress, interest groups, ethnic constituencies within the United States, and others all aimed to shape U.S. foreign policy objectives. Presidents are also forced to deal with more executive agencies that take an interest in foreign policy as well as with an "information revolution" that has enabled ordinary citizens and political elites to have increased access to, and increased understanding of, foreign policy. Hamilton also describes how the diversity and individualism of members of Congress have lead the institution to be less bashful when it comes to foreign policy making. Hamilton concludes his chapter with a critique of how Congress has comported itself in foreign policy and offers a list of suggestions for how the president and Congress should behave when it comes to foreign policy making. He advocates a relationship between the branches based on consultation with key interests outside government as the best way to create sound foreign policy.

As a complement to Lee Hamilton's chapter on Congress and foreign policy, in chapter 11, "Clinton's Military Actions: No Rivals in Sight," Louis Fisher examines in careful detail the difference between the formality and the reality of the president's war-making powers. Fisher argues that the Framers feared concentrating war-making power in the hands of a single person and, as a result, gave Congress the authority to authorize military action. Fisher argues that this constitutional design has been fundamentally transformed and that presidents today enjoy the monarchical power in war making that the Framers feared. He argues that, although Congress issues nonbinding resolutions surrounding these actions, in practice these resolutions do little to curtail the president. Using the actions in Panama, Somalia, Bosnia, Afghanistan, the former Yugoslavia, and various actions against Iraq to illustrate his point, Fisher argues that President George H. W. Bush expanded the scope of presidential power, especially with the claim that he could go to war against Iraq without seeking authorization from Congress. President Clinton built on this precedent in Bosnia and Serbia. The examples detailed suggest that international and regulatory organizations such as the U.N. Security Council and the North Atlantic Treaty Organization have become instruments by which presidents can circumvent the constitutional role of Congress in authorizing military action. Yet members of Congress have facilitated this shift in institutional power by being all too willing to rally behind nonbinding resolutions for military actions.

The complex relationship between the president and Congress is at the core of American government, yet it is one of the most misunderstood relationships in contemporary politics in the United States. *Rivals for Power* attempts to improve understanding of presidential–congressional relations by combining the firsthand experiences of former members of Congress and White House staff with academic analyses from scholars who have worked in the White House and Congress and have been studying these two institutions for many years. *Rivals for Power* chronicles the complex tandem and dynamic nature of the policy-making relationship between the White House and Congress. The evolving pattern of institutional interrelationships over time, which often promotes opposing dynamics such as conflict and cooperation, reciprocity and combat, cordiality and hostility, or even benign neglect, is explained in this volume. Whether by design, good fortune, or a combination of both, the Founding Fathers crafted a system that safeguards the people of the United States from the corruption of power and abuse of authority. As a lingering rebuke of the authoritarianism of King George III, the presidential–congressional tensions described in *Rivals for Power* have become a brilliant and workable model for other governments in the world that are attempting to limit unbundled executive authority.

NOTES

1. James A. Thurber, "Thunder from the Right: Observations about the Elections," *The Public Manager* (winter 1994–95): 13–16.

2. On 27 September 1994, Republican congressional candidates signed the Contract with America, pledging that if elected they would support changes in congressional procedures and bring votes in the House on a series of proposals such as a balanced budget amendment, a line-item veto, and term limits for members of Congress. For more on the Contract with America, see Ed Gillespie and Bob Schellhas, eds., *Contract with America* (New York: Times Books, 1994).

3. For more on the 1992 elections, see Michael Nelson, ed., *The Elections of 1992* (Washington, D.C.: CQ Press, 1993).

4. Beth Donovan, "Maverick Chairman Forgiven as Clinton Reworks Bill," *Congressional Quarterly Weekly Report*, 12 June 1993: 1251–52.

5. Erwin C. Hargrove, "The Presidency: George Bush and the Cycle of Politics and Policy," in *The Elections of 1988*, ed. Michael Nelson (Washington, D.C.: CQ Press, 1989), 175.

6. Quoted in James A. Barnes, "Political Focus," *National Journal*, 11 February 1989: 377.

7. For a description of presidential–congressional policy battles, see Lance T. LeLoup and Steven A. Shull, *Congress and the President: The Policy Connection* (Belmont, Calif.: Wadsworth Press, 1993).

8. See chapter 6 for a full discussion of how presidential support scores are measured.

9. Janet Hook, "Bush Inspired Frail Support for First-Year President," *Congressional Quarterly Weekly Report*, 30 December 1989: 3540.

10. For more discussion of this rivalry, see Gary Andres, Patrick Griffin, and James A. Thurber, "The Contemporary Presidency. Managing White House–Congressional Relations: Observations from Inside the Process," *Presidential Studies Quarterly* 30, no. 3 (2000): 553–63.

11. See James A. Thurber, "Congress and the Constitution: Two Hundred Years of Stability and Change," in *Reflections on the Constitution*, ed. Richard Maidment (Manchester: University of Manchester Press, 1989), 51–75.

12. For a discussion of this constitutional basis of conflict, see Louis Fisher, *Constitutional Conflicts between Congress and the President* (Lawrence: University Press of Kansas, 1991); Louis Fisher, *The Politics of Shared Power: Congress and the Executive* (Washington, D.C.: CQ Press, 1993); and Charles O. Jones, *The Presidency in a Separated System* (Washington, D.C.: Brookings Institution Press, 1994).

13. Richard E. Neustadt, *Presidential Power and the Modern Presidents: The Politics of Leadership from Roosevelt to Reagan* (New York: Free Press, 1990), 317.

14. A pocket veto is the act of the president withholding his approval of a bill after Congress has adjourned. See Harold W. Stanley and Richard G. Niemi, *Vital Statistics on American Politics*, 5th edition (Washington, D.C.: CQ Press, 1995), 258. For vetoes and overrides from the 80th to the 103d Congresses (1947–94), see Norman J. Ornstein, Thomas E. Mann, and Michael J. Malbin, *Vital Statistics on Congress, 1995–1996* (Washington, D.C.: CQ Press, 1996), 167.

15. Todd S. Purdum, "President Warns Congress to Drop Some Budget Cuts," *New York Times*, 29 October 1995: 30.

16. See Jones, *The Presidency in a Separated System*.

17. See George C. Edwards III, *Presidential Influence in Congress* (San Francisco: Freeman, 1980); and Cecil V. Crabb Jr. and Pat M. Holt, *Invitation to Struggle: Congress, the President, and Foreign Policy*, 4th edition (Washington, D.C.: CQ Press, 1992).

18. James Madison, *Federalist*, no. 46, in *The Federalist Papers*, ed. Clinton Rossiter (New York: New American Library, 1961), 296.

19. See Stephen Wayne, *The Legislative Presidency* (New York: Harper and Row, 1978).

20. David R. Mayhew, *Congress: The Electoral Connection* (New Haven: Yale University Press, 1974).

21. Thomas E. Mann, "Breaking the Political Impasse," in *Setting National Priorities: Policy for the Nineties*, ed. Henry J. Aaron (Washington, D.C.: Brookings Institution Press, 1990), 302.

22. On divided party control of government, see David R. Mayhew, *Divided We Govern: Party Control, Lawmaking, and Investigations, 1946–1990* (New Haven: Yale University Press, 1991); James A. Thurber, ed., *Divided Democracy: Cooperation and Conflict between the President and Congress* (Washington, D.C.: CQ Press, 1991); and Gary C. Jacobson, *The Electoral Origins of Divided Government* (Boulder: Westview Press, 1990).

23. Ornstein, Mann, and Malbin, *Vital Statistics on Congress*, 49.

24. Nelson Polsby, quoted in *Congress and the Nation*, vol. 7: *1985–1988* (Washington, D.C.: Congressional Quarterly, Inc., 1990), 21–22.

25. Mayhew, *Divided We Govern*, 198.

26. For more on Speaker Cannon, see Ronald M. Peters, *The American Speakership: The Office in Historical Perspective* (Baltimore: Johns Hopkins University Press, 1990).

27. See Stephen J. Wayne, "Great Expectations: What People Want from Presidents," in *Rethinking the Presidency*, ed. Thomas E. Cronin (Boston: Little, Brown, 1982), 185–99; and Glen R. Parker, "Some Themes in Congressional Opportunity," *American Journal of Political Science* 21 (February 1977): 93–119.

28. See Committee on the Constitutional System, *A Bicentennial Analysis of the American Political Structure* (Washington, D.C.: Committee on the Constitutional System, 1987).

29. James A. Thurber, "The 104th Congress Is Fast and Efficient: But at What Cost?" *Roll Call*, 4 March 1995: 16.

30. See Joel H. Sibley, "The Rise and Fall of American Political Parties," in *The Parties Respond: Changes in American Parties and Campaigns*, ed. L. Sandy Maisel (Boulder: Westview Press, 1994), 3–18.

31. See Jonathan Rauch, *Demosclerosis* (New York: Times Books, 1994).

32. See James G. March and Herbert A. Simon, *Organizations* (New York: Wiley, 1958).

33. See Jones, *The Presidency in a Separated System*.

2

The President and Congress at the Turn of the Century: Structural Sources of Conflict

James P. Pfiffner

Even in the best of times the president and Congress will have difficulty getting along. The primary reason for this is that the Framers intended that "ambition must be made to counteract ambition," as Madison argues in *Federalist* no. 51. But in the final decade of the twentieth-century, relations between the two branches were particularly contentious, with a 1995 showdown between parties with sharply conflicting policy priorities and the impeachment of President Clinton by the House of Representatives.

At one level the causes of these battles were the conflicting ambitions of two men of opposite parties and opposing policy views. President Bill Clinton and Speaker of the House Newt Gingrich fought each other in the headlines and backrooms of U.S. politics. But the roots of their personal, partisan, and policy clashes were much deeper than their contrasting personalities and the tactics they employed. It is the argument of this chapter that even if these two individuals had not been leading their respective political parties and branches of government, the current era of presidential–congressional relations would have been highly conflictual.

This chapter examines the sources of the highly volatile politics of the turn of the century in the structural underpinnings of political change in the 1960s and 1970s. It addresses first the breakup of the "Solid South" and its effects on the distribution of power in Congress and then the impact of divided government. It then examines the consequences of these structural underpinnings in the increasingly polarized behavior in Congress over the past several decades. Voting in Congress has become more partisan; the use of delaying tactics such as the filibuster has become more common; and the level of civility has declined. Finally, it looks at some of the policy and partisan battles between President Clinton and Congress that have added their own flavor to the conflict between the branches. The chapter concludes that the relatively high level of partisan and institutional conflict is not likely to go away soon, regardless of which party controls the two branches.

STRUCTURAL AND ELECTORAL UNDERPINNINGS OF POLITICAL CHANGE

The 1994 elections marked the culmination of a long and bitter fight by the Republicans to take control of the House. The 1994 congressional victories of the Republicans were impressive, but in emphasizing the individual efforts of Newt Gingrich, the problems of the Democrats, and the strategic and tactical skill with which Republican Party leaders acted, it is possible to lose sight of the longer term trends on which they built. The building blocks of the Republican majority in the House can be traced to the partisan reversal in the South over the past three decades. This transformation led to the increasing ideological cohesiveness of both parties and polarization in Congress that is examined in the second section of this chapter. When the voters repudiated the Democrats in the 1994 elections, these trends culminated in Republican control of Congress and the stormy relationship between President Clinton and Congress that marked the end of the century.

The Breakup of the Solid South Transforms Congress

After the harsh Republican Reconstruction after the Civil War, the South remained firmly Democratic for the next century. The "Solid (Democratic) South" retained its loyalty to the Democratic Party and was a major component of Franklin Roosevelt's New Deal coalition. The coalition began to crack in 1964 when archconservative Barry Goldwater won the Republican presidential nomination, despite his defeat by Lyndon Johnson, who won in a landslide. Goldwater's conservatism fit with the social conservatism of southern white voters: support of the military, suspicion toward Washington, and racial conservatism.

National policies in the 1960s led to increasing participation by African Americans in the electoral process. The Voting Rights Act of 1965 and the registration of many more black voters in the South began the slow change that led to a Republican majority in Congress. Through the mid–twentieth century southern Democratic members of Congress had been quite conservative in their voting and electoral appeals to voters. But the increasing numbers of black voters led Democratic candidates to become less conservative and more in line with the rest of the Democratic Party. Because of this, many conservative southern voters began to elect Republicans to Congress. What happened was not that the South necessarily became more conservative but, rather, that conservatives came to see the Republican Party as the conservative party of the South.[1]

In addition, increased black voting and the creation of majority minority districts (in which a majority of the voters were African American) led to increased numbers of African American representatives from the South.[2] As black members of Congress tended to reflect the liberal orientation of their constituents, they reinforced the liberal wing of the Democratic caucus; but the new Republican representatives from the South tended to be more conservative than their Democratic predecessors had been. Conservative Democrats and liberal Republicans could no longer hold their own against the more ideologically committed candidates in their parties' primary elections. This caused increased cohesion of both parties in the House (and Senate) and contributed to the increasing polarization of Congress.

The consequences of these dynamics can be seen in a number of electoral trends in the South. Party identification of southern whites changed steadily over the past four decades; in 1952, 80 percent of white voters identified themselves as Democrats, but by 1992 that number had fallen to 43 percent, and the Republicans enjoyed a majority of white voter identification. Similarly, of those southerners who considered themselves conservative in 1974, half identified with the Republican Party; by 1994 that had increased to 80 percent.[3] As party identification changed in the South, Republicans began to mount challenges for House seats much more consistently. In 1966 forty House races went unchallenged, but by 1994 only five went unchallenged.[4] In addition, the Republican challengers came to be more experienced politicians and thus more serious challengers to the Democratic incumbents.[5]

As the party identification of southern whites changed, so did the number of House seats from the South held by Republicans. From 1945 through 1962 Republicans held fewer than 10 percent of House seats from the South. In 1968 Republicans won 26 percent of southern House seats; in 1984 they held 36 percent; and by 1996 they held 60 percent of House seats. At the same time the South came to make up a larger portion of the Republican Party: southerners made up 37 percent of the Republican membership of the House in the 105th Congress.[6]

The conservative trend and increasing strength of the Republican Party were not the exclusive result of the political dynamics of the South. Ronald Reagan's election in 1980 signaled a nationwide conservative trend that

Table 2.1 Party of Members of Congress from Southern States, 102d–105th Congresses

	102d Congress (1991–1992)	*103d Congress (1993–1994)*	*104th Congress (1995–1996)*	*105th Congress (1997–1998)*
Senate				
• Democrats	17	15	10	8
• Republicans	9	11	16	18
House				
• Democrats	85	85	64	54
• Republicans	44	52	73	83

Source: Lawrence C. Dodd and Bruce I. Oppenheimer, "Congress and the Emerging Order: Conditional Party Government or Constructive Partisanship?" in their *Congress Reconsidered* (Washington, D.C.: CQ Press, 1997), 396–97.

helped the Republicans throughout the country and moved their national partisan identification much closer to the level that the Democrats enjoyed. The consequences of this trend for the House were intensified by the redistricting following the 1990 census. States in the South and West tended to be Republican and gained seats at the expense of states in the Northeast and Midwest, which tended to lean to the Democrats.

Nevertheless, the conservative trend was most striking in the South, and the changes in the South had the largest impact on Congress. In the 102d Congress the Democrats enjoyed a margin of eighty-five to forty-four seats in the House; in the 105th Congress the margin had reversed to an eighty-three to fifty-four Republican advantage. In the Senate, southern seats were dominated by the Democrats in the 102d Congress by a margin of seventeen to nine; by the 105th Congress the Democrats were at an eighteen to eight disadvantage (see table 2.1). Partisan representation in the other three regions of the country stayed relatively stable over the same period.[7] Thus, the Republican capture of Congress in 1994, in addition to short-term factors such as Democratic vulnerability and effective Republican strategies, was a culmination of longer term trends in national and particularly southern electoral politics.

Divided Government

The occurrence of divided government—the control of one or both houses of Congress by a political party other than the president's—is not new in U.S. politics. But its incidence has increased in recent decades, and it has resulted in strained relations between the executive and legislative branches. From 1887 to 1945 divided government was present 12 percent of the time, and from 1946 to 1992 it existed 67 percent of the time. But from 1981 to 2001, divided government was the result in nine out of ten elections, that is, it was the case 90 percent of the time.[8]

The reason why divided government is problematic for the U.S. political system is expressed cogently by Woodrow Wilson: "You have an arrested government. You have a Government that is not responding to the wishes of the people. You have a Government that is not functioning, a Government whose very energies are stayed and postponed. If you want to release the force of the American people, you have got to get possession of the Senate and the Presidency as well as the House."[9] Political scientist James Sundquist sees the problem as one of accountability and coherent policy. The concept of responsible party government holds that if one political party controls both branches, the citizenry can hold its members responsible for the policy actions taken while they were in office. One party will have been in control of the government and would thus be responsible for the actions taken on its watch. The members of that party will deserve credit or blame for the outcome, and voters can hold them responsible at the next election. On the other hand, if control of the government is divided between the two branches, each party can blame the other for things that have gone wrong and try to take credit for what has gone right. In addition, each party has enough power to block the other party from acting, and this mutual veto can lead to deadlock, with neither party able to take action to confront pressing problems.

Sundquist has argued:

> For coherent and timely policies to be adopted and carried out—in short, for government to work effectively . . . the president, the Senate, and the House must come into agreement. When the same party controls all three of these power centers, the incentive to reach such an agreement is powerful despite the inevitable institutional rivalries and jealousies. The party *does* serve as a bridge or the web, in the metaphors of political science.[10]

Proponents of the responsible party government model argue that unified party control makes cooperation between the two branches more probable. They believe that the forces of fragmentation in the U.S. political system are so strong that the unifying factor of party is essential to coherent national policy making. If the same party controls both branches, there is a common long-term interest in producing a successful record to run on for reelection. But with opposing parties in charge of the two institutions, there is an incentive for each to frustrate the other's policy initiatives.[11]

When Sundquist made his argument, the evidence for the negative effect of divided government on policy making seemed plausible; the 1980s were a time of high conflict between the parties. David Mayhew, however, decided to take a longer time perspective; he has examined the period from 1948 to 1990 with respect to the likely consequences of divided government. He hypothesized that periods of divided government should produce less important legislation and that there should be more hostile investigations of the executive branch by Congress during such times. But what he found was that it makes no difference whether the government is divided or unified; the production of significant legislation and investigations critical of the executive branch occur just as often in either situation.

As impressive as the evidence that Mayhew has amassed is, the problem with the data is that there was no control for the mood of the country or the demand for new laws. That is, in periods of high political demand for government action, we should expect that more laws would be passed. And during periods of relative quiescence, or in an era of cutting back government programs, we should expect that there would be fewer laws passed. Given these reasonable expectations (however one defines the differing periods) the real question is: What effect does divided government have relative to the political times? Thus, a true measure of divided government would be the ratio of laws actually passed to those that the political system seriously considered during that time period—in Mayhew's words, "some actually-did-pass numerator over some all-that-were-possibilities-of-passage denominator."[12] Mayhew does a very credible job of measuring the numerator of the ratio, that is, those laws that actually were passed. But, by his own admission, he does not make any estimate of the denominator, that is, all of the laws that might have been passed.

But other scholars have come to the rescue by devising ways of measuring how many laws were seriously considered and might have been passed, making it possible to determine the relative percentage of laws that actually were passed in relation to those that might have been. Comparing periods of divided government with unified government would then give us an idea of whether divided government has an effect on the ability of the system to produce significant public policy appropriate for the times, whether activist or quiescent. Their conclusions have been that the conditions of divided government have had a greater impact than Mayhew's study indicates.

George Edwards and his colleagues reasoned that they might approximate the denominator to the ratio by calculating the number of bills that were seriously considered in Congress. If the percentage of such potential laws that were finally enacted is significantly less during periods of divided government, then divided government can be seen to have a negative impact on the ability of the system to make policy. They made their approximation of the number of potential laws that were seriously considered by counting the number of proposed laws that failed to pass in each session according to the account by *Congressional Quarterly*'s yearly almanac and, from among those selected, those that were important enough to be the subject of a hearing by a committee or subcommittee.[13]

The authors find that, when the number of laws that were finally passed is compared with the number of those that were seriously considered by each Congress from 1947 to 1992, the presence or absence of divided government does in fact make a difference. They find that the presence of divided government increases the number of bills that presidents opposed from 12 to 37 percent. They also find that the odds that potentially significant legislation will fail are increased by 45 percent. Divided government does not, however, affect the ability of presidents to block laws they oppose, which they can do more than 90 percent of the time in any case. Nor does it affect the ability of presidents to get measures that they endorse passed, for divided government is only one of several factors that affect presidential success.

Sarah Binder also has found that divided government has an impact on the proportion of potential policy proposals that eventually become law. In determining how the proportion should be calculated, Binder determines a plausible denominator by trying to calculate a broad system agenda composed of those issues that are considered important by members of the political community. She operationalizes this by using the editorials of the *New York Times* as an indicator of those issues that were important enough to be considered by Congress, including both those issues the *Times* favored and those it opposed. The assumption is that the *Times* would write about the most important issues of the day. She thus calculates the "demand" for legislation so that she may compare it with the "supply," that is, laws that were actually passed.[14]

Binder also concludes that the presence of divided government does make a difference. That is, the proportion of potential policy enactments considered important at the time that were actually enacted is greater during periods of unified government than during periods of divided government. But she also concludes that several other factors have an even greater impact on the proportion of potential policy changes that made it to fruition. According to her systematic comparisons of the ratio of actual enactments to important issues considered by the political system, two factors outweigh the effect of divided government: the ideological gap between the parties and the ideological distance between the two houses of Congress. Thus, if one is concerned with the problem of "gridlock" (which Binder defines as "the share of salient issues on the nation's agenda left in limbo at the close of each Congress"), ideological polarization in Congress is even more important than the division of the institutions of government between the two parties.[15] These factors, among others, are considered in the next section.

THE CONSEQUENCES OF STRUCTURAL CHANGE: PARTISAN POLARIZATION IN CONGRESS

The Waning Center

In the middle of the twentieth century the two political parties in Congress were not ideologically monolithic. That is, each party had a significant number of members who were ideologically sympathetic to the other party. The Democratic Party contained a strong conservative wing of members, the southern "Boll Weevils," who often voted with the conservative Republicans. The Republican Party contained a noticeable number of moderates, mostly from the Northeast, the "Rockefeller Republicans," who would often vote with the Democrats. These cross-pressured members of Congress made up between one-fifth and one-third of each house of Congress from 1950 to the mid-1980s.[16]

In the last fifteen years of the twentieth century, the cross-pressured members of each party all but disappeared. Bond and Fleisher have calculated the number of liberal Republicans and conservative Democrats in Congress from the 1950s through the 1990s and have documented their decline. The number of conservative Democrats in the House has decreased from a high of ninety-one in 1965–66 to a low of eleven in 1995–96. In the Senate the high of twenty-two in the early 1960s was reduced to zero in 1995–96. Liberal Republicans similarly fell from a high of thirty-five in the early 1970s to a low of one in 1993–94 in the House and a high of fourteen in 1973–74 to a low of two in 1995–96 in the Senate.[17] This disappearance of the middle is a convincing demonstration of ideological polarization in Congress.

It used to be that the most conservative Democrats would have ideological preferences closer to average Republican preferences than to the Democratic mean, and the most liberal Republicans would be closer to the Democratic mean than the Republican ideological average. But the area of overlap in the center had almost disappeared by the end of the century. The *National Journal* developed its own ideological scale of liberal and conservative voting and has calculated individual scores for members of Congress. Since 1981, most House Democrats would be on the liberal end of the spectrum, and most Republicans, on the right end. There has always been a number of members of each party whose voting records put them in the middle, overlapping ideological space. In 1999, however, only two Republicans and two Democrats shared the middle ground.

Up to the mid-1990s the Senate had a middle group of ten to seventeen centrists from both parties who often voted with the opposite party. But in 1999, for the first time since the *National Journal* began calculating the scores in 1981, all of the Republicans had a score to the right of the most conservative Democrat, and all of the Democrats had a score to the left of the most liberal Republican.[18] The polarization in the Senate was exacerbated in 1996 by the retirement of fourteen Senate moderates who contributed significantly to the civility of the Senate and who could reach across party lines in policy deliberations, among them Republicans Alan Simpson (Wyo.) and Hank Brown (Colo.) and Democrats Sam Nunn (Ga.) and Bill Bradley (N.J.).[19]

What the above data mean in a practical sense is that each of the political parties in Congress is more ideologically homogeneous. Thus, there is less need to compromise in a moderate direction when reaching a consensus within each party. And it is correspondingly more difficult to bridge the ideological gap between the contrasting perspectives of the two parties. So finding middle ground where compromise is possible becomes much more difficult. It is more likely that votes will be set up to highlight partisan differences and will be used for rhetorical and electoral purposes rather than to arrive at compromise policies.[20]

Another measure of partisan conflict that reflects the polarization in Congress is the "party vote," in which a majority of one party opposes a majority of the other party in a roll-call vote. This measure of polarization has been increasing in recent years, especially in the House. From 1955 to 1965 the votes in the House that were party votes averaged 49 percent; from 1967 to 1982 the percentage was 36 percent. But after 1982 it began to climb, and in the 1990s it reached 64 percent for the 103d Congress.[21] Party voting reached a record 73.2 percent in 1995.[22] Senate scores on party voting roughly paralleled those in the House though at slightly lower levels, reaching a Senate record of 68.8 percent in 1995.[23] Party unity scores, in which members of the two parties vote with their majorities on party line votes, also increased to unusually high levels.[24]

Representative John Tanner (D-Tenn.) expressed the problem this way: "Democratic districts become more Democratic and Republican districts become more Republican. There are fewer and fewer districts in the middle. . . . Because the districts in Congress are more and more one-party dominant, the American Congress is more extreme."[25] There is some evidence that the electoral constituencies of members of Congress have become slightly more polarized since the 1970s.[26] But it is unlikely that the polarization of voters caused the polarization of members of Congress. It is more probable that increasingly extreme candidates for Congress chosen by party activists in primary elections forced voters to choose between more ideologically opposite candidates.[27]

Partisan differences in the Senate are often registered by the threat of members of the minority party to filibuster. The filibuster is a time-honored convention (formalized in Rule XXII) in which any member (or members) can hold the floor as long as he or she wants in order to delay the consideration of legislation. Before the 1970s the filibuster was used occasionally when senators felt strongly about an issue and were willing to block Senate business in order to achieve their goals. In the 1950s filibusters were occasionally used to keep the majority from enacting civil rights legislation. In the early decades of the twentieth century use of the filibuster would occasionally peak at ten per Congress, but in the 1970s and 1980s the use of the filibuster exploded to twenty-five or thirty-five per Congress (see table 2.2).[28] The increased use of the filibuster and other dilatory tactics, such as "holds" on nominations, has amounted to a "parliamentary arms race" in which each side is willing to use the extreme tactic because the other side has used that tactic against it.[29]

In addition to actual filibusters, the mere threat of a filibuster can slow the legislative process. As Barbara Sinclair has calculated, threats to filibuster major legislation have increased significantly in the past two decades (see table 2.3). Presidential threats to veto bills also increased sharply in the 1990s.

The dynamics of recent congressional elections are such that political elites, who are more committed to their positions and thus more polarized than most voters, participate in politics disproportionately. These are the voters who turn out for primary and midterm elections and support more

Table 2.2 Average Number of Filibusters and Cloture Votes per Congress, 1951–1998

Years	*Filibusters per Congress*	*Cloture Votes per Congress*
1951–1960	1.0	0.4
1961–1970	4.6	5.2
1971–1980	11.2	22.4
1981–1986	16.7	23.0
1987–1992	26.7	39.0
1993–1994	30.0	42.0 (103d)
1995–1996	25.0	50.0 (104th)
1997–1998	29.0	53.0 (105th)

Source: Richard E. Cohen, "Crackup of the Committees," *National Journal,* 31 July 1999: 2212.

Table 2.3 Veto and Filibuster Threats in Congress, 1969–1998

Congress	*Veto Threats (%)*	*Filibuster Threats (%)*	*Actual Vetoes*
91st (1969–1970)	14	12	5
97th (1981–1982)	23	22	4
101st (1989–1990)	52	28	9
103d (1993–1994)	4	47	0
104th (1995–1996)	60	49	10
105th (1997–1998)	69	50	5

Source: Barbara Sinclair, "Hostile Partners: The President, Congress, and Lawmaking in the Partisan 1990s," in *Polarized Politics: Congress and the President in a Partisan Era,* ed. Jon R. Bond and Richard Fleisher (Washington, D.C.: CQ Press, 2000), 145.

conservative Republicans and more liberal Democrats. Once candidates have been elected, they use all the advantages of incumbency effectively to keep themselves in office. These polarizing dynamics are reinforced by redistricting in all of the states and the creation of majority minority districts in the South. It should come as no surprise, given the partisan polarization documented above, that interpersonal relations among members of the opposing parties have suffered.

The Decline of Civility

Eric Uslaner argues that the traditional norms of courtesy, reciprocity, and comity that marked the 1950s and 1960s in Congress began to break down in the 1970s.[30] Reflecting broader divisions in U.S. politics over the Vietnam War and Watergate, life in Congress became more contentious. Legislative language had traditionally been marked by overly elaborate politeness in order to manage partisan and sometimes personal conflict. But instances of harsh language and incivility became more common and more partisan in the 1970s and 1980s. In the House the Republicans felt increasingly suppressed by the majority Democrats through the rules of debate and legislative scheduling and, under the leadership of Newt Gingrich, began to use obstructionist tactics to clog up the legislative process.[31] The predictable Democratic response was to tighten up the rules even more to deal with disruptive tactics.

Even the usually more decorous Senate suffered from declining civility. In the early 1980s Senator Joseph Biden remarked, "There's much less civility than when I came there ten years ago. There aren't as many nice people as there were before. . . . Ten years ago you didn't have people calling each other sons of bitches and vowing to get at each other."[32] Uslaner argues that "there is a powerful downward trend for all four congressional parties beginning with the 89th Congress (1965–66). . . . At least since the mid-1960s, then, *there is a single syndrome of incivility for all four congressional parties. Ideological extremism shows the same basic time path in the Senate as it does in the House for both parties*."[33] Even though the Senate was markedly more civil in its trial than the House had been in the impeachment of President Clinton, the probable reason was that the outcome was virtually certain; reaching a two-thirds majority to convict the president was highly unlikely.[34] Scholars David Brady and Morris Fiorina summarize the political context:

> In a context in which members themselves have stronger and more distinct policy preferences, where they scarcely know each other personally because every spare moment is spent fund-raising or cultivating constituents, where interest groups monitor every word a member speaks and levy harsh attacks upon the slightest deviation from group orthodoxy, where the media provide coverage in direct proportion to the negativity and conflict contained in one's messages, where money is desperately needed and is best raised by scaring the bejesus out of people, is it any wonder that comity and courtesy are among the first casualties?[35]

Near the end of the 106th Congress, even the leadership in both houses was not able to restrain the harsh feelings that had been building up. Speaker of the House Dennis Hastert, who had taken over the speakership at the beginning of the 106th Congress, had a reputation (in contrast to his predecessor, Newt Gingrich) as a mild-mannered and workmanlike legislator who was more concerned with making deals and legislating than with making symbolic points through hostile rhetoric. Yet, one year into his speakership, the level of hostility between Hastert and Minority Leader Richard Gephardt was quite high.

The two leaders seldom talked with each other, even on necessary procedural issues, and they held each other in contempt. According to Gephardt, "Frankly, the relationship is really no different than it was with Newt Gingrich. . . . Their definition of bipartisanship is, 'My way or the highway.' "[36] According to Hastert, Gephardt's "sole purpose is to try to make this House fail."[37] Hastert went so far as to campaign in Gephardt's district for his Republican challenger, a very unusual breach of the usual leadership decorum.[38] Hastert even seemed to have much better relations with President Clinton than his House colleague Gephardt, meeting with the president almost as many times as he met with Gephardt.[39]

The Senate has not been spared the leadership animosities that plagued the House in 2000. Senate Majority Leader Trent Lott and Minority Leader Tom Daschle became particularly bitter in the second session of the 106th Congress as the Senate struggled with passing legislation during an election year. In early June 2000, Majority Leader Lott complained, "The last couple of weeks before we went out have been the most obstructionist I've ever seen them."[40] According to Daschle, "No Majority Leader in history has attempted to constrain the Senate debate as aggressively as Senator Lott has chosen to do"; it amounted to "a Senate version of dictatorship that I think is unacceptable."[41] Lott replied, "I have to go on the record saying I do believe I have been maligned unfairly . . . to come in here and think we have to have a right to offer non-germane amendments to every appropriations bill that comes through, and then criticize us for not getting our work done—Oh, boy, that is really smart, really smart."[42]

From the perspective of the Democrats, the Republican majority was refusing to confirm the nominees of President Clinton and was preventing them from offering amendments to legislation so they could have their priorities voted on. From the perspective of the Republicans, the Democrats were trying to obstruct the flow of legislation with their amendments so that they could blame the Republicans for being a "do nothing Congress" in the election campaign. The unusual personal bitterness and intemperate language reflected election-year politics in which much was at stake, but it was also a product of the polarization of the Congress over the past several decades.

CONGRESS DURING THE CLINTON ERA: POLARIZED POLITICS

The Clinton era was a contentious time for relations between the president and Congress. At one level the conflict reflected a personal rivalry between Bill Clinton and Newt Gingrich. Clinton, a self-described "New Democrat," pulled the Democratic Party in a more moderate direction and "captured" some issues from the Republicans, for example, support for crime control, fiscal prudence, and family values (at least in rhetoric). Gingrich, on the other side, had led the Republicans from the wilderness of minority status to the promised land of majority control of Congress and sought to dismantle much of the liberal "Great Society" legislation that Democrats had passed.

Policy Conflict

In the 103d Congress (1993–95) the Democrats still held a majority in Congress and had high hopes that they would achieve a positive policy record that would mark a resurgence of Democratic hegemony after twelve years of Republican control of the presidency.[43] But the dream was not to come true. Clinton's first major policy push was for deficit reduction, which he won with no Republican votes but which was bitter medicine for congressional Democrats who would rather have pushed new programs. Then, Clinton's big initiative for universal health care coverage was defeated by the Republicans in 1994. The huge and complex plan favored by the administration was framed by the Republicans as more "big government" and too costly. In 1994 the Republicans were able to use the Clinton record to "nationalize" the midterm congressional elections and take control of Congress for the first time in forty years.

The Gingrich-led Republican victory was so overwhelming that at the beginning of the 104th Congress they were able to push the "Contract with America" agenda through the House in spring 1995 and roll over the Democrats in doing so. The national agenda was so dominated by the Republican "contract" that on 18 April 1995 President Clinton had to argue that he was "relevant" to the policy process: "The President is relevant. . . . The Constitution gives me relevance; the power of our ideas gives me relevance; the record we have built up over the last two years and the things we're trying to do give me relevance."[44] But when much of the contract proposals foundered in the Senate, the Republicans decided to build into the appropriations process provisions that would go far beyond the contract in trying to reduce severely many of the government programs of which they disapproved. They wanted to abolish three Cabinet departments and severely cut back programs in education, environmental protection, Medicare, and Medicaid as well as eliminate smaller programs such as the National Endowment for the Arts and the National Endowment for the Humanities.

Many of these priorities were packaged in omnibus legislation in fall 1995, and President Clinton vetoed the bills several times. When the Republicans did not change the provisions, much of the government was shut down for lack of appropriations. When it became clear that the public saw the Republican Congress rather than President Clinton as responsible for the shutdown, Robert Dole, who was running for president, convinced Congress to pass appropriations bills and negotiate the budget bills. Clinton was reelected in 1996, and the Republicans retained control of Congress by narrow margins.[45]

The 105th Congress (1998–99) began with Clinton's plans to propose a number of "small bore" policy proposals that would be acceptable across the political spectrum, but in late January the Monica Lewinsky scandal hit. The rest of the spring was dominated by the efforts of Kenneth Starr to investigate the scandal, and the fall was dominated by the bitterly partisan battle to impeach the president. Many Democrats and moderate Republicans would have preferred to condemn the president's behavior rather than impeaching him and trying to remove him from office. The key to President Clinton's impeachment was the ability of the House Republican leadership to invoke party discipline on a procedural vote to prevent a vote on censoring the president. The articles of impeachment passed on party line votes, with only a few members from each party defecting on the two articles that were adopted.

The 106th Congress began with the Senate trial of the president and its decision not to remove him from office. The rest of the session was taken up with the aftermath of the impeachment trial and partisan battles over policy priorities. The second session began in an election year (2000) and was not marked by major policy victories or an impressive legislative record. Each party was more concerned with its efforts to prevail and win a slim majority in the fall elections. Even issues with broad bipartisan support could not be passed in the corrosive atmosphere. Representative Jim McDermott (D-Wash.) has characterized the 106th Congress: "Everything was crafted on their side to win the election. And everything we tried to do was [to] derail them from winning the election. . . . It was the most unproductive public policy year I've spent in my life." Senator John Breaux (D-La.) puts it this way: "We've entered into a pattern of blaming each other for failure. People were actually in some cases afraid to compromise because they would lose the issue. On both sides."[46]

As bitter as the battles between Clinton and Gingrich were, the argument of this chapter is that the fundamental causes of the partisan battles that dominated the four Congresses of the Clinton era have been driven by the polarization of Congress rather than by the personalities of the two men. The structural underpinnings of polarization lie in the demise of the "Solid South" and the division of Congress, especially in the House, into a more conservative Republican Party and a more liberal Democratic Party (recognizing that the whole political spectrum shifted in a conservative direction in the 1980s, just as it shifted in a more liberal direction in the 1960s). This polarization, as documented above, has led to a more contentious atmosphere in Congress with more party voting and use of obstructionist tactics in both the House and the Senate. It has also led to greater use of the veto by the president.

Partisan conflict and battles between the president and Congress, however, do not mean that no important legislation gets passed. *Stalemate* is a relative term, and the government keeps operating (even during a shutdown) during intensely partisan periods. Thus, President Clinton and Congress were able to pass a number of important policy initiatives. In 1993 Clinton fought for congressional approval of the North American Free Trade Act (NAFTA). But he was able to get it passed only by knitting together a coalition of more Republicans than Democrats, and he was opposed by Majority Leader David Bonnier in the House. Democrats in Congress were not pleased that Clinton backed the Bush-initiated NAFTA legislation, but free trade was a Clinton "New Democrat" issue.

Similarly, President Clinton decided to sign the Republican welfare reform bill in the summer of 1996, despite opposition from the Democrats in Congress (and some in his own administration). Although Clinton thought the bill was too harsh, it did move in the direction he favored. But it was also an election year, and Clinton did not want to give Republicans the issue of arguing that he had vetoed three welfare bills after promising to "end welfare as we know it."

In 1997 President Clinton and the Republican Congress were able to compromise in order to come to an agreement that would balance the budget within five years. This impressive agreement was achieved by the willingness of each side to set aside partisan warfare and negotiate an outcome in which each side could claim victory. The 1997 deal was followed by a fiscal year 1998 budget that was actually balanced—four years earlier than had been projected.[47] The surplus in fiscal year 2000 was more than $200 billion. This historic turnaround was based on the groundwork laid by President Bush in 1990 and President Clinton in 1993, with their deficit-reducing agreements and spending constraints. But it was made possible by a booming economy and historically high stock market.[48]

In spring and summer 2000, President Clinton was able to work with Republicans in Congress to win approval of permanent normal trade relations with China. In the House more than twice as many Republicans as Democrats supported the measure, echoing the coalition that passed NAFTA in 1993. The above policy achievements were possible only through bipartisan cooperation and the willingness to share credit. But such cross-party victories have been unusual; the primary pattern has been one of partisan rancor and stalemate.

Patterns of Partisanship

The pattern that emerges from the above analysis is that of a president in the middle of the political spectrum, unable to depend on support from his own party, needing to cobble together separate coalitions of policy support from both political parties. The problem, of course, is that the parties are polarized, so finding moderates on both sides of the aisle is a challenge. In addition, the president is liable to alienate the more partisan wing of his own party and can count on opposition from the more partisan wing of the opposition party. This limits severely the policy options of the president. Most issues in Congress will be contentious, and there is no natural coalition of congressional support for the president.

The structural causes of this lie in the different ideological orientations of the president and members of Congress. In order to be elected, presidents must appeal to voters in the middle of the political spectrum, that is, moderates or independents. They may have to appeal to the core constituencies of their political parties in the primaries, in which only the more committed turn out to vote. But once the nomination has been won, they must move quickly back to the center to appeal to the broader electorate that votes in the general election.

This need to appeal to the center is why most presidential nominees locate themselves in the middle of the ideological spectrum; it is necessary for victory, as the landslides in 1964 and 1972 demonstrate.[49] The 1980 election was somewhat of an exception, though President Carter was saddled with unusually difficult conditions—with hostages in Iran, high gas prices, double-digit inflation, and interest rates approaching 20 percent. But the presidential races in 1988, 1992, 1996, and 2000 all reinforce the maxim that president candidates must appeal to the middle if they hope to win. In the 2000 campaign George W. Bush and Al Gore moved so decisively toward the middle that they may have passed each other at times, with Bush emphasizing his "compassionate conservatism" and Gore arguing for fiscal responsibility.

The reality that presidents are elected by support from the middle of the political spectrum runs into the reality that congressional politics have become polarized. President Johnson was able to rely on large majorities of Democrats in Congress, and President Reagan was able to call on southern Boll Weevils (conservative Democrats) in the House to support his initial agenda. Presidents at the turn of the century have no natural coalitions they can count on in Congress. Divided government is part of the problem facing presidents, though, as David Mayhew has demonstrated, the problem is not overwhelming; important legislation still gets passed regularly. But George Edwards has shown that divided government does make a difference, and Sarah Binder has shown that the ideological distance between the parties in Congress and between the House and Senate are even greater obstacles to productive legislative sessions than divided government.

CONCLUSION

In order to win legislative victories in the early twenty-first century, presidents will have to appeal to a coalition across partisan boundaries, even though the ideological gap between the parties has increased in distance. In doing this, they will necessarily alienate the wings of their own parties. When President Clinton tried this approach in the 1990s, it was called "triangulation" by his adviser Dick Morris, that is, locating the president in a dimension "above" the Left–Right spectrum in order to appeal to a coalition of the middle in Congress.[50] Clinton was attacked by Democrats and ridiculed by Republicans for his efforts; but given the polarized structure of Congress, that was one of the few options open to him if he wanted to win legislative victories.

In addition to polarization, the narrow partisan majorities in Congress at the turn of the century make appeals across party lines more difficult because of the strategic situation facing the parties. If the margins are lopsided, the outcome of important votes is clear. It is easy for minority members to vote their consciences, and it is not costly if a member of the majority defects. But if margins are narrow, each vote counts, and the costs of defecting become much higher. This is illustrated by the House vote on censuring the president before the vote on impeachment in 1998. The Senate trial was less rancorous than the House impeachment proceedings in part because the probability of achieving a two-thirds majority to remove the president from office was quite low; the stakes were lower for individual senators. Similarly, when the margins are narrow, just a few defections can give victory to the other party. So there is tremendous pressure for party discipline and less slack for voting one's conscience. With narrow margins the stakes are also higher in terms of the next election. Each vote must be evaluated not just on the merits of the issue at hand but also for its implications for the next election. Thus, partisanship is more intense, and stalemate is more likely.

The elements of the partisan configuration in the early years of the new century—a polarized Congress, narrow margins in both houses, party line voting, and an extraordinarily close presidential election—are a recipe for gridlock. As Mayhew points out, important legislation will be passed, but the president will be frustrated. He will be forced to seek votes from the other party and will alienate some of his co-partisans. Goodwill on the part of a president is admirable and may lead to some victories; but personal civility and a willingness to reach out to the other party will only take a president so far. The fundamentals of the strategic context, with polarized parties, narrow majorities, and the lack of a presidential mandate, will ensure that any president will have a frustrating time with Congress and that most important policy issues will be contentious. Even unified government will not solve these problems, as President Clinton's experience in 1993 and 1994 demonstrates. The unusual circumstances surrounding the 2000 presidential election only exacerbated this state of affairs.

NOTES

For comments on an earlier draft of this essay, I would like to thank colleagues Sarah Binder, Timothy Conlan, Hugh Heclo, Burdett Loomis, Thomas Mann, Donald Wolfensberger, and members of my doctoral seminar in American government: Alberto Figueroa-Garcia, William Clark Thomas, and Nikhilesh Prasad.

1. Earl Black and Merle Black, *The Vital South* (Cambridge, Mass.: Harvard University Press, 1992); Bruce Oppenheimer, "The Importance of Elections in a Strong Congressional Party Era," in *Do Elections Matter?* ed. Benjamin Ginsberg and Alan Stone (Armonk, N.Y.: M. E. Sharpe, 1996); Benjamin Ginsberg and Alan Stone, eds., *Do Elections Matter?* (Armonk, N.Y.: M. E. Sharpe, 1996); Gary C. Jacobson, "The 1994 House Elections in Perspective," in *Midterm: The Elections of 1994 in Perspective*, ed. Philip A. Klinker (Boulder: Westview Press, 1996); Paul Frymer, "The 1994 Electoral Aftershock: Dealignment or Realignment in the South," in *Midterm: The Elections of 1994 in Context*, ed. Philip A. Klinker (Boulder: Westview Press, 1996); and Philip A. Klinker, ed., *Midterm: The Elections of 1994 in Context* (Boulder: Westview Press, 1996).

2. Gary C. Jacobson, *The Politics of Congressional Elections* (New York: HarperCollins, 1992), 3.

3. Frymer, "The 1994 Electoral Aftershock," 103.

4. Frymer, "The 1994 Electoral Aftershock," 105.

5. Gary C. Jacobson, "Reversal of Fortune: The Transformation of U.S. House Elections in the 1990s," paper presented at the Midwest Political Science Meeting, Chicago, 10–12 April 1997, 8.

6. Barbara Sinclair, "Transformational Leader or Faithful Agent? Innovation and Continuity in House Majority Party Leadership: The 104th and 105th Congresses," paper presented at the Annual Meeting of the American Political Science Association, Washington, D.C., 1997.

7. Dodd and Oppenheimer, "Congress and the Emerging Order," 396–97.

8. James A. Thurber, "Representation, Accountability, and Efficiency in Divided Party Control of Government," in *Understanding the Presidency*, 2d edition, James P. Pfiffner, ed. (New York: Addison Wesley Longman, 2000), 265.

9. Lloyd N. Cutler, "The Cost of Divided Government," *New York Times*, 22 November 1987.

10. James Sundquist, "Needed: A Political Theory for the New Era of Coalition Government in the United States," *Political Science Quarterly* 103 (winter 1988–89): 629.

11. Gary W. Cox and Samuel Kernell, *The Politics of Divided Government* (Boulder: Westview Press, 1991), 4–8.

12. David R. Mayhew, *Divided We Govern* (New Haven: Yale University Press, 1991), 34.

13. George C. Edwards, Andrew Barrett, and Jeffrey Peake, "The Legislative Impact of Divided Government," *American Journal of Political Science* 41, no. 2 (April 1997): 545–63.

14. Sarah A. Binder, "The Dynamics of Legislative Gridlock, 1947–96," *American Political Science Review* 93, no. 3 (September 1999): 519–33.

15. Sarah A. Binder, "Going Nowhere: A Gridlocked Congress?" *The Brookings Review* (winter 2000): 17.

16. Binder, "Going Nowhere," 17.

17. Jon R. Bond and Richard Fleisher, "The Disappearing Middle and the President's Quest for Votes in Congress," *PRG Report* (fall 1999): 7.

18. Burdett A. Loomis, "Civility and Deliberation: A Linked Pair," in *Esteemed Colleagues: Civility and Deliberation in the U.S. Senate*, ed. Burdett A. Loomis (Washington, D.C.: Brookings Institution Press, 2000), 9.

19. Richard E. Cohen, "A Congress Divided," *National Journal*, 26 February 2000: 4.
20. Binder, "The Dynamics of Legislative Gridlock," 526.
21. Sinclair, "Transformational Leader or Faithful Agent?" 5.
22. It was the highest since *Congressional Quarterly* began keeping data in 1954; see *CQ Weekly Reports*, 27 January 1996: 199. According to John Owens's calculations, party voting was the highest since 1905–06. See John Owens, "The Return of Party Government in the U.S. House of Representatives: Central Leadership–Committee Relations in the 104th Congress," *British Journal of Political Science* 27 (1997): 265.
23. Richard Fleisher and Jon R. Bond, "Congress and the President in a Partisan Era," in *Polarized Politics: Congress and the President in a Partisan Era*, ed. Jon R. Bond and Richard Fleisher (Washington, D.C.: CQ Press, 2000), 4.
24. Sinclair, "Transformational Leader or Faithful Agent?" 5.
25. Eric M. Uslaner, *The Decline of Comity in Congress* (Ann Arbor: University of Michigan Press, 1993); Eric M. Uslaner, "Is the Senate More Civil than the House?" in *Esteemed Colleagues: Civility and Deliberation in the U.S. Senate*, ed. Burdett A. Loomis (Washington, D.C.: Brookings Institution Press, 2000), 45.
26. Gary C. Jacobson, "Party Polarization in National Politics: The Electoral Connection," in *Polarized Politics: Congress and the President in a Partisan Era*, ed. Jon R. Bond and Richard Fleisher (Washington, D.C.: CQ Press, 2000), 25–29. See also Gary C. Jacobson, *The Politics of Congressional Elections*, 2d edition (New York: Longman, 2001).
27. David Brady and Morris Fiorina, "Congress in the Era of the Permanent Campaign," in *The Permanent Campaign and Its Future*, ed. Norman Ornstein and Thomas Mann (Washington, D.C.: American Enterprise Institute and Brookings, 2000), 152; David C. King, "The Polarization of American Parties and Mistrust of Government," in *Why People Don't Trust Government*, ed. Joseph S. Nye Jr., Philip D. Zelikow, and David C. King (Cambridge, Mass.: Harvard University Press, 1997), 156.
28. Sarah A. Binder and Steven S. Smith, *Politics or Principle?* (Washington, D.C.: Brookings Institution Press, 1997), 10.
29. Binder and Smith, *Politics or Principle?* 16.
30. Uslaner, *The Decline of Comity in Congress*.
31. Uslaner, "Is the Senate More Civil than the House?" 32–55.
32. Uslaner, "Is the Senate More Civil than the House?" 39.
33. Uslaner, "Is the Senate More Civil than the House?" 48.
34. Loomis, "Civility and Deliberation: A Linked Pair," 6.
35. Brady and Fiorina, "Congress in the Era of the Permanent Campaign," 147.
36. Quoted in Eric Planin and Juliet Eilperin, "No Love Lost for Hastert, Gephardt," *Washington Post*, 20 March 2000: A4.
37. Quoted in Karen Foerstel, "Hastert and the Limits of Persuasion," *CQ Weekly Reports*, 30 September 2000: 2252.
38. Foerstel, "Hastert and the Limits of Persuasion," 2252.
39. Lizette Alvarez and Eric Schmitt, "Disarming Leader at Battle on the Hill," *New York Times*, 9 October 2000: A10.
40. Lizette Alvarez and Eric Schmitt, "Undignified and Screaming, Senate Seeks to Right Itself," *New York Times*, 7 June 2000: A26.
41. Quoted in David Baumann, "The Collapse of the Senate," *National Journal*, 3 June 2000: 1758.

42. Quoted in Erich Schmitt, "When Senators Attack: 'Why, I Oughta . . . ,' " *New York Times*, 11 June 2000: wk7.

43. James P. Pfiffner, "President Clinton and the 103rd Congress: Winning Battles and Losing Wars," in *Rivals for Power: Presidential–Congressional Relations*, ed. James A. Thurber (Washington, D.C.: CQ Press, 1996), 170–90.

44. Quoted in Joe Klein, "Eight Years: Bill Clinton and the Politics of Persistence," *New Yorker*, 16 and 23 October 2000: 209.

45. See James P. Pfiffner, "President Clinton, Newt Gingrich, and the 104th Congress," in *On Parties: Essays Honoring Austin Ranney*, ed. Nelson W. Polsby and Raymond E. Wolfinger (Berkeley: Institute of Governmental Studies, 1999), 135–68.

46. Quoted in Andrew Taylor, "Symbolism and Stalemate Closing Out 106th Congress," *CQ Weekly Report*, 28 October 2000: 2519, 2521.

47. Allan Schick, *The Federal Budget: Politics, Policy, Process* (Washington, D.C.: Brookings Institution Press, 2000), 26–30.

48. Louis Uchitelle, "Taxes, the Market and Luck Underlie the Budget Surplus," *New York Times*, 20 October 2000: 1.

49. Jacobson, "Party Polarization in National Politics," 28.

50. Dick Morris, *Behind the Oval Office* (Los Angeles: Renaissance Books, 1999), 80.

3

Presidential Leadership of Congress: A Functional and Institutional History

Stephen J. Wayne

THE CONSTITUTIONAL DESIGN

The Framers of the American Constitution did not expect or want the president to be chief legislator. They did not expect the president to set Congress's policy agenda except in times of crisis, particularly in situations when Congress is not in session. The emergency triggering mechanism devised by the delegates gives the president the authority to call a special session, provide the Congress with the information it needs on the state of the union, and then, if the president thinks it is desirable, recommend necessary and expedient legislation.

Nor did the Framers anticipate or want the president to be chief domestic policy maker, although, in conjunction with the Senate, the executive was given responsibility to formulate treaties and alliances, that is, participate in the making of foreign policy. But Congress has a role here as well: to enact any implementing legislation including appropriations.

The veto power, a traditional executive prerogative and the president's only other legislative weapon, was intended primarily as a defensive check on a Congress that might intrude into the executive's sphere of authority or as a device the president may use to negate unwise and ill-conceived legislation. It was not intended as a tool for imposing a presidential policy judgment on the legislature. In *Federalist* no. 73, Hamilton writes: "The primary inducement to conferring the power in question [the veto power] upon the Executive is, to enable him to defend himself; the secondary one is to increase the chances in favor of the community against the passing of bad laws through haste, inadvertence, or design."[1] As a hedge against misuse by the president, an overwhelming majority in Congress, a minimum of two-thirds of each house, can override the veto. In this sense, a unified Congress has the last word.

Legislative draftsperson, congressional lobbyist, coalition builder, both inside and outside the government—there is little indication that the Framers expected or wanted the president to assume any of these roles on a regular basis. In fact, there is much more indication that they did not. The policymaking authority of the national government appears in the same constitutional article that gives the Congress "*all legislative powers herein granted.*" Although a president may affect the legislature's exercise of its authority through information, recommendations, and, as a final resort, the veto, the executive cannot assume legislative powers by virtue of any inherent or implied constitutional grant.

Nor did the concept of separation of powers anticipate a major, ongoing legislative role for the president beyond the sharing of appointment and treaty-making powers with the Senate. George Washington, chair of the Constitutional Convention, had limited contact with Congress, and much of it was formal: his State of the Union Addresses, several dinners and events at which members of Congress were present, and three legislative proposals submitted to Congress.[2] Washington even refused a House committee's request for his advice on the grounds that it would violate the constitutional separation.

As far as the roles of lobbyist and coalition builder are concerned, there was no expectation and no formal or informal authority by which the president should or could exercise these roles. The debate over presidential selection suggests that the Framers were fearful of demagogues, equated popular leadership with them, and saw the constitutional structure as a hedge against a plebiscitary president. Going public was viewed as undesirable, even dangerous.[3]

The good news is that the Constitution and the framework it established are alive and well. The bad news is that this framework inhibits presidential leadership of Congress in an era when the public, press, and to some extent the Congress itself expect and want that leadership.[4] Herein lies the president's legislative leadership dilemma.

THE NINETEENTH CENTURY: EXERCISING INFORMAL INFLUENCE

Despite the constitutional investiture of legislative powers in the Congress, the president's legislative role has increased. Jefferson and Jackson used their party leadership to influence Congress. Jefferson met informally with his partisans, had his representatives attend congressional caucus meetings, used the appointment process to satisfy some of their personnel requests, and engaged in social lobbying. Jackson too exerted partisan influence in Congress, but he also threatened and used the veto to get his way. He exercised twelve vetoes, two more than all his predecessors combined. By doing so, he opened up the veto as an instrument of presidential power.

Lincoln too enhanced the president's legislative role, but he did so in times of crisis. So his actions, which include the first bill actually drafted in the White House and sent to Congress as well as emergency measures that he initiated on his own, were not seen as precedents by those who followed him in office. In fact, by the end of the nineteenth century the conventional wisdom, as described by Professor Woodrow Wilson, was that ours was a "congressional government."[5] Wilson saw the president's legislative powers as no greater than his prerogative of the veto.

THE TWENTIETH CENTURY

The President as Policy Initiator

The policy initiatives of Theodore Roosevelt, his Square Deal program, and later Woodrow Wilson's New Freedoms program had much to do with modifying Wilson's initial view of the balance between Congress and the president. But so did the consequences of World War I, particularly budget deficits at home and a larger international role abroad. Although the Senate rejected the Versailles Treaty and League of Nations, it could not prevent future presidents from assuming more active policy-making roles in foreign affairs if they chose to do so, a role that the Supreme Court acknowledged they had the power to exercise in 1936.[6] Legislators did turn to the president for imposing fiscal responsibility. The enactment of the Budget and Accounting Act of 1921 made it a presidential responsibility to provide Congress with an annual executive branch budget.

Franklin Roosevelt's new economic initiatives,[7] his lobbying of Congress, and his public appeals added a new dimension to presidential leadership of Congress, while the Executive Office of the President provided an institutional structure to facilitate the president's expanded legislative presence.[8] Both Truman and Eisenhower continued these roles, also depending on units in the new Executive Office to perform them. Truman converted the State of the Union message into an annual agenda setter for Congress and political address to the country. Eisenhower created the first White House legislative affairs office to explain his program to members of Congress and later, after the Democrats gained control of both houses, to dissuade them from enacting proposals he opposed.[9]

Kennedy and Johnson expanded the president's domestic policy-making sphere to include civil rights and social welfare legislation. They also created policy staffs in the White House to develop priority policy initiatives. Outside task forces generated ideas that were "staffed out" by executive branch personnel under the coordination of the White House, while an expanded congressional legislative operation, working out of the East Wing of the White House, pushed these initiatives on Capitol Hill. In coordination with the Democratic leadership, the White House liaison staff counted heads, twisted arms, and involved the president with committee chairs and other critical members of Congress.[10]

Prioritizing Legislative Proposals

In effect a two-track legislative system had been created with priority legislation on track one, initiated, coordinated, and pushed by the White House, and less important legislation on track two, initiated by the departments, coordinated by the Bureau of the Budget, and monitored by the departments' legislative affairs offices. There was considerable presidential involvement in track one lobbying activities. Johnson, especially, enjoyed the give and take of legislative relations and, according to most reports, was very good at it.[11]

Whether Johnson's civil rights and Great Society programs were enacted because of the president's legislative skills, the Democrats' overwhelming majority in both houses, or public support is difficult to determine. It is clear, however, that the structure of power in Congress in the 1960s, the committee system, controlled by southern Democrats, Johnson's personal relations with them, and the closed-door style of decision making facilitated presidential influence in a way that today's more decentralized, more individualistic, more public congressional decision-making process, particularly the opening of markup sessions to full public view, does not.

From the perspective of the president's legislative goals and operations, the Nixon–Ford presidency was transitional. The White House, enlarged and more centrally managed, particularly under Nixon, continued to have its policy staffs develop, coordinate, and oversee track one legislation. A more politicized, management-oriented, and newly named and structured Office of Management and Budget (OMB) ran the executive clearance processes. The liaison operation continued in much the same manner as it had during previous Democratic administrations.

Differentiating Executive Responsibilities

The centralization of policy making and legislative liaison in the White House permitted the administration to focus its efforts on major priorities, track one, while the OMB coordinated and monitored track two, with the executive departments and agencies expected to shoulder the principal burden of policy formulation, congressional liaison, and if successful, implementation. During the Ford administration, the person who functioned as head of White House operations did not as general practice get involved with congressional matters. Although Donald Rumsfeld had served in Congress and his deputy, and later White House successor, Dick Cheney had worked for him on the Hill, neither played a major legislative role in their capacity as chief of staff.

Carter's refusal to designate a chief of staff at the beginning of his term in office, combined with his own personal reluctance to lobby members of Congress, left legislative liaison initially to Frank Moore, a non-Washingtonian with few congressional contacts and a very small staff. Hamilton Jordan, who served as the president's de facto assistant, functioned briefly as a contact person between the president-elect, and later the White House, and the congressional leadership. But relations were chilly. From the perspective of the Democratic leadership, Jordan's "holier than thou" attitude combined with his and the president's refusal to do politics as usual got Carter's congressional relations off to a very poor start.[12]

Jordan did get involved with the ratification of the Panama Canal Treaty. He was instrumental in organizing and operating from his office an administration task force that coordinated a public education campaign with the administration's lobbying effort in the Senate. The task force operation was eventually institutionalized by Carter in the form of a public liaison office that organized interest and community groups in support of the president's legislative initiatives.

The chief of staff's involvement in legislative relations, however, remained ad hoc until Carter restructured his White House in 1979 and placed Hamilton Jordan in charge. One of Jordan's principal responsibilities was to improve the administration's relations with Congress. He tried but without much success. By then, even Democratic members of Congress were leery about getting too close to the White House, and Jordan became increasingly involved with the president's reelection campaign.[13]

THE CONTEMPORARY PRESIDENCY

Centralized Coordination in the White House

James Baker III, Reagan's first chief of staff, was heavily involved in the formulation and promotion of the president's legislative policy initiatives. Throughout Reagan's first term, Baker ran a legislative strategy group out of his own office to monitor and move the administration's program on Capitol Hill. In addition to the chief of staff, the group included one of Baker's deputies, the policy director from the appropriate Cabinet council, the head of congressional liaison, the president's chief political adviser, and the director of the White House. Meetings, which occurred almost daily, were designed to coordinate the administration's contacts with members of Congress, involving Cabinet members as needed, and link these efforts with the administration's outreach and public relations activities, which were occurring simultaneously. Baker also made it a practice to stay in close touch with the congressional leadership. He promoted the president's program in his daily contacts with the press, with which he would speak on an *off-the-record basis*.[14] Routine legislative matters continued to be handled by the congressional liaison staff.

Donald Regan, Baker's successor as chief of staff, had poorer relations with Congress and limited patience for negotiating with the Republican leadership. Nonetheless, he tried to keep his hands in an array of legislative matters. Regan's penchant for tightly filtering congressional input to the Oval Office proved to be his downfall. Frustrated members of Congress who could not reach the president because of Regan and his aides took a back channel to the Oval Office in the form of anonymous leaks to the press that undercut and infuriated Regan and quickly reduced even further his tolerance for dealing with Congress. The result was a chilly separation that lasted until a new chief of staff, Howard Baker, was named. Baker and his deputy and later successor, Ken Duberstein, both had extensive Hill experience, many contacts, and were well liked, so relations improved even though the Congress fell under complete Democratic control.

George Bush was not as successful in dealing with Congress. Part of the reason stemmed from his lack of a comprehensive legislative agenda and his focus on foreign affairs. But part also stemmed from chief of staff problems. As in the Reagan White House, Bush's top aides, including Chief of Staff John Sununu, were heavily involved in legislative matters that affected the president's initiatives on the budget, education, and the environment. According to one senior official who was also involved in these issues, "Sununu got right down into the weeds with the Clean Air Act. He participated in practically every aspect of the policy from interagency lobbying to lobbying the Congress."[15] Similarly, he was also a major participant in the deficit reduction compromise that forced Bush to recant his "read my lips, no new taxes" pledge. In fact, Sununu's interest in the domestic agenda was so great that a high White House official has noted sarcastically, "We had to remind him [Sununu] of the Cabinet's role in the domestic arena."[16]

But Sununu developed a congressional problem similar to Regan's. He antagonized members of Congress who perceived him as frequently abrasive, condescending, and intolerant. After Sununu fell from grace, he was replaced by Sam Skinner, former secretary of transportation. Having little congressional experience of his own and lacking a close relationship to the president, Skinner had difficulty mediating between Congress and the president. W. Henson Moore, a former member of Congress and Skinner's deputy, became in practice the principal White House liaison, particularly for Republicans who knew him from his days on the Hill.[17] After the Persian Gulf War ended, however, Bush's relations with Congress deteriorated. Skinner and Moore were replaced by James Baker, who was forced to focus almost entirely on the president's reelection campaign, not congressional affairs as he had during the Reagan administration.

Despite the difficulties Bush's chiefs of staff encountered in their dealings with Congress, members continued to look to the chief of staff, not the head of liaison, as the principal go-between with the president on the priority issues. This presented a problem in the early months of the Clinton administration because of the disorder in the White House. In addition to the president, who was heavily involved in policy formulation and promotion, Chief of Staff Mac McLarty, Head of Communications George Stephanopoulos, Liaison Head Robert Paster, economic adviser Robert Rubin, Treasury Secretary Lloyd Bentsen, and Vice President Al Gore also participated in congressional negotiations on the economic stimulus and deficit reduction plans, often working at cross-purposes with one another.

It was not until the defeat of the economic stimulus bill by a Senate filibuster that the White House tried to impose order on its legislative operations. Bentsen was designated as point man to deal with the House and Senate tax committees on the deficit reduction bill, Assistant Treasury Secretary Robert Altman was put in charge of a "war room" to forge and promote a coherent public position, and Clinton continued to engage in behind-the-scenes lobbying for the measure. In fact, the president attributed the defeat of his economic stimulus bill in the Senate to his delegation of Senator Robert Byrd as floor leader for the bill. According to David Gergen, the lesson Clinton learned from this experience was to keep control himself and get the bills through on his own.[18]

In addition to Clinton, Bentsen, and Altman, McLarty also dealt with representatives and senators whom he knew from his days as an oil executive. Stephanopoulos has also reported that he too was a critical cog in the congressional operation: "My official function was to get the right people on the phone, to record the deals and ensure they got done, to pass bulletins back to the Hill and relay the responses back to Clinton. But I also served as coach and companion, prompting the president during his calls with handwritten notes, gingerly urging him to do a little less listening and a little more demanding, helping him decipher the hidden meanings in a member's words."[19] Meanwhile, Paster and his staff continued to scout Congress and lobby on behalf of the president. Paster maintains that his efforts were continually undercut by others in the White House, notably McLarty and Bentsen. He was blindsided by their deals.[20] Bentsen saw the problem differently. Bob Woodward writes that the treasury secretary "felt Clinton had made it too desirable for congressmen to hold out, to appear to make up their minds in the end game when they had maximum leverage. Clinton needed more discipline and should not keep paying off the holdouts."[21]

The legislative affairs office lost credibility during this period. It was clear that Paster was not speaking for the president. As a consequence, end runs were encouraged; partisan support turned to neutrality in order to "roll" Clinton. The president's reputation suffered. Health care had to be delayed.

Although an amended deficit reduction bill was finally enacted, the costs, measured in terms of the president's relations with Congress, were very high. House Democrats, forced to vote in favor of an energy usage tax, were livid when the administration backed off it in the Senate.[22] Democratic divisions in the Senate, heightened by the deficit reduction negotiations and debate, exploded into full public view. Clinton's relationships with Senators Boren, Kerrey, Moynihan, and Shelby turned into personal animosities that lasted well through the administration. Rolling Clinton continued to be the most popular sport on Capitol Hill. In fact, it assumed bipartisan dimensions, which is one of the few times that Democratic and Republican members of Congress seemed to have a common political objective.

In late spring 1994, Clinton began the restructuring of his White House operation with the appointment of Leon Panetta as chief of staff. Panetta attempted to impose order on the administration's relations with Congress. He personally played a key role in negotiations with the congressional leadership, especially on budget matters that were salient from 1995 on. Panetta has described his contact in the following way: "I knew most of the players up there. I would go up and brief our caucus. . . . I would go to their luncheons. I would go to their meetings. Usually we tried to tie it to major issues [and votes] that were coming up so that we could make the case for why they should support the administration."[23] Panetta was also conscious of the need to coordinate his activities with the legislative affairs office: "I had to be very careful that I didn't just go out there and do it on my own without coordinating with the people who had a responsibility. And they also had a lot of responsibility to come up with a lot of the backup material, . . . they had a responsibility to provide all the material and supporting documents every time we developed policy."[24]

Clinton continued to stay heavily involved in legislative matters. He used the White House to lobby legislators in order to maximize his persuasive advantage. Panetta noted, "If you bring a member down to the White House into the Oval Office, one on one with the president, it's a much more effective way to lobby a member than to have your presidential assistant for legislative affairs go up there or even the secretary of state go up there. It's just much more powerful, . . . and there's the ambiance. There aren't a lot of people who tell the president to go to Hell when they are in the Oval Office."[25] Besides, he added, "the people that come down from the Hill . . . always like to be able to ride up there and have the press see them walk into the West Wing. So if you want to give the meeting a higher profile, . . . you usually have it at the White House. If you want to low key it and really talk business, I found that it was just much better for me to go up to the Hill."[26]

Panetta's successors as chief of staff, Erskin Bowles and John Podesta, tried to operate in much the same manner. They too engaged in negotiations with the congressional leadership; they too acted as spokespeople for the administration; they too coordinated the president's legislative operation on major initiatives, continuing the practice of recent administrations of centralizing control of the legislative operation on major policy issues in the White House, at or near the Oval Office.

Mobilizing Public Opinion

The development of institutional mechanisms to build public support for the president's legislative proposals began during the Nixon administration. Nixon was the first president to have an office of communications in the White House to control the flow of information into and out of the White House. He was also the first to appoint a liaison to business and labor. The president saw these outreach efforts as essential to leverage the Democratic Congress, buttress the administration against its real and imagined political enemies, and provide a broad constituency on which to build his reelection campaign.

The communications office, business and labor liaison, and a more coordinated media operation worked in tandem with one another to build support for the president's legislative priorities, both domestic and foreign. This institutional structure, based in the White House, provided the president with a mechanism for "going public."[27] However, continuing public divisions over the Vietnam War and the events of Watergate prevented the Nixon administration from reaping the benefits of these outreach activities in the president's abbreviated second term.

Nonetheless, the foundation had been set. And the communications technology was available. The representational expansion of the Washington political community with its proliferation of single-issue interest groups, weaker political parties, and partisan division between the White House and Congress all provided incentives for presidents to reach beyond Congress to influence it.

Expanding Outreach Activities

Ford and Carter, however, took limited forays into the public arena. After his approval as vice president, Nelson Rockefeller hosted a series of public forums around the country to formulate a domestic legislative agenda for the administration in anticipation of the president's 1976 State of the Union Address and his subsequent election campaign. Rockefeller's proposals, however, were too liberal and government oriented for most congressional Republicans who refused to sponsor or even support the proposed legislation. Their rejection of the Rockefeller agenda combined with their criticism of him personally, and Ford's unwillingness to back his vice president led to Rockefeller's decision not to run as the Republican vice presidential candidate in 1976.

Carter's election in 1976 combined with continued Democratic control of Congress promised a return to the halcyon days of the 1960s with unified party government, but in practice Carter faced many of the same difficulties that his two Republican predecessors faced and for many of the same reasons. Congress had decentralized power; powerful single interests had organized, professionalized, and proliferated; parties had become weaker; and the press was more critical. All of these developments worked to inhibit presidential leadership of Congress. Carter's own failings as a legislator, his refusal to play the game of politics, his unwillingness to lobby individual members of Congress, and his comprehensive agenda, introduced at the same time, which got stuck in the labyrinth of committees and subcommittees, also contributed to his problems with Congress.

These problems, well publicized by the news media, forced the administration to modify the way it dealt with Congress. Not only did the coordination of key legislative lobbying become more centralized in the White House, but outreach activities were expanded. By 1978, the Carter White House had two additional liaison offices concerned directly or indirectly with Congress: the public liaison office, which linked and coordinated interest group activity for the president, and the intergovernmental affairs office, which had a similar mission for and with state and local governments. A political affairs office was added during the Reagan administration to help mobilize partisan support for the president.

Establishing the Permanent White House–Based Public Relations Campaign

The people who advised Ronald Reagan understood the lessons of Ford's and Carter's legislative experiences. Setting priorities, cycling issues, packaging proposals, and going both inside and outside simultaneously were seen as key to the president's policy successes. Moreover, Reagan needed to adopt a hands-on style for selling his policy even though he had not utilized a hands-on approach for making it. To achieve these objectives, the Reagan White House brought in skilled media managers to develop and implement a communications strategy. Michael Deaver, deputy chief of staff, oversaw the operation and was the key aide for coordinating the public relations campaign with the administration's other legislative activities on major presidential priorities.

Using the president as the key salesman, the Reagan "PR" campaigns consisted of speeches, travels, and appearances before organized groups, all choreographed for television. The objective was to mount a dual campaign in pictures and words that the news networks would feel compelled to air. Much preparation and coordination characterized these campaigns. Here is how political scientist Samuel Kernell describes the components of the Reagan media-oriented operation:

> Polls were taken; speeches incorporating the resulting insights were drafted; the press was briefed, either directly or via leaks. Meanwhile in the field, the ultimate recipients of the president's message, members of Congress, were softened up by presidential travel into their states and districts and by grass-root lobbying campaigns, initiated and orchestrated by the White House but including the RNC [Republican National Committee] and sympathetic business organizations.[28]

Major speeches were timed to coincide with key votes. Prior to the speeches, the public liaison office working with outside groups, such as the Business Roundtable, would establish telephone banks that went into action the moment the speech ended. By generating a seemingly spontaneous and favorable public response and by doing so on a constituency-by-constituency basis, the White House was able to provide Democrats with political cover to support the president.

The Reagan model has set the tone for today's public legislative presidency, although it was Clinton, not Bush, who followed the strategy most closely. The Bush administration was much less desirous of conducting permanent PR campaigns. Much of the reason lay with the president himself. Bush lacked Reagan's skills and confidence as a communicator. He was critical of his predecessor's scripted presidency. Moreover, with fewer domestic priorities and an emphasis on foreign affairs, Bush had less need to play the outside game with Congress. He could and did let his actions and the press coverage of them speak for themselves. The president's numerous trips abroad, his diplomatic initiatives, his administration's responses to international humanitarian crises, and its use of force in Panama and the Persian Gulf presented the presidency in a way that worked to Bush's advantage so long as there were no pressing domestic issues. His approval ratings, which exceeded Reagan's during most of their first two years in office, suggest that the public was content with his nontelegenic presidency. However, as economic conditions began to deteriorate after the war in the Persian Gulf was concluded, the president was unable to change his style of governing. Lacking a domestic agenda, influence in Congress, and a strategy to build public support, the Bush administration floundered. A president who had used his actions and events, as highlighted by the news media, to define his presidency now found his inactions and the out-of-control economic events, also highlighted by the news media, leading to a very different conclusion about his leadership skills.

Clinton should have learned from Carter and Bush. At the beginning of his presidency, he claimed to be following Reagan's legislative strategy, but his fragile political mandate (he was elected with only 43 percent of the vote), his own inexperience, magnified by his White House's blunders, the administration's circumvention of the White House press corps, and the diverse and often conflicting economic policy proposals that were made or leaked to the press indicated a presidency in chaos and a White House that lacked central coordination. The president's first two legislative priorities suffered as a consequence. His economic stimulus bill was defeated by a Senate filibuster, and his deficit reduction plan was significantly and publicly modified before it passed the Democrat-controlled Congress by the narrowest margins, two votes in the House and one vote in the Senate (the vice president's, which broke the tie). Although the administration did have some legislative successes in its first year, the North American Free Trade Agreement (NAFTA) being the most noteworthy, most of the policy achievements resulted from Democratic congressional initiatives that the president supported, not the other way around.

Although Clinton managed to gain approval for NAFTA, he paid a heavy price for his arm-twisting and political trading. In order to secure sufficient Democratic support to ensure the bill's passage, Clinton and his legislative aides literally had to go door to door in the House, making promises to on-the-fence Democrats. In some case, exemptions from the treaty for crops grown in their districts were made; in others, financial help was pledged for the next election cycle. The horse-trading, accompanied by a public relations campaign, concluded with a 234 to 200 vote in favor of the agreement. In the end, 102 Democrats voted with the president despite opposition from many of their key constituents: organized labor, public interest, and environmental groups. But Clinton's legislative reputation was tarnished in the process, particularly among those who were associated with the liberal wing of his party. His attempt to placate this wing by holding fast to the major components of the administration's health care reform package contributed to the latter's defeat.

The second year of Clinton's legislative presidency, marred by the demise of health care reform and the subsequent Republican takeover of Congress, forced the administration to reinvent itself, the president to change his policy priorities and positions, and the White House to modify the way it did business with Congress. Instead of setting the congressional agenda, the president was forced to react to the Republicans' "Contract with America." Instead of operating as head of government, the president was forced into the role of head of state, a role in which public relations are emphasized. Instead of continuing to focus on domestic policy, the president turned to foreign affairs. In making these adjustments, as painful as they were, Clinton and his aides finally figured out how to use the president's bully pulpit, presidential seal, and White House communications office to better advantage. What followed was a public relations extravaganza, as calculated and as orchestrated as Reagan's, but one that was very different.

Whereas the Reagan White House used its outreach and public relations to build support for the president's congressional initiatives, the Clinton White House used them to build support for the president's legislative vetoes. Whereas the Reagan White House emphasized the distinctiveness of the president's legislative goals, the need to reverse the course of government, the Clinton White House repositioned the president on Republican issues, claimed the middle ground for itself, and put the president in a position to take credit for legislative successes such as the balanced budget, welfare reform, and incremental health care policies while blaming the Republicans for its legislative failures.

The Reagan and Clinton models are similar in that both used foreign travel to enhance the president's image, particularly in light of the scandals that afflicted both presidents in their second terms. Both PR campaigns showed an active and powerful president, thereby countering the allegations that they would be crippled as lame ducks with the opposition party controlling both houses of Congress. Clinton also took advantage of man-made and natural disasters to play the role of crisis manager and empathic leader, a people-oriented president. In short, both White Houses used the public relations presidency to offset their policy weaknesses and enhance presidential images. The public responded with high approval ratings.

The Rebirth of the Permanent Campaign as an Instrument of the Legislative Presidency

In 1995, the Clinton presidency was redesigned within the context of public opinion and public relations. A new team of political operatives joined with ongoing White House staff to recast Clinton as a plebiscitary president. With the pulse of the public measured by continuous polling, the administration repositioned itself within the political center and used its presidential podium to cast the congressional Republicans as extreme and mean-spirited and to stereotype their policy orientation as one designed to benefit the rich. Focus groups were used to capture emotionally laden words and phrases, while presidential travels, meetings, and events highlighted the active, publicly oriented Clinton presidency.

Much of the White House–generated public activity was intended to benefit Clinton politically, to set the stage for his reelection, maintain his high approval ratings, and shield him from personal scandal. Occasionally, however, public campaigns were designed to help the president with legislative policy goals. Clinton had attributed the defeat of his health care initiative and, later, fast-track authority to the administration's failure to mount and maintain a successful public relations campaign for these issues, while in the case of health care, opponents of the Clinton plan, such as the Health Insurance Association of America, spent in excess of $13 million on advertising to defeat his plan. Obviously, there were other factors that contributed to their defeat, but the president saw public relations as the key variable.[29] The lessons of these failures were not lost on the administration when the president proposed normalizing trade relations with China in 2000.

THE PUBLIC RELATIONS CAMPAIGN FOR NORMALIZING TRADE WITH CHINA: DID IT MAKE THE DIFFERENCE?

It was Clinton's last year in office. Not only was he a lame duck, but he had suffered through a fourteen-month impeachment ordeal. China had made threatening statements toward Taiwan prior to the Taiwanese elections in 1999; the Chinese government had repressed a religious movement within the country and forced Tibet's Dalai Lama into exile; it had a terrible human rights record and an abysmal one on the environment. Yet Clinton stressed the importance of this initiative and tied it to his legacy as well as to his remaining political clout. The White House deemed a major public campaign as critical to the success of the China initiative.

The campaign began with the president's State of the Union Address given on 23 January 2000. In the lengthy speech in which the president provided a laundry list of domestic and foreign policy goals, he said, "Passing normal trade relations will open China's markets to the United States and will promote the cause of change in China." Six weeks later, the administration introduced legislation to grant normal trade status to China. An accompanying letter from the president stated the administration's principal argument—that trade would benefit the United States and at the same time give China incentive for improving labor conditions, respecting human rights, and promoting sounder environmental policies.

In the quiet phase of the China campaign, the president began a series of meetings with members of Congress to make the case for extending permanent most-favored-nation trading status to China. These meetings continued and accelerated as the public phase of the campaign got under way in April 2000. Altogether, the president met with over 100 members of Congress, some on a one-to-one basis in the days before the vote. In these meetings Clinton let it be known that Democrats would *not* be let off the hook on the basis of their constituency interests, as he had let them off on the issue of fast-track authority.

A special White House task force was created to coordinate the initiative. It was led by Commerce Secretary William Dailey, who had run the NAFTA campaign, and included John Podesta, chief of staff; Steve Richetti, one of his deputies; and Charles Brain, the head of legislative affairs. Other members of the group were Cabinet Secretaries Dan Glickman (Agriculture), Madeleine Albright (State), and Alexis Herman (Labor) and U.S. Trade Representative Charlene Barshefsky. All were charged with working with their organized clienteles on the issue as well as using their congressional contacts to build support for the administration's position. Staffs from their departments as well as from the White House operated a twenty-four-hour "war room" to react to events and monitor the leanings of members of Congress.[30] Even Federal Reserve Chairman Alan Greenspan was called into action to present pro-normalization arguments in speeches he gave before various economic groups. Furthermore, over the course of the public relations effort, the White House released nineteen statements by Cabinet secretaries and administration officials as well as twenty-one letters and supporting statements by congressional leaders, former presidents, former secretaries of commerce, former trade representatives, and other former governmental officials, plus thirteen editorials and op-ed pieces, all of which appeared on a separate website created for the China initiative (http://www.chinapntr.gov) and linked to the White House site (http://www.whitehouse.gov).

Inside Congress, many deals were struck. The administration promised to support an executive commission to assess the plight of American workers hurt by freer trade and another one to monitor human rights in China; to win the backing of the Congressional Black Caucus, the administration supported a bill to expand trade with Africa and the Caribbean basin. Democratic members of Congress who claimed that a vote in favor of normalizing relations would hurt them politically and financially received promises of business or White House–facilitated fund-raising events, some to include the president. Invitations for trips on Air Force One, state dinners, even a new zip code for a reluctant representative were offered (and accepted) as inducements for a pro-China vote.

Dailey organized the outreach activities. Early in the campaign, he put together a working group, consisting of representatives of the public and private sectors, to lobby for the legislation. Pro-business groups such as the Business Roundtable and Chamber of Commerce spent upward of $15 million on advertisements and lobbying efforts, which included coordinated telephone and mail campaigns and the use of professional lobbyists to speak to members with whom they knew and did business. *Washington Post* reporter John Burgess describes the effort as "one of the biggest lobbying extravaganzas in memory. The Business Roundtable targeted 88 congressional districts, hiring 60 trade organizers to work the issue full time. The U.S. Chamber of Commerce got to work in 66 districts."[31]

Remembering the controversy over laundered Chinese contributions that found their way into the 1996 Clinton reelection campaign and not wanting anti-Chinese feelings to be an excuse for opposing the trade bill, the administration urged the Chinese government to maintain a low profile during the campaign. American businesses, which stood to benefit from increased trade with China, took up the slack and made the case for normalizing trade.

The opposition to the trade agreement was similar to that of NAFTA and fast track. It came from labor unions, especially the teamsters and United Auto Workers, fearful that the trade would cost them jobs and critical of labor conditions in China; it also came from human rights advocates, public interest groups, and pro-democracy and environmental groups angry with China's policies on child and prison labor, its disregard for safety and environmental concerns, and its policies regarding Taiwan and Tibet. These groups argued that the United States would exercise more leverage on these issues with the Chinese government if the trade issue came up annually.

A large campaign was mounted by these diverse groups. Their experts testified against the legislation; 5,000 teamsters descended on Washington to protest the bill; union organizers and labor lobbyists contacted Democratic members of Congress who had large labor constituencies. But the efforts of anti-normalization groups paled by comparison with those of the proponents. In the end, seventy-three Democrats joined 164 Republicans to pass the bill in the House. Although the number of Democrats fell short of the administration's goal of 100, it was still thirty more than the forty-three Democrats who voted to give the president fast-track authority.

How important was the PR campaign to the enactment of the legislation? It is difficult to answer this question without candidly interviewing all the members of Congress. But candor is a tricky commodity. Those in elected office tend to give certain "legitimate" explanations for their votes. For example, presidential arm-twisting is not usually perceived as a valid reason for voting for the president's position, but presidential concessions that impact on a legislative district may be seen as a more legitimate factor. Similarly, strong constituency opinion as expressed in congressional correspondence, in telephone calls, or by groups with large membership bases within the district are deemed acceptable reasons to give for voting a certain way, but the data on which these opinions are based are often incomplete and without a basis for ascertaining representativeness. Public opinion polls in which accuracy can be estimated are usually too expensive to be done on a constituency-by-constituency basis on most issues. National surveys are available, although their influence on congressional voting seems tenuous at best.

On the China question, the polls reveal considerable ambiguity. Gallup polls show a small increase in the level of public interest on the news about China and the World Trade Organization, a related but not identical issue, during the month preceding the House vote.[32] Support for normalizing trade relations also increased. Gallup asked the following question three times in 2000: "Would you favor or oppose Congress passing a law that would normalize trade relations between China and the United States and that would allow China to join the World Trade organization—or are you unsure?" The responses are given in table 3.1.[33] However, when people were asked to choose one of the two positions that were debated in Congress—(1) the United States should increase trade with China *now* because doing so will promote more economic, political, and religious freedoms in the country versus (2) the United States should *not* increase trade with China until the Chi-

Table 3.1 Responses to the Following Gallup Poll Question: "Would you favor or oppose Congress passing a law that would normalize trade between China and the United States and that would allow China to join the World Trade Organization—or are you unsure?"

Date	Favor	Oppose	No Opinion
25–26 January 2000	50	40	10
7–9 April 2000	43	45	12
18–21 May 2000	56	37	7

Source: http://www.gallup.com/poll/indicators/IndChina.asp.

nese government gives more economic, political, and religious freedom to its citizens—they chose the second by a substantial margin, 62 to 33 percent.[34]

The polling data hardly indicate a groundswell of public support that would compel members, whatever their motivation, to vote for the president's position. So why, then, was the president successful? Was it the amount of Republican support or the Democratic votes that were critical? Did the president win because of the substance of the issue, the policy area, or foreign affairs, or was it his own personal resolve and lobbying that did the trick? Was it the inside game or the outside public relations campaign that mattered most? The safest guess is that it was probably some combination of these factors that contributed to the president's victory.

CONCLUSION

Are administrations correct in believing that major public relations campaigns are part and parcel of today's legislative presidency? Although it is impossible to generalize from this one example, I believe that they are. What follows is a speculative conclusion. The public relations campaign seems important for several reasons:

1. It signifies to Congress the high priority that the president places on an issue. Members of Congress cannot mistake it for just another vote or just another issue on which the president has a position.
2. It brings the issue to the attention of more people than would otherwise be the case, thereby upping the ante for members of Congress.
3. It enables the president to use his "bully pulpit" to advantage, to define the issue in favorable terms and then have others, including himself, reinforce that definition. The other side is usually unable to argue as

loudly and clearly because it lacks the reach and status of the president's pulpit.

4. In the particular area of foreign policy, the president maximizes his advantage by going public because it puts the burden of proof on those who would go against the president in an area in which he is expected to lead.

The negative side of going public, however, is that compromise may be made more difficult; electoral calculations may become more salient; interest group participation may unleash forces that an administration cannot control, as was the case with health care reform; and raising the stakes may make defeat more politically, and perhaps psychologically, devastating.

NOTES

1. Alexander Hamilton, "Federalist, No. 73," in *The Federalist* (New York: Modern Library, 1961), 477.

2. Louis Fisher, *The Politics of Shared Power* (Washington, D.C.: Congressional Quarterly, 1993), 18, 29.

3. See Jeffrey K. Tulis, *The Rhetorical Presidency* (Princeton: Princeton University Press, 1987), 25–49.

4. Charles O. Jones, in his book *The Presidency in a Separated System* (Washington, D.C.: Brookings Institution Press, 1994), draws the opposite conclusion: it is good news that the Constitution constrains the president's legislative leadership but bad news that the public, Congress, and the president do not understand, much less appreciate, a more constrained presidential role.

5. Woodrow Wilson, *Congressional Government* (New York: Meridian Books, 1885).

6. In *United States v. Curtiss Wright Corporation* (299 U.S. 304, 1936) the Supreme Court acknowledges the president as "sole organ of the federal government in the field of international relations" with constitutionally based "plenary and exclusive power" within the realm of foreign affairs.

7. In the first phase of the New Deal, Roosevelt submitted to Congress an emergency banking bill, Truth in Security Act, Agricultural Adjustment Act, National Industrial Recovery Act, and Federal Deposit Insurance Corporation Act, to name but some of his initiatives, to deal with the exigencies of the Great Depression. In the second phase, from 1934 to 1936, Roosevelt got a Democratic Congress to enact the Wagner Act, Social Security Act, and Soil Conservation and Domestic Allotments Act, as well as the National Labor Relations Act. New bureaucracies were also created to implement this legislation and provide for ongoing regulatory activities.

8. It was during this period that the legislative clearance and enrolled bill processes were established by the Bureau of the Budget to coordinate and control the executive departments and agencies. See Stephen J. Wayne, *The Legislative Presidency* (New York: Harper and Row, 1978), 70–107.

9. Wayne, *The Legislative Presidency*, 41–42.

10. The liaison office also began to service members' constituency needs, thereby necessitating an increase in size.

11. However, George C. Edwards III has found that Johnson's legislative success on a whole (as measured by the percent of legislative support he received on all bills in which he took a public position) was not much greater than Carter's even though Carter was seen as a much less effective legislator by Congress, the press, and the public. As a consequence, Edwards contends that legislative skills are overrated as an instrument of presidential power and that they do not have a systemic effect on increasing congressional support for the president, although he admits that in individual cases they may matter. See George C. Edwards III, *At the Margins* (New Haven: Yale University Press, 1989), 176–89.

I contend that Edwards's methodological assumptions and his aggregate analysis of roll-call voting patterns force these conclusions. For a discussion of the limitation of this type of analysis of presidential influence in Congress, see my response in *The Legislative Presidency*, 168–72.

12. Speaker Tip O'Neill derisively referred to Jordan as "Hamilton Jerkin" and refused to have anything to do with him after a much publicized incident in which Jordan cavalierly refused to satisfy the speaker's request for seats to inaugural activities.

13. Charles O. Jones, *The Trusteeship Presidency* (Baton Rouge: Louisiana State University Press, 1988), 114.

14. Interview, Presidency Research Group's Transition Project. Note that the description of the role of the chief of staff's office in legislative policy making is based in large part on interviews conducted by Martha Kumar for the Presidency Research Group's Transition Project. Interviewees were promised that there would be no quotations with attribution unless and until they consent to allow their interviews to become part of the public record. Accordingly, I have identified only those officials who had provided that consent at the time this chapter was written.

15. Interview, Presidency Research Group's Transition Project.

16. Interview, Presidency Research Group's Transition Project.

17. W. Henson Moore, interview, Presidency Research Group's Transition Project, 15 October 1999.

18. David Gergen, *Eyewitness to Power* (New York: Simon and Schuster, 2000), 278.

19. George Stephanopoulos, *All Too Human* (Boston: Little, Brown, 1999), 177.

20. Bob Woodward, *The Agenda* (New York: Simon and Schuster, 1994), 194–95, 231–32, 319.

21. Woodward, *The Agenda*, 297.

22. Woodward, *The Agenda*, 231.

23. Leon Panetta, interview, Presidency Research Group's Transition Project, 4 May 2000.

24. Panetta, interview. Panetta added: "Anytime I was dealing with something on Capitol Hill, I would normally call that person (the president's assistant for legislative affairs) into my office so that they would know what I was doing and were supportive of it."

25. Panetta, interview.

26. Panetta, interview.

27. For an extended discussion of the ongoing public phenomenon, see Samuel Kernell, *Going Public*, 3d edition (Washington, D.C.: Congressional Quarterly, 1997).

28. Kernell, *Going Public*, 169–70.

29. Health care reform lost in part because the administration did not mount a coordinated effort. A separate health care group, which did not include most of the president's principal West Wing aides, managed the bill and oversaw the public relations campaign. Although President Clinton delivered a major address on health care before Congress in September 1993, the actual legislation did not arrive until almost one month later. The bill, large and complex, made it difficult to sell but easy to attack. Meanwhile, as the president's focus was diverted by foreign policy matters, Mrs. Clinton became the public advocate for the bill and the major critic of those industries that opposed it. Her involvement, her advocacy, and her criticism made compromise difficult. No single person coordinated the administration's campaign as the opposition to the plan mounted, the Harry and Louise ads were aired, and Congress was increasingly divided over various health care proposals. With the opponents of the plan spending heavily to defeat it, with the administration unable to organize a counterattack, and with the 1994 election approaching and the Republicans seeing the demise of health care as the road to their electoral success, the proposal died on the floor of Congress, and with it, Democratic control of both houses.

The fast-track problem was also magnified by the absence of a public relations campaign amid the bitter politics of the Monica Lewinsky affair. The administration claimed that it was surprised by events that brought the legislation to the floor of the Senate earlier than expected. Without the time to mount a full-scale public relations campaign, the president was forced to lobby for it, mostly behind closed doors. Because he had forced many reluctant Democrats to vote for NAFTA against their own best political judgment, Clinton let it be known that he would not do so for fast track. This concession weakened his position; he could not gain sufficient votes by simply making deals. Besides, the publicizing of such deals by those who benefited from them made the president look like he was buying votes, an undesirable public perception.

30. Alex Simendinger, "Inside the White House Trade 'War Room,' " *National Journal*, 25 March 2000: 941.

31. John Burgess, "A Winning Combination: Money, Message and Clout," *Washington Post*, 25 May 2000: A4.

32. Gallup asked the following question in two national surveys, the first conducted on 5–7 May and the second conducted on 18–20 May 2000: "How closely have you been following the news about China and the World Trade Organization?" The results are as follows:

Date	*Very closely*	*Somewhat closely*	*Not too closely*	*Not at all closely*	*No opinion*
5–7 May	7	22	31	39	1
18–21 May	8	33	34	24	1

Source: http://www.gallup.com/poll/indicators/IndChina.asp.

33. See http://www.gallup.com/poll/indicators/IndChina.asp.

34. The poll was conducted on 18–20 May 2000, and it is available on the Gallup website, http://www.gallup.com/poll/indicators/IndChina.asp.

4

The Presidency and Congressional Leadership

Roger H. Davidson

One has only to study a map of Washington to learn how the Founders envisioned the business of governing that was to be conducted in the capital city they had conceived. After consulting with several of the Constitution's authors, Major Pierre l'Enfant, their French architect, laid out the spaces where the governmental branches would operate. As the first branch of government, Congress was at the city's apex—occupying a single large building on the highest promontory, Jenkins Hill. On a flat area a mile or so to the northwest, the executive mansion would form the hub of a neighborhood of departments and their employees. A stately avenue would link the two parts of the city, permitting ceremonial meetings and exchanges of communications. Characteristically, the Capitol building faced east, and the executive faced northward, their backs turned on each other.[1]

Collaboration between the two elective branches lies at the heart of the successes—and failures—of our government. The relationship has often been stormy; rarely has it been wholly benign. The two branches are charged with distinctive duties and serve divergent constituencies. When constitutional scholar Edward S. Corwin described the Constitution as an "invitation to struggle," he was referring to foreign policy; the phrase applies even more to domestic policy making.[2]

The constitutional powers of the two branches are distinctive but not actually separated. The assent of both branches is normally required for major policy enactments; neither can function without the other. Presidents help set the congressional agenda and influence the content of laws through a combination of persuasion and veto threats. By the same token, the executive branch—its size, organization, and mission—is shaped by Congress.

BOTH ENDS OF THE AVENUE

Following the Framers' design, presidents and legislators have repeatedly struggled to bridge the distance between the two branches. Alexander Hamilton, the first treasury secretary, sought mastery over Congress in order to enact his plans for financial stability and economic growth. Thomas Jefferson criticized such efforts to exercise influence over Congress; but as president he sought mastery by courting his fellow partisans, especially in the House of Representatives.

Most, though not all, of Jefferson's successors followed his example. Indeed, presidents with activist agendas cannot avoid asserting their prerogatives in the legislative process. During the nineteenth century, presidents and Congresses tended to work at arm's length, although strong presidents—Jefferson, Andrew Jackson, and Abraham Lincoln—actively pushed legislation. Lincoln's death in 1865 brought on an era of presidential eclipse—"congressional government," Woodrow Wilson called it—that lasted for more than a generation; but post–Civil War trends, including economic growth, social complexity, and an expanding public sector, laid the groundwork for later legislative activism.

The modern model of the president as legislative leader is primarily a twentieth-century innovation. Wilson and the two Roosevelts, Theodore and Franklin, all sent lengthy legislative agendas to Capitol Hill. Wilson revived the practice of delivering his State of the Union Addresses in person to ensure public attention and press coverage. For more than half a century—indeed, ever since the end of World War II—everyone has come to expect that presidents will lay out their legislative priorities. Presidents who fail to present legislative agendas or who appear simply to defer to congressional initiatives invite criticism that they are weak or ineffective.

Framing national agendas, in fact, is what the presidency is all about. Within the White House, priorities have to be established for using the president's precious commodities of time, energy, and influence. Setting a national policy agenda poses the same problem writ large: how to guide other players rather than be swept along by their initiatives. This is the essence of leadership for all presidents with ambitious programmatic goals—Wilson, the two Roosevelts, Lyndon Johnson, Ronald Reagan, and even Bill Clinton. Reagan's first year in the White House in 1981, for example, provides a modern-day model of leadership through agenda control. Clinton's first year, in contrast, yielded mixed results: by setting forth a broad array of initiatives, Clinton dissipated his energies and gave opposing coalitions multiple opportunities for obstruction.

Presidents communicate their agendas in a variety of ways—not only in State of the Union Addresses but in special messages, reports, and required documents such as the annual budget. Through these devices presidents strive to highlight priorities, provoke public debate, stimulate congressional deliberation, and exhort for attention and support.

For congressional leaders, maintaining at least minimal working relationships with incumbent presidents is an important element of their jobs. For one thing, leaders are expected to handle presidential requests and initiatives. This expectation is underscored when the president and the leader are of the same party or when a crisis arises that threatens the nation's security. For another thing, leaders' access to the White House can provide extra leverage for dealing with colleagues. Knowledge of the president's intentions and the ability to get the president's ear are valuable attributes that set leaders apart from most of their colleagues most of the time and help them build coalitions within their respective chambers.

Presidents have consulted informally with prominent senators ever since the first Congress, and regular meetings have been held since Theodore Roosevelt's time. Historians tend to believe that modern leadership posts, at least in the Senate, emerged in response to the need for a regular channel of communication between the White House and Capitol Hill. Strong leadership has been more urgent in the larger House of Representatives, and liaison with the White House is a key element in the de facto job descriptions of the speaker and the majority and minority floor leaders.

THE EVOLUTION OF CONGRESSIONAL LEADERSHIP

After the 2000 elections, there was much beating of breasts and rending of garments among commentators about the expected stalemate resulting from the public's mixed verdict. For those who are concerned about such electoral indecision, I propose that we examine another era of political stalemate and instability: the nineteenth century's Gilded Age, which eventually led to reforms and the advent of modern congressional party leadership.

The Congress described by Woodrow Wilson in 1885 was all-powerful but failed to provide leadership for the nation. Whereas it hoarded power and diligently passed laws on all manner of subjects, Congress had utterly failed to clarify great public issues and engage the public in its deliberations: What was lacking in public debates was "the instruction and guidance in political affairs which the people might receive from a body which kept all national concerns suffused in a broad daylight of discussion."[3]

The reason for Congress's failure, in Wilson's eyes, was a dearth of leadership. Congress relied on standing committees rather than political party caucuses to identify issues and formulate policies. Standing committees had been a fixture on Capitol Hill since the early decades of the republic; in the post–Civil War years they proved ideal arenas for bargaining over the particularized benefits that marked the era that has been described as "the great barbecue"—pensions, government contracts, land deals, patronage, and the like.

Wilson's denunciation of "government by the standing committees of Congress" might seem peculiar in light of the robust grassroots strength of nineteenth-century parties. "Outside of Congress," Wilson writes, "the organization of the national parties is exceedingly well-defined and tangible, . . . but within Congress it is obscure and intangible."[4] Without crisp partisanship in floor debates that could illuminate Congress's work, legislation was crafted within the often inaccessible committee rooms, which Wilson called the "dim dungeons of silence."[5] Little wonder, then, that the public seemed so estranged from the bewildering mechanics of lawmaking on Capitol Hill.

Even before Wilson himself entered the White House, his assessment of the state of national decision making had dramatically shifted. Now he saw the president as the single spokesperson for the nation: "His is the only national voice in affairs. Let him once win the admiration and confidence of the country, and no other single force can withstand him."[6] Influenced by momentous changes in American life and politics, Wilson's focus had moved from the Gilded Age's congressional supremacy to a new-century vision of presidential leadership.

Nor was the reinvigorated presidency and its "bully pulpit" the only transformation that occurred around the turn of the twentieth century. On Capitol Hill, shifting coalitions set the stage for historic changes in the leadership and organization of both the House and the Senate.

Although they had no place in the constitutional blueprint, political parties soon became stable and institutionalized elements of congressional life. Regional conflicts, along with social and economic upheavals produced by rapid industrialization, nurtured long-standing partisan cleavages. The years between the Civil War and World War I mark the boundaries of an era of pervasive partisanship in the country at large and even on Capitol Hill. Party organizations at all levels were massive and militant by American standards; at the grassroots, they were divided along class, occupational, and regional lines to a degree unmatched even by today's partisan standards.

In the nation's capital, divided party control and wafer-thin legislative majorities characterized the years between the collapse of Reconstruction in 1876 and the Republicans' landslide victory twenty years later.[7] From 1876 to 1896, Senate majority party control changed hands no less than seven times; in the House there were five party turnovers. Major party margins were unusually small during those years: 5.5 seats on average in the Senate (including an even split in 1881–83) and 23.5 seats in the House. Minor party lawmakers were somewhat more numerous than they are today—an average of four in the House and at least one in the Senate. It was not until the early 1890s that Republicans gained solid control of the House and, after 1896, the Senate as well. This enabled the GOP to push forward a partisan agenda and, not incidentally, to consolidate its leadership in both chambers.

The Republicans' partisan dominance remained intact until 1910, when internal dissention and then midterm electoral defeat destroyed their hegemony. In 1912, party divisions cost the GOP the White House as well as Congress.

THE RISE AND FALL OF THE STRONG LEADERSHIP

During the Gilded Age—the period described in Wilson's *Congressional Government*—the House was often a chaotic place. Centrifugal forces dominated; the two parties battled to stalemate and alternated in power. Legislative outputs were small and insignificant.[8] The House was the object of ridicule; in full public view, small minorities were able to bring the House to a halt by interposing dilatory tactics. Newspapers and reformers clamored for changes in the rules.

Out of this stalemate there eventually emerged a vigorous party leadership. One precondition, of course, was the advent of a more or less stable partisan majority. Another impetus for more hierarchical leadership was structural: the growing size of the body. Between the reapportionments following the 1860 and 1900 censuses, the chamber grew by more than 60 percent, from 243 to 391 members. Later in this period, another factor came into play: the rise of careerism on Capitol Hill, which led members to insist on privileges based on their seniority.

From at least the time of Henry Clay in the early nineteenth century, the House speakership was a partisan as well as a procedural office. Following the Civil War a series of forceful speakers, most but not all of them Republicans, established precedents that eventually formed the superstructure of party government in the House.[9] These include the speaker's power to recognize members during floor deliberations and to appoint committee members with an eye to legislative priorities. A critical landmark is the 1890 revision of the

House rules—the handiwork of Speaker Thomas Brackett Reed (R-Me.), one of the chamber's true parliamentary masters. The "Reed rules" completely revised the order of business in the House, outlawing dilatory motions, reducing to 100 the quorum in Committee of the Whole, authorizing that body to close debate, and requiring every member present in the chamber to be counted in determining whether a quorum is present.

Reed greatly expanded the powers of the speakership as both a partisan and a procedural leader. Most of the precedents he established were passed on to his successors, especially Illinois Republican Joseph G. Cannon (1903–11). If his predecessors had selectively enlarged the speaker's powers, Cannon exploited all of them to their limits and even beyond. In addition to the prerogatives bequeathed by Reed, Cannon used the party caucus to bind Republicans to vote with their party. He chaired and dominated the Rules Committee, and occasionally he reported out "special rules" to shape debate or even suspend House rules. Taken individually, Cannon's powers were little different than Reed's; taken together, they bordered on the dictatorial.[10]

As the years went by, grumbling over Cannon's regime became increasingly belligerent. His downfall in 1910—one of the singular events in the history of American political institutions—was a combination of structural and partisan factors. One factor was the heightened careerism of House members.[11] Congress's enlarged role as overseer of a growing governmental apparatus rendered federal service ever more attractive and rewarding. As members stayed in office for longer periods of time, they insisted on commensurate institutional rewards. Careerism thus led to almost universal application of the seniority "rule" to reward lengthy service.

Careerism triumphed in both chambers at about the same time. In the Senate there was no decisive event; seniority, in fact, was largely unchallenged after 1877. The House "revolt" of 1910 occurred in large part because Speaker Cannon, who chaired and controlled the Rules Committee, had stifled progressive legislation, passed over senior members for committee assignments, and behaved arbitrarily in other ways. The anti-Cannon forces numbered not only the minority Democrats but also a group of Republican progressives, called "Insurgents." From reform-minded districts of the Upper Midwest, they urged an activist federal government far beyond that condoned by the orthodox conservatives who controlled the congressional GOP. The minority Democrats, for their part, were grasping for leverage, the ability to forge bipartisan coalitions that could prevail on the floor. In March 1910 the bipartisan coalition launched a direct assault on Speaker Cannon, and eventually it prevailed. The new rule diluted the speaker's power by removing him from the Rules Committee and depriving him of his power to appoint that committee's members. Appointment of committee members became the prerogative of the party caucuses.

Taken together, the changes that followed from the 1910 revolt thwarted the development of strong centralized leadership and enlarged the role of the committee chairs. It was not until the 1970s that the institutional powers of the party leaders were again aggregated.

THE SENATE BEGETS PARTY FLOOR LEADERS

The Senate has always had its leaders, even though none was formally elected until early in the twentieth century. During its first century, the Senate was a smallish body whose members were chosen indirectly by state legislatures. A few—like the "great triumvirate" of Henry Clay, John C. Calhoun, and Daniel Webster—possessed singular intellectual or rhetorical gifts and became national figures and champions of sectional interests at the same time. The Senate was full of local or state party bosses who controlled statewide political machines and blocs of delegates to national party conventions. Most of them were agents for dominant economic interests within their states, sent to the nation's capital to gather all forms of government largesse. Thus, the Senate was "a great gathering (and bargaining) place of the major party organizations that so dominated late-nineteenth-century politics."[12] As Woodrow Wilson put it in 1885, "No one is *the* senator. . . . No one exercises the special trust of acknowledged leadership."[13]

By the end of the nineteenth century, however, Senate party organizations—the Republican Caucus and the Democrats' Steering Committee—brought a modicum of procedural discipline to committee assignments and scheduling. The caucus chairs who emerged in the 1890s—not all of whom were powerful figures outside the chamber—drew influence from their ability to take care of the Senate's legislative business. A group of strong-willed senators—among them Republicans Nelson W. Aldridge of Rhode Island, William Allison of Iowa, Orville H. Platt of Connecticut, and John C. Spooner of Wisconsin and Democrat Arthur Pue Gorman of Maryland—used their experience and parliamentary expertise, combined with party discipline, to regulate the flow of legislation.

"Party leadership for the first time dominated the chamber's business," David Rothman relates. The rise of clearly identifiable party leaders in the Senate, Rothman argues, reflected a "new breed" of senator who valued party unity and "the machinery of [party] organization," especially the party caucus.[14] Soon those senators who chaired their respective party caucuses acquired levers of authority over senatorial business. They chaired important party panels, shaped the Senate's schedule, and mobilized votes to buttress party positions. Reflecting on the new era of Senate leadership, Woodrow Wilson stated in 1907: "The leader of the Senate is the chairman of the majority caucus. Each party in the Senate finds its real, its permanent, its effective organization in its caucus, and follows the leadership, in all important parliamentary battles, of the chairman of that caucus."[15] From the Senate's early caucus chairmanships, the position of majority floor leader informally emerged by 1913. In that year Democrats selected the first formally designated floor leader, John Worth Kern of Indiana. It has been argued that the advent of activist presidents such as Woodrow Wilson and Franklin D. Roosevelt demanded Senate leaders who could confer with the White House and manage the president's legislation.[16] Another explanation is that directly elected senators, mandated by the Seventeenth Amendment (1913), found it necessary to function as individual political entrepreneurs, which obliged them to deputize seasoned leaders to take care of housekeeping matters and, incidentally, to adjust the Senate's schedule and workload to serve their own political schedules and goals. From today's vantage point, these two functions—dealing with the White House and serving individual senators' needs—are at the core of the floor leaders' jobs.

The floor leader's job was not always held in high esteem. "The office is one that requires no gifts of a high order," once declared so astute an observer as reporter Richard Rovere: "It has generally been held as a reward for enterprising mediocrity."[17] At midcentury several floor leaders faced criticism and even rejection at the polls as a result of their Senate duties.

The post really came of age in 1953. In that year, Robert A. Taft of Ohio, "Mr. Republican," took over as majority leader after nearly a decade of being GOP leader in everything but name. Across the aisle, the Democrats, temporarily in a minority, chose as their floor leader someone elected only four years earlier. Two years later, that senator, Lyndon B. Johnson of Texas, became majority leader. Taft, in his brief tenure, revitalized the floor leader's job; Johnson wholly redesigned it.

Personal characteristics and skills, of course, have always exerted a powerful force on Senate floor leadership, and leaders have differed considerably in approaching their duties. On the Democratic side of the aisle, Johnson was the flamboyant persuader and deal maker; Montana's Mike Mansfield (1961–76) was the quiet conciliator and backroom facilitator; and Robert C. Byrd of West Virginia (1977–86) was the procedural specialist. In the Senate GOP, there were Everett M. Dirksen of Illinois (1959–69), the wily strategist and old-fashioned orator; Howard Baker of Tennessee (1977–84), the agenda coordinator and strategist; and Robert Dole of Kansas (1985–96), the deal maker and public spokesman.

The successors of Taft and Johnson, however, have without exception served as true party leaders and key players within the chamber; some, like Republicans Dirksen and Dole, were national leaders as well. Taft installed a centralized leadership; he and his immediate successors dominated their party's policy-making bodies and played an active role in scheduling and floor strategy. Over the years some decentralization of leadership functions has occurred in both parties, but the floor leaders (and assistant floor leaders) cannot escape being active promoters of their party's agendas as well as facilitators of their colleagues' individual agendas.

Congressional Party Regimes

With the end of Cannonism and turn-of-the-century Republican hegemony, party instability returned to Capitol Hill. In the last century, in fact, eras of true legislative–executive harmony—party government in more or less the parliamentary sense of the term—have occurred only rarely. By general consensus there have been only three of them: Woodrow Wilson's first administration (1913–17), Franklin Roosevelt's celebrated "New Deal" (1933–36), and the high-water mark of Lyndon Johnson's "Great Society" (1963–66). These periods of high legislative productivity flowed from unique convergences of a forceful chief executive, a popular but unfulfilled policy agenda, and a Congress responsive to the president's leadership. These were periods of frantic lawmaking, which produced landmark legislation and innovative government programs.

For the post–New Deal period, I have identified at least four distinct regimes, or eras, viewed from the Capitol Hill vantage point. These periods are delineated not only by partisan margins but also by internal structure and politics.[18] Roosevelt's seeming mastery of Congress in the early New Deal years soon gave way to a long period of *bipartisan conservative dominance*, which lasted roughly from the second Roosevelt administration through the early 1960s. Both parties were split internally between a progressive, internationalist wing and a reactionary wing.[19] Although the progressives tended to dominate presidential sections, the conservatives held sway on Capitol Hill. An oligarchy of senior leaders, often called "the old bulls," wielded the gavels and commanded the votes in committees and on the floor. Whichever party was in power, congressional leaders overrepresented safe one-party regions: for Democrats, the rural South and inner-city machines (known as the "Austin–Boston" alliance); and for Republicans, the rural Northeast and Midwest. Such leaders pursued the limited legislative agenda of the bipartisan conservative majority that dominated most domestic policy making. This bipartisan conservative era outlasted several presidents of widely varying goals and skills—from Roosevelt through Kennedy.

The cozy world of the committee barons was eventually overturned by the advent of a *liberal activist regime* (1964–78). With its huge liberal working majorities in both chambers of Congress, this regime spanned the period from Lyndon Johnson through Jimmy Carter. Internally, the period saw a series of reforms that pointed Congress in the direction of more open and participatory processes that in turn encouraged legislative innovation and productivity. The prerogatives of the committee barons were reined in and redirected both upward to the party leaders and downward to the rank-and-file members—many of whom chaired subcommittees or enjoyed access to other levers of influence. Legislative activity soared by whatever measure one uses; the processing of freestanding bills and resolutions became the centerpiece of committee and subcommittee work. That the liberal juggernaut survived during the more conservative presidencies of Richard Nixon and Gerald Ford is a phenomenon that ought to persuade political historians and policy analysts to give special focus to the years 1969–76. This legislative outpouring formed a gigantic "bulge in the middle," which David Mayhew notes in his study of lawmaking between 1946 and 1990.[20] This pattern, in my judgment, is largely responsible for his counterintuitive conclusion that party control made little difference in the output measures he examined.

In the 1980s Congress entered what is called its *postreform* period. Lagging economic productivity and changing intellectual fashions supported the idea that the federal government should review, refine, and cut back existing programs rather than designing new programs or establishing new agencies. In an era marked by cutback politics, legislative productivity was markedly curtailed: fewer freestanding bills were sponsored, huge legislative "megabills" were fashioned, budgetary politics became paramount and constraining, and individual legislators engaged in "blame avoidance" tactics to shield themselves from the adverse effects of curtailing or cutting off government services or facilities.

During this period, congressional party leaders continued to recover power that had been lost ever since the anti-Cannon revolt. Not only did leaders benefit from powers conferred on them by reform-era innovations of the 1960s and 1970s; they also responded to widespread feelings that they were the only people who could, and should, untangle committee jurisdictional squabbles and manage the legislative schedule.

The Republicans' unexpected 1995 takeover of both chambers was a singular event in the history of Congress. At the time it appeared also to signify a new congressional regime, in which a dominant party with a set of policy ideas would be able to dictate the agenda and floor proceedings on Capitol

Hill. This was true in the most obvious sense: the Republicans controlled the House for the first time in forty years and the Senate for the first time in nearly a decade. But although the GOP retained its majority status in the next three elections, it failed to consolidate or enlarge its position. Indeed, its margins have progressively narrowed, and the verdict in 2000 was virtually bipartisan. (The instability of the Senate's situation resulted in a singular "power-sharing" pact when the Senate split fifty–fifty, with the GOP in charge solely on the vice president's party affiliation. Five months later the baton was passed to the Democrats—when Vermont's Jim Jeffords switched from Republican to independent, changing the party ranks to fifty to forty-nine to one.) Are we seeing the advent of a new Republican-dominated Congress? Or, as seems increasingly likely, are we merely in an era of fierce *party competition and instability*? At the very least, the true character of the current congressional regime has yet to make itself clear.

Presidential Regimes

Just as patterns of congressional operations do not always conform to presidential administrations, so too, we have learned, White House politics are not necessarily delineated by a given president's term of office. We commonly speak of, say, the Roosevelt era or the Reagan presidency. However, as Charles O. Jones has pointed out, patterns of executive–legislative relations do not always follow given presidencies or even presidents' four-year terms. From the foregoing discussion of congressional eras, it can at least be plausibly argued, for example, that Kennedy–Johnson and Nixon–Ford represent single periods in terms of interbranch relations.

By the same token, presidencies may evolve through several distinct stages in dealing with Congress. Franklin Roosevelt's most productive period of New Deal lawmaking did not last much beyond his first reelection and the disastrous "court-packing" fight of 1937; his wartime administration (1941–45) bears even less resemblance to his earlier concentration on domestic matters. Ronald Reagan also found congressional cooperation over his first two years. After that period, his hold on Congress was more tenuous, especially during his final two years after his party lost control of the Senate.

THE STRENGTH OF CONGRESSIONAL PARTIES

Whatever the state of party organization in the nation at large is, partisanship and factionalism remain very much alive on Capitol Hill. Through the workings of the four congressional parties, policy platforms are put together, agendas are negotiated, campaign funds are raised and dispersed, nonincumbent challengers are encouraged and tutored, floor leaders are chosen, committee assignments are made, floor debates are scheduled, and members' votes are rounded up. The range of functions, and their attendant organizational apparatus, dwarfs all previous congressional partisan efforts. The current state of affairs, in fact, stands Woodrow Wilson's observation on its head: congressional parties are robust, whereas grassroots parties are all-too-often atrophied.

The Capitol Hill parties' formal structures are extensive. Within both chambers, there are policy committees, campaign committees, research committees, elaborate whip systems, and countless task forces. Nearly 400 staff aides are employed by party leaders, and perhaps an equal number is employed by assorted party committees.[21] Party-oriented voting bloc groups (such as the Conservative Democratic Forum or the Republicans' Mainstream Coalition), "class clubs" (such as the Republican Freshman Class or the Democratic First-Term Class), and social groups complement and reinforce partisan ties.

On the House and Senate floors, party affiliation is the strongest single predictor of members' voting behaviors; in recent years party-line voting has reached levels nearly as high as a century ago. Of the nearly 2,000 floor votes cast by individual representatives and senators on the articles of impeachment against President Clinton, for example, 92 percent followed partisan battle lines—Republicans favoring impeachment, Democrats resisting it.

Given the presumed individualistic tendencies of today's elected politicians, what can account for the strength of party leadership and the prevalence of party-line voting in the two chambers? One answer lies in the members' constituencies and in the long-term partisan realignment in the nation at large. Among Democrats, increasing numbers on their southern flank are African Americans. The dwindling cadres of Democrats elected from conservative districts—mostly southern and rural—strive to put distance between themselves and their national leaders. By the same token, Republicans are more uniformly conservative than they used to be. In the South, conservative areas with white majorities now tend to elect Republicans, not Democrats. In the Northeast, many districts once represented by GOP liberals have fallen to the Democrats. The long-term decline of archconservative southern Democrats and liberal northeastern and progressive-state Republicans underlies much of the present ideological cohesion within the two parties. At the same time, it has widened the ideological chasm between the congressional parties.

This partisan realignment has shrunk the ideological center in the two chambers. The proportion of centrists—conservative Democrats and moderate Republicans—hovered at about 30 percent in the 1960s and 1970s, according to Sarah A. Binder.[22] (Binder's centrists are those members who are closer to the ideological midpoint between the two parties than to the ideological centers of their own parties.) Only about one in ten of today's lawmakers falls into this centrist category.[23]

Another source of today's partisanship is institutional: the congressional parties and their activities to promote party loyalty. New member socialization is dominated by party organizations. Incoming members attend party-sponsored orientations, rely on party bodies for their committee assignments, and often organize into partisan "class clubs." When seeking out cues for voting, therefore, lawmakers tend to rely on party colleagues to guide their own behavior.

FOCUS ON PARTY LEADERS

A by-product of cohesive congressional parties is strengthened leadership prerogatives. Insofar as members are confident that a caucus broadly reflects their own views, and that it promotes their own policy and career goals, they are more willing to cede powers to the caucus's elected leaders. By the same logic, when members realize that the opposing party poses an immediate threat that must be overcome, it is easier for them to adopt the party line and to articulate partisan rhetoric. By no means are elected leaders given blank checks as they go about their work. Rather, they hold power only so long as they pursue strategies that advance their members' individual and collective goals.

The roller-coaster career of Speaker Newt Gingrich of Georgia serves as Exhibit A for what political analysts call "principal-agent theory." Gingrich, conceded to be the architect of the GOP triumph in 1994, exploited a range of prerogatives reminiscent of nothing so much as the era of "Uncle Joe" Cannon. He chose committee chairs and demanded that their committees send to the floor elements of the party's "Contract with America" in the first 100 days of the 104th Congress. Leadership-controlled committees—Rules, Budget—and leadership task forces often drafted or perfected legislation in competition with the authorizing committees. The tenuous equilibrium between committee and party prerogatives tilted away from the former and toward the latter.

Following the triumphant early months of the Republican regime, the power and credibility of the party leaders, especially Gingrich, came under fire. Gingrich's alleged weakness in bargaining with the White House also came in for criticism. When ethics problems led to his reprimand by the

House in 1997, he was forced to cede certain powers to rival leaders (especially the committee chairs) in order to ensure their support. The next year, the speaker was inevitably identified with the House Republicans' Clinton impeachment and a midterm election effort that reminded voters of that effort. The party's poor showing in the 1998 elections—losses instead of the expected big gains—along with further revelations pertaining to Gingrich's personal conduct, made it clear that his continued leadership would be a liability for House Republicans. Soon thereafter, Gingrich withdrew from the speakership and resigned his House seat.

In the 106th Congress, Senate Majority Leader Trent Lott (R-Miss.) became the target of similar criticism. As the Congress opened, his leadership was tested as the Senate considered President Clinton's impeachment. Although many conservatives, most notably the House impeachment managers, decried the Senate's seeming haste to rid itself of the issue and acquit the president, it is clear that Lott was acting to implement the will of a great majority of the senators. Even senators who voted to convict the president were eager at the same time to rid themselves, and the Senate, of the corrosive issue. Seen in that light, Lott's strategy was impressively successful. However, the GOP leader's troubles later in the 106th Congress were, if anything, more complex and more difficult to cope with. It was a classic leadership dilemma in an era of competitive parties. Struggling to expedite "must-pass" legislation, Lott had to use all the parliamentary weapons he possessed. Democrats in turn were outraged at what they considered high-handed tactics that deprived them of their floor rights.[24] Some of Lott's Republican colleagues, too, expressed restiveness at his leadership. Lott and his deputy leader, Don Nickles (R-Okla.), faced an even tougher job in view of the GOP losses in the 2000 elections: five incumbents defeated and one open-seat loss, offset by only one Democratic defeat and one open-seat turnover. Senate Republicans, unlike their House counterparts, have no history of removing their leaders after electoral setbacks; but the results hardly burnished Lott's leadership record.

House and Senate party leaders exploit each chamber's rules and procedures to encourage favorable outcomes on the floor. House procedures sharpen partisanship, inasmuch as a cohesive party majority can normally work its will. By controlling key committees, employing scheduling powers, and using special rules to structure floor debate and voting, majority party leaders can arrange votes they are likely to win and avoid those they are apt to lose. Senate leaders have fewer opportunities to engineer victories because that chamber's rules and procedures distribute power more evenly between the parties and among individual senators. Yet Senate floor leaders can regulate the timing of debates to their advantage and (through their right to be recognized first to speak or offer amendments on the floor) shape the order and content of floor deliberation.

One outgrowth of robust partisanship is the advent of congressional party "platforms" designed to attract voters and validate the party's bid for power. The House Republicans' manifesto, the "Contract with America," was by no means the earliest such document, but it was shrewdly drafted, aggressively marketed, and then employed as the party's working agenda during its first months in power.[25] Four years later, the Clinton impeachment became a pitched battle along party lines, dividing not only lawmakers but also their constituents. Virtually the same cleavages appeared in the 2000 presidential and congressional elections. The current appeals to partisan loyalty, and the close competition of the major parties, would be all too familiar to politicians and voters of a century ago.

DIVIDED PARTY CONTROL

The volatile mixture that marked the nineteenth century's Gilded Age—intense partisanship coupled with divided and shifting party control of government—is replicated in the recent history of Congress and the presidency. As all are aware, divided government has become a normal part of the contemporary political landscape. In almost two-thirds of the Congresses elected since the end of World War II, one or both houses were in the hands of the party opposed to the president. So-called divided government marked two stormy years of Truman's presidency, all but two years of Eisenhower's and Clinton's, and all of Nixon's, Ford's, Reagan's, and Bush's years.

Slender partisan majorities have also marked the Congresses controlled by the Republicans (1953–54 and 1995–2002). Since the GOP takeover of the House in 1995, the gap between the two parties has averaged 16.75 seats—which means that a shift of nine votes would make the difference. Rather than building on its strength, the Republican Party has seen its majorities in the House dwindle with succeeding elections. In the Senate, the Republicans' majorities have never approached or exceeded the decisive number of sixty—the number needed to invoke cloture and end debate.

The 2000 elections raised serious short-term and long-term questions about presidential–congressional relations. As for the White House, George W. Bush, the victor in the presidential contest, has brought to his office less legitimacy than any president in modern times. For one thing, there is the extreme closeness of the election—both nationally and in a number of battleground states. For another, the popular vote and the electoral college vote offered a split decision for the first since 1888. There was no talk of a popular mandate of any kind—except perhaps to practice bipartisanship and lower the volume of political rhetoric. No doubt we will hear numerous appeals to cooperation and civility. It was President George H. W. Bush who in 1989 promised a "kinder, gentler" brand of conservatism. His son employs the phrase "compassionate conservatism." Democrats have countered with similar pleas for bipartisanship. To no one's surprise, calls for bipartisanship are heard from those leaders most in need of votes from the other side of the aisle.

But in rendering their bipartisan verdicts, the American voters may have precluded the actual practice of bipartisanship. A presidency devoid of a clear victory, much less a mandate, coupled with a Congress composed of two parties of virtually equal strength, is most apt to produce a continuation of the trench warfare that marked executive–congressional relations in the 1990s. The 2002 and 2004 campaigns will dominate congressional, if not presidential, leadership strategies in the 107th Congress. Let the political games continue.

CONCLUSION

Like our counterparts of 100 years ago, we live in an era of noisy, combative partisanship. But the kinds of partisanship of the two eras contrast radically in character and structure. Party loyalties were deeply ingrained in nineteenth-century political life, mirroring not only ideological beliefs but social and regional differences. Local party organizations were powerful and extensive, whereas the national parties were just beginning to erect structures.

Today, the Republican and Democratic parties organize Congress and dominate its proceedings more thoroughly than they did a century or so ago. In the country at large, voters profess to dislike both parties and their propensity to quarrel with one another. (One is entitled to be skeptical of citizens' antipathy toward the parties: at least among the voting public, nine out of ten professed partisans do in fact vote for the presidential and congressional candidates of their own parties.[26]) Both parties, however, are well organized and generously funded. Leadership structures are extensive and well staffed. But as long as neither party commands a working majority on Capitol Hill, party leaders will be focused more on compiling records for the next campaign cycle than on negotiations aimed at resolving substantive policy questions. Campaigning thus becomes a permanent element in Capitol Hill politics. As a result, legislative outputs are inevitably going to be relatively few and extremely hard fought.

NOTES

1. James Sterling Young, *The Washington Community, 1800–1828* (New York: Columbia University Press, 1966).

2. Edward S. Corwin, *The President: Office and Powers, 1787–1957* (New York: New York University Press, 1957), 171.

3. Woodrow Wilson, *Congressional Government: A Study in American Politics* (New York: Meridian Books, 1956), 170.

4. Wilson, *Congressional Government*, 80.

5. Wilson, *Congressional Government*, 63.

6. Woodrow Wilson, *Constitutional Government in the United States* (New York: Columbia University Press, 1908), 56–61.

7. Mark W. Summers, "History of Congress: The Age of the Machine," in *Encyclopedia of the United States Congress*, vol. 2, ed. Donald C. Bacon, Roger H. Davidson, and Morton Keller (New York: Simon and Schuster, 1995), 1006–07.

8. Summers, "History of Congress," 1006–07.

9. Mary Parker Follett, *The Speaker of the House of Representatives* (New York: Longmans, Green, 1896).

10. Charles O. Jones, "Joseph G. Cannon and Howard W. Smith: An Essay on the Limits of Leadership in the House of Representatives," *Journal of Politics* 30 (August 1968): 617–46.

11. The seminal work on congressional careers is Nelson W. Polsby, "The Institutionalization of the House of Representatives," *American Political Science Review* 62 (March 1968): 146–47.

12. Summers, "History of Congress," 1006.

13. Wilson, *Congressional Government*, 223.

14. David J. Rothman, *Politics and Power: The United States Senate, 1869–1901* (Cambridge, Mass.: Harvard University Press, 1966), 5–7.

15. Wilson, *Constitutional Government in the United States*, 133.

16. Margaret Munk, "Origin and Development of the Party Floor Leadership in the United States Senate," *Capitol Studies* (winter 1974): 23–41.

17. Richard Rovere, "What Course for the Powerful Mr. Taft?" *New York Times Magazine*, 22 March 1953: 34.

18. See Roger H. Davidson, "The Presidency and Congressional Time," in *Rivals for Power: Presidential–Congressional Relations*, ed. James A. Thurber (Washington, D.C.: CQ Press, 1996), 19–44.

19. See James MacGregor Burns, *The Deadlock of Democracy: Four-Party Government in America* (Englewood Cliffs, N.J.: Prentice-Hall, 1963).

20. David R. Mayhew, *Divided We Govern: Party Control, Lawmaking, and Investigating, 1946–1990* (New Haven: Yale University Press, 1991), especially 76.

21. Norman J. Ornstein, Thomas E. Mann, and Michael J. Malbin, *Vital Statistics on Congress, 1999–2000* (Washington, D.C.: AEI Press, 2000), 129.

22. Sarah A. Binder, "The Dynamics of Legislative Gridlock, 1947–1996," *American Political Science Review* 93 (September 1999): 519–33.

23. Sarah A. Binder, "The Disappearing Political Center," *Brookings Review* 15 (fall 1996): 37.

24. See, for example, the bitter exchange between Lott and Democratic Senator Robert C. Byrd (W.V.) during expedited debate over the Comprehensive Test Ban Treaty, in *Congressional Record* 145 (106th Congress, 1st session, 13 October 1999): S12505–S12506.

25. See John B. Bader, *Leadership Agendas in Congress and the "Contract with America"* (Washington, D.C.: Georgetown University Press, 1996).

26. See Marjorie Connelly, "Who Voted: A Portrait of American Politics, 1976–2000," *New York Times*, 12 November 2000: B4.

5

The Impact of Campaigns on Presidential–Congressional Relations

Richard E. Cohen

Elections and governing naturally are related in a democracy. In recent decades, however, how we select our presidents has become less related to how those presidents attempt to shape policy once they are in office. Is that because campaigns have become theatrical exercises that are less relevant to the affairs of state? Or has legislating on Capitol Hill become so much more complex that even the most skillful politicians have encountered more obstacles to success? Surely, there has been some of each. More to the point, participants in presidential campaigns plus those who observe these contests often have lost sight of the fact that elections—and the mandates that may result—have consequences for what follows in the political system.

Modern presidential campaigns have become complex and exhausting operations that typically demand major commitments of time and resources. The candidates appeal for voters' support through a combination of personal attributes, party identification, and public relations salesmanship. But then what for the winner? For most of the past century, a major element for judging presidents' success after they have been elected has been their ability to work with Congress and achieve policy changes. But students of this relationship—including scholars, journalists, and other observers of Washington's sausage making—have typically paid scant attention to the connection between how presidents win office and how they fare legislatively. Why the topic has received so little attention is beyond the scope of this chapter. But a review of presidential candidates and their subsequent accomplishments during the past forty years reveals clear predictors of the electoral victors' early legislative prospects.

Some conclusions are intuitively logical:

1. The more comprehensive and specific the candidate's agenda with the voters, the stronger his position in dealing with Congress following the election.
2. The greater the winning candidate's electoral mandate from the voters, the more likely that he scores significant legislative achievements.
3. The more closely the eventual president has worked with congressional allies during his campaign, the more likely that he secures a positive relationship to work with them in office.

In short, inclusive candidates and big election winners become inclusive presidents and skillful legislators in office.

But recent elections also make clear that many factors potentially imperil a successful contender's ability to get the job done legislatively after the election. First, with presidential candidates of both parties increasingly running as outsiders who win office by distancing themselves from Washington and its political establishment, some have found it more difficult to effectively exercise the perquisites of their office. Second, no matter how specific their campaign agendas are, narrow outcomes leave the winners with less of an electoral mandate—regardless of the presidential party's strength in the House and Senate. And third, some presidential candidates succeed in their campaigns without devoting much attention to a legislative agenda, or they decide to move cautiously after taking office. In such cases, not surprisingly, their success with Congress inevitably will be more limited than would otherwise be the case.

The dynamics of the 2000 election—which featured, for the first time since 1952, the confluence of the president not seeking reelection and partisan control of both the House and Senate up for grabs—focused special attention on the shaping of party messages during the campaign. George W. Bush and Al Gore and their respective parties were circumspect in defining partisan themes and in responding to those pressures. Although each presidential candidate made some efforts to rally behind the themes of his congressional team, both nominees took only limited steps to publicly engage their putative allies. Bush, for his part, offered a few significant proposals during his campaign and acknowledged that once elected he would need to reach out to members of Congress in both parties to achieve his policy goals. Whether he was well positioned to succeed as president was uncertain during his initial months in office, though the conditions of his victory appeared likely to limit the scope of his governing agenda. In any case, maintaining Republican unity appeared to be essential to his legislative success.

The limited policy discussion during the campaign was an indication that the nation and its elected representatives lacked agreement on a compelling set of national priorities and appeared content to maintain the status quo. Politicians, of course, find it difficult to rally a public that is not eager for action. In contrast to some previous elections, in which there was an obvious demand for either an increase in federal programs or a decrease in spending and taxes, the relative "peace and prosperity" at the start of the twenty-first century produced an election without a call for obvious new policy directions. So, too, neither Democrats nor Republicans in Congress had prepared a broad set of initiatives for their parties' candidates to embrace. Those factors added to the limited political mandate that appeared to flow from the election, even apart from the extraordinarily narrow outcome of both the Bush–Gore contest and the battles for House and Senate control.

Still, the results of the first election since 1952 in which Republicans won control of the White House and both chambers of Congress—regardless of their razor-thin margins—left both sides aware that the public typically holds a party accountable in such a situation. Whether or not Republicans were prepared or unified to govern, they may not have many excuses for inaction—even with the subsequent shift to Democratic control of the Senate. Following six years of virtual gridlock between a Democratic president and a Republican-controlled Congress, the outcome further increased the pressure on Bush and GOP legislative leaders to define an agenda and demonstrate progress.

The 2000 election plus the two prior campaign victories by Bill Clinton also were reminders that it is the exception, rather than the rule, for sweeping legislative mandates to emerge from an election. As this chapter describes, only two campaigns since 1960 have yielded a clarion call for action. In each of those cases, the president took advantage of that opportunity in Congress and scored major legislative triumphs that had lasting national impact. Significantly, however, the period of those Capitol Hill successes was of limited duration. In less than a year, the White House and Congress returned to slogging as usual.

MEASURING A CANDIDATE'S LEGISLATIVE AGENDA

The two presidents who achieved short-term mastery in moving their agendas through Congress were Lyndon B. Johnson in 1965 and Ronald Reagan in 1981. To be sure, there were marked differences between them.

One was a liberal Democrat and a proven Capitol Hill wheeler-dealer; the other was a conservative Republican and a self-styled political outsider. Johnson was working with huge Democratic majorities in both the House and Senate—slightly more than two-thirds control in each case, the largest majorities since Franklin Roosevelt's New Deal. Reagan, on the other hand, had only a narrow Republican majority in the Senate, and he had to work with a House that was nominally under Democratic control. But the similarities in the election campaigns of those two successful presidents were far more important to their legislative prospects.

First, each defined clear-cut objectives for his presidency. Johnson ran in 1964 with promises of the "Great Society," an unprecedented expansion of federal programs to assist the public during good economic times. For the poor, he offered urban renewal and expanded federal housing. For racial minorities, he promised to build on the 1964 Civil Rights Act with what became the Voting Rights Act, which guarantees every citizen's political franchise. For the broad middle class, the goals were federal aid to education and medical care for the aged—which ultimately became the centerpiece of Johnson's legacy. Reagan's promises in the 1980 campaign were very different but equally comprehensive. Chief among them was an across-the-board tax cut of 10 percent for each of the next three years. But he also made less specific promises to scale back the federal role in daily lives, through both less government spending and regulation.

Second, in each case, members of the president's party on Capitol Hill had defined and promoted the ideas extensively for years. What became the Medicare program had been the topic of liberal Democrats' promises for many years and of unsuccessful legislative efforts under President Kennedy. Prior to the 1964 election, however, Democrats lacked the congressional votes to achieve their goal. Reagan's tax cut originally was known as "Kemp–Roth." Representative Jack Kemp of New York and Senator William Roth of Delaware, the tax cut's two hard-charging proponents, had convinced many initially reluctant Republicans to sign on during the late 1970s; but with Democrats holding firm House and Senate majorities at the time, the tax plan had no chance of passage before the 1980 election, even with the preponderance of Republican support.

Third, both Johnson and Reagan in those campaigns scored huge electoral victories, which transcended their own contests. Johnson won 61 percent of the popular vote against Barry Goldwater and carried 486 electoral votes, losing only five states in the Deep South and Goldwater's home state of Arizona. In 1980, Reagan won 51 percent of the popular vote against President Jimmy Carter, who won 41 percent, and independent John Anderson, with 7 percent; Reagan won 489 electoral votes and all but six states scattered across the nation. Equally significantly, Democrats in 1964 gained thirty-six House seats and two Senate seats—giving Johnson firm control on Capitol Hill; Republicans in 1980 won thirty-three House seats and twelve Senate seats—yielding their first Senate majority in twenty-six years—and left many conservative Democrats reluctant to buck Reagan's legislative initiatives. In each case, members of the president's party overwhelmingly fell in line behind his agenda.

Other presidential candidates have prevailed in a variety of different circumstances. In some cases, the victories were personal mandates rather than calls for sweeping policy agendas or clearly partisan mandates. In 1960, for example, John Kennedy promised a "New Frontier." But his victory, though an important political turning point, was largely a matter of style. He wanted to inject renewed vigor into Washington more than he sought to propose an endless string of new programs. As was the case with other presidents during that era, he and the nation also became consumed by Cold War conflicts around the world, leaving less time for domestic issues. Jimmy Carter succeeded in his 1976 campaign on his promise to restore integrity in government in the wake of President Richard Nixon's 1974 resignation amid the Watergate scandal. Carter, who had little background in Washington, defeated several senior congressional Democrats to win the presidential nomination. Even though Democrats retained large House and Senate majorities following his election, and the "conservative coalition" had all but disappeared from Congress, they struggled with Carter throughout his presidency.

Other presidents have won election on nonlegislative issues. Nixon's 1968 victory was based largely on his unspecified pledges to end the Vietnam War, which had badly divided the nation. With Democrats retaining firm control of Congress, Nixon did not offer a campaign agenda to make significant changes in Johnson's recently enacted domestic program. Winning only 43 percent of the vote in the three-way contest against Democrat Hubert Humphrey and George Wallace, Nixon was not positioned for major legislative initiatives.

As for Nixon's 1972 reelection, in which he swept forty-nine states, that too was largely a personal triumph, which was not accompanied by a broad party manifesto or by significant changes in the Democrats' congressional majority. (Plus, Nixon would soon become entangled in the Watergate scandal.) Likewise, when Reagan won reelection with forty-nine states in 1984, his campaign theme was a nonpartisan evocation of "Morning in America"; as it turned out, his chief legislative initiative in his second term was tax reform, which had a bipartisan genealogy. In their landslide reelections, neither Nixon nor Reagan emphasized his cooperation during the prior four years with congressional Republicans or extended himself to ensure their election success. In both 1972 and 1984, ironically, Republicans won about a dozen House seats and actually lost two Senate seats.

The 1988 and 1992 elections meshed the policy and personal approaches. Neither produced a resounding political victory. In the former, Vice President George Bush carefully sought to distance himself from Reagan without disavowing his leadership and broad goals of the previous eight years ("Read my lips, no new taxes!"). Bush used both policy proposals (environment and education, for example) and personal style ("kinder and gentler") to draw those contrasts. His approach, which implicitly acknowledged the likelihood that Democrats would retain their House and Senate majorities, gave him a less than overwhelming 53 percent of the popular vote. In challenging Bush four years later, Bill Clinton used stylistic points ("the man from Hope," with a focus on "the economy, stupid") to underline how he would offer more vigorous policies than the incumbent. But neither Clinton nor congressional Democrats during the campaign were specific on their budget or health care proposals, which eventually brought major political headaches for both the new president and the party. The winners in the 1988 and 1992 elections received sizable electoral college majorities, but that factor proved insignificant for the winner, especially with the modest congressional changes in each case.

Clinton's 1992 campaign had some similarities to Carter's in 1976: the southern governor running as a political outsider to defeat a Republican president while keeping his distance from the Democrat-controlled Congress. In contrast to Carter, Clinton had more interest and background in federal policy debates. But his victory was hampered by the fact that he won only 43 percent of the vote in the three-way race that included independent Ross Perot; and Clinton entered office with notably fewer congressional Democrats (258 in the House and 57 in the Senate) than Carter had when he took office (292 in the House and 62 in the Senate).

In his 1996 reelection, Clinton's success was substantially based on his success in running *against* the Republican-controlled Congress that had been led by his campaign opponent, former Senate Majority Leader Robert Dole, and by still-controversial House Speaker Newt Gingrich. Running as a "New Democrat," whose support of welfare reform and a balanced budget was not enthusiastically embraced throughout his party, Clinton won a victory that was more personal than partisan. Despite a major effort, Democrats failed in their goal of regaining House control.

This brief history of the ten presidential campaigns from 1960 to 1996 demonstrates the significance for governance of how the candidates posture themselves as the nation's prospective chief policy advocates and legislative agenda setters, both before and after an election. Indeed, even though many presidential campaigns have been thin in their discussion of policy, they have provided the chief focal point for a broad discussion of issues. (When they subsequently seek to take legislative action on controversial proposals that were not discussed, or even were rejected, during their campaigns, presidents usually are inviting trouble; Carter's calls to limit energy consumption, Reagan's 1981 proposal to revise social security benefits, and Bush's approval of the 1990 tax increase in contravention of his "no new taxes" campaign pledge are examples.) Although presidents must recognize limits in how much they can affect the actual drafting of legislation, as is discussed in the following section, they have gained a unique role in determining what topics will be the focus of national debate and action. That role has evolved significantly since the Founding Fathers drafted the Constitution and envisioned the president mainly as the chief executive.

In addition, it has become clear during the past century that only the president has the political standing and leadership authority in our representative democracy to define the national agenda and advocate it from his bully pulpit. Notwithstanding Gingrich's limited success in supplanting Clinton in setting the policy agenda following the 1994 election, in which House Republicans made their "Contract with America" the national political focus, the ensuing two years demonstrated that the president's veto power and his ability to command the executive branch with a single voice gave him huge advantages in dealing with a Congress led by the opposite party. Even strong Democratic congressional leaders who have been in the majority, such as House Speaker Jim Wright and Senate Majority Leader George Mitchell during the Reagan–Bush years, were mostly reactive in seeking to urge—or thwart—presidential initiatives.

A PRESIDENT'S FIRST-YEAR DEALINGS WITH CONGRESS

When a president emerges from an election with a clear mandate from the voters and has shown agreement with a substantial number of congressional lawmakers on key issues, those logically are the ideal circumstances for seeking speedy legislative action. Although success is not guaranteed, such a step gives strong momentum to a presidency. Plus, although the significance of political honeymoons probably has been overblown in any case, it is also true that delay hardly strengthens a president's hand with Congress.

In the initial weeks and months following a convincing victory, a new president typically will meet with his party's congressional leaders—both during the transition period and soon after the inauguration—and will agree on a clear set of objectives, usually in a limited number of areas. Then, they move to achieve those goals; this period was once known as the "first 100 days," but more recently it has become a six-month legislative blitz leading to the August recess. After that period, business as usual typically begins to settle in, especially among House members who become less receptive to presidential entreaties as they prepare for the midterm election.

The most successful practitioners of the intensive early start, not surprisingly, were Johnson and Reagan, with their sweeping campaign agendas and convincing electoral mandates. Despite their contrasting styles, each showed the political wisdom of moving quickly after his election to implement his campaign agenda.

Johnson proposed a laundry list of social and economic development legislation and remained personally engaged in keeping the pressure on his Democratic allies—both his longtime colleagues from the House and Senate and the many new members elected on his coattails. For most of 1965, Congress moved at a relentless pace as Johnson virtually dictated the terms of his legislation. With a House majority of 295 to 140 and Senate control of 68 to 32, plus some support from moderate Republicans for his programs, the president could not be stopped: "Members of Congress were like mere stage props for LBJ's initiatives, making few changes before returning the finished bills to the president for his signature."[1] The intense pace continued through the October end of the legislative session. But 1966 proved to be a different story, as Republicans became more aggressive in counterattacking and Democrats grew concerned about reelection.

In 1981, with Democrats holding a 243 to 192 majority and still chairing House committees, Reagan and his team were forced to adopt a more indirect route to secure passage of their program. With weaker leverage over day-to-day operations, they essentially circumvented the House Rules Committee—which is typically the House's scheduler and traffic cop—and instead concentrated their efforts on a handful of bills, which they prepared outside the committee process. They were immeasurably aided by the procedures in the 1974 Congressional Budget Act. First, they defined the outlines of their tax and spending goals in the annual budget resolution; then, they used the budget "reconciliation" process to achieve their specific objectives for tax cuts (which were reduced slightly to 25 percent over three years) and changes in entitlement programs. In each case, Republican control of the Senate—where their majority of fifty-three to forty-seven was firm—became a useful management device, especially given the occasionally slapdash quality of the legislative drafting by Reagan's House allies. Assisted by occasional timely presidential speeches and private persuasion, Reagan achieved by the August recess the principal legislative goals that defined his presidency. As was the case for Johnson's second year, Reagan's second year was far less active legislatively as his allies grew concerned about the coming election.

In each case, the presidential team's electoral fears proved warranted. House Democrats in 1966 suffered a forty-six-seat loss, with thirty-nine members losing their seats, and many conservative Democrats returned to their more comfortable alliance with resurgent House Republicans. In 1982, Democrats picked up twenty-six seats and regained effective control of the House; in the Senate, Republicans retained their majority until their large incoming class faced the voters in 1986, but the party's loss of the House also reduced the previously iron-clad discipline in the Senate.

Despite their relatively brief legislative dominance and subsequent electoral setbacks, the Johnson and Reagan whirlwinds left major marks on the nation. Most of the Great Society expansion of the federal government withstood not only Nixon but also the conservative victories led by Reagan and Gingrich, and none of them seriously challenged the core of civil rights and Medicare protections. True, some of the "poverty program" did not survive; but, collectively, federal support for low-income groups has grown sizably in other, probably more effective programs and benefits. As for Reagan's tax cuts, opponents sought to reverse them and later criticized their role in creating huge federal deficits during the following decade. But they remained in place. Whether or not there is a link is for others to determine, but it is a fact that the nation experienced only one brief and modest recession during the seventeen years after Reagan's economic program fully took effect.

Other presidents—notably, Carter and Clinton—have sought quick legislative starts with Congress, especially when their party was in control. Lacking an electoral mandate, however, their results from the start have been less impressive. Carter entered office with nearly as many congressional Democrats as did Johnson, but he was poorly positioned to take advantage of the opportunity. He did not have a well-defined agenda, he had few dependable legislative allies, and he had little experience in dealing with Congress. From the start, the Carter team's legislative efforts proved disastrous. They offended the newly elected House Speaker Thomas P. O'Neill Jr. on matters as mundane as distribution of inauguration tickets. Carter's early economic-stimulus proposal of a $50 rebate for all taxpayers became a laughing stock. In extended battles on various issues, he ended with a mixed scorecard on economy, energy, and health care proposals, with congressional Democrats frequently fighting each other as well as the White House. Carter's government reform proposals, such as the independent counsel statute and tighter financial disclosure rules for federal employees, gained broader legislative support, but their lasting impact was more dubious.

Clinton, too, sought a quick legislative start. With few close allies, he found himself beset with problems within his own party on Capitol Hill. In his early weeks in office, he backed down on a proposal to permit gays in the military, his first two nominees for attorney general were forced to withdraw after they ran into confirmation problems, and his economic-stimulus plan to send dollars to chiefly Democratic constituencies bogged down and in the Senate eventually became the victim of a Republican filibuster and objections by moderate Democrats. But his biggest setback came on his health-reform proposal, which was planned as the centerpiece of his legislative agenda. Lacking a specific proposal from his campaign or from congressional Democrats, Clinton and his White House staff—led by First Lady Hillary Rodham Clinton—spent most of 1993 in an elaborate process to produce a complex proposal that few understood which was designed to give federal guarantees of medical coverage to all Americans. By the time that House and Senate committees began to work on the proposal, Republican and industry opposition was deep-seated and Democrats were divided on their best legislative approach. With the bill bogged down in the House and the Senate amid the election campaign and with no agreement for votes in either chamber, the exercise became a legislative debacle. The chief political result was that Democrats lost the majority in both chambers in the 1994 election and never regained control during Clinton's presidency.

In other cases, presidents have moved cautiously, either because of a divided government in which they faced a hostile political environment with the other party controlling Congress or because their own forces held a weak hand. When John F. Kennedy took office in 1961, for example, his limited legislative goals were an acknowledgment of the reality on Capitol Hill. With Republicans having gained twenty-two House seats in the 1960 election, Kennedy was forced to do battle during his presidency with what was termed the "conservative coalition" of Republicans and southern Democrats, especially in the House. Although he was a product of Congress, Kennedy clearly distanced himself from the conservative Democratic chairmen in control of most committees; they largely represented an earlier political generation that was out of sync with the president's "New Frontier." And, unlike Johnson, Kennedy had little interest or skill in working the legislative machinery to advance his program.

Nixon's 1968 victory had little to do with domestic policies, and the new president was reluctant to disrupt Johnson's Great Society achievements. Nixon's presidency witnessed the activist Democrat-controlled Congress's significant expansion of domestic spending and regulation. Nixon's chief initiatives dealt with his politically popular attention to "law and order" issues. That resulted in several major pieces of legislation and, perhaps more importantly, led to major showdowns with the Senate on Supreme Court nominees, two of whom were defeated.

After his 1988 election, Bush was duly warned of the dilemma he faced with Congress when the Democrat-controlled Senate rejected his nomination of John Tower for defense secretary. In addition, the House was consumed that spring by an ethics investigation of Speaker Jim Wright that was spurred by Republican backbencher Newt Gingrich and led to Wright's resignation under fire in June 1989. The Bush team moved deliberately to prepare and advocate a legislative agenda, with emphasis placed on a capital gains tax cut and clean air amendments. Unexpectedly, Congress spent much of the year consumed by what became a successful bipartisan move to repeal a 1988 law to provide catastrophic insurance coverage to Medicare beneficiaries. Not until 1990 did Bush and Congress begin to seriously engage, chiefly in a budget summit that lasted for months and ultimately led the president to his politically fateful decision to abandon his "no new taxes" pledge.

The political shoes were reversed following the 1996 election when Clinton won a second term but faced a continuation of the Republican-controlled Congress. Once again, ethics conflicts poisoned the climate. The House began the new year with a virtually unanimous vote to reprimand Speaker Gingrich for improprieties in his personal finances. Then, in January1998, reports of Clinton's dealings with Monica Lewinsky led to an independent counsel investigation and ultimately to House impeachment, shutting down most serious legislative work for that year. Between those two events, Clinton and the Republican-controlled Congress reached agreement in 1997 on the Balanced Budget Act, which was designed to achieve its goal in 2002. But that deal was chiefly a political cessation of the budget war that had dominated the previous two years; in economic terms, it was little more than a ratification of the booming economy, which actually placed the federal budget into surplus in 1998, four years ahead of the once-optimistic schedule. In any case, this divided government became a synonym for paralysis.

As for the overwhelming reelections of Nixon and Reagan, the fact that they scored the biggest margins of any presidential candidates during the past forty years had minimal residual impact and offered the winners little political cover on Capitol Hill. Within a year, Nixon was deeply enmeshed in investigations of the Watergate scandal involving the cover-up of a burglary of Democratic headquarters. Two years after Reagan's landslide, Congress launched its extended investigation of the Iran–Contra affair concerning the administration's allegedly illegal transfer of funds to rebel forces in Nicaragua. In each case, some members of the president's own party were among his most severe critics. Would it have mattered if each president had campaigned more actively on behalf of candidates from his own party? Perhaps. But the larger factor, in all likelihood, is that the limited congressional Republican gains on Election Day in each case meant that there was little political loyalty for a president who, not coincidentally, became a lame duck on the next day.

As this chronology reveals, election results create a climate of expectations in Congress. Successful and cooperative candidates breed successful and cooperative legislating. While it is not quite that simple, of course, most members of Congress are shrewd politicians who are ever mindful of the shifting political winds. Except for those on the ideological extremes, they would rather not have to explain to constituents why they have cast votes against the program of a popular president. Achieving that state of equilibrium is an appropriate presidential goal, though it is easier said than done.

THE 2000 CAMPAIGN

From the start of his two-year bid for the presidency, George W. Bush and his election team appeared to be well aware of and responsive to these political dynamics. Bush laid out a well-defined campaign agenda—with a limited series of specific goals. He said that he planned to work closely with members of Congress in both parties. And his lead in public opinion polls throughout much of the contest gave him hope of winning a convincing victory on Election Day. But he encountered a series of setbacks and other bumps in the road that may frustrate his ability to deliver his campaign promises.

The most obvious limitation of Bush's victory, of course, was his unprecedented close margin: 271 to 267 in the electoral college, which took thirty-five days to become official because his victory in Florida was so narrow and so hotly contested that it required two U.S. Supreme Court decisions for it to be finally resolved. The fact that Bush trailed Gore by several hundred thousand in the nationwide popular vote count had no bearing on the official outcome; among many voters as well as other politicians, however, it enhanced the sense of how tenuous his victory was. As for the congressional results, the good news for Bush and the Republicans was that they retained their House and Senate majorities, at least in the postelection numbers. The bad news was that the fifty/fifty balance in the Senate when the 107th Congress convened, plus the 221 to 211 margin in the House (with two independents and one vacancy), not only represented electoral setbacks for the party but gave the new administration and its team virtually no room for error. The results created additional handicaps for Bush. In contrast to the case after the 1964 and 1980 presidential elections, few if any of the new lawmakers felt that they owed their local election to the new president or his coattails. In addition, although Bush regularly discussed his governing themes and priorities in his campaign speeches, there appeared to be little indication that they had caught fire during the campaign; nor was his victory a strong mandate for action.

Still, there was a striking consistency to Bush's campaign message and its focus on a few ideas. The campaign's textbook approach to legislative agenda setting began during the quest for the nomination. "Mr. Bush is the GOP nominee largely because of his agenda. [John] McCain was the character-only candidate," writes *Wall Street Journal* columnist Paul A. Gigot: "Mr. Bush is the Republican who wanted to cut taxes and who realized his party had to compete on education, Social Security and health care."[2]

Of all those issues, his Social Security initiative probably was the boldest and had the potential for the greatest public impact, though it carried significant political risks. Presidents and candidates generally have kept their distance from the issue, which has been termed the "third rail" in U.S. politics because politicians who touch it pay a big price. But generational pressures to fix the long-term financing shortfalls in the retirement system, plus many younger Americans' desire for greater control of their investments, led Bush to embrace proposals that allow individuals to allocate some of their Social Security funds to personal retirement accounts. The political balance could be dicey. In campaign speeches, Bush told seniors that their savings were secure: "No changes, no reductions, no way." At the same time, he told younger workers that he would advocate reforms so that the system would not go bankrupt in the longer term and that they would have the choice of higher returns on their funds. "We will give you the option to put a part of your payroll taxes into sound, responsible investments you control" became his campaign mantra.

Many Democrats, including Gore campaign advisers, not only opposed Bush's ideas in this area but were convinced that they could turn the Social Security debate in their favor, as past candidates have done. (Gore had proposed a more limited plan—which nonpartisan critics said lacked coherence—to use federal budget savings to extend the life of the Social Security trust fund.) They ran television commercials late in the campaign that claimed that Bush's plan would jeopardize either older retirees or younger workers. Bush responded that the Democrats were trying to scare seniors at Halloween time. Although Social Security reform became a routine part of his campaign speeches, Bush did not offer a specific proposal. Instead, he and his advisers cited half a dozen proposals that had been introduced by members of Congress from both parties and suggested that their own proposal would be consistent with those earlier versions. Bush also raised the possibility that he would convene a commission with private citizens to lay the groundwork for legislative action. In the end, it appeared, Bush's Social Security discussion had been a political plus and had opened the door to a major legislative initiative. Major action would not come early in the Bush presidency, but in spring 2001 Bush named a commission to make recommendations, and such reforms have the potential to become his defining legacy in domestic policy.

Bush approached his takeover with a commitment to his agenda and confidence that he could achieve it. At the center of this approach was the campaign's view that his goals were popular with the public and that lawmakers in both parties were eager to break the legislative logjam of the Clinton years and address these national priorities. Election Day exit polls showed support for those goals, including Social Security reform, said Representative Rob Portman, an Ohio Republican who has been a key player on Capitol Hill and was a close policy adviser to the Bush team during the campaign. Likewise, public opinion polls showed support for Bush's proposed tax cuts. With near-lockstep Republican unity, their enactment in June became Bush's first major legislative accomplishment.

Regardless of his narrow election mandate, Bush and his advisers were hoping that widespread public support for his ideas would pave the way to bipartisan action. For example, his proposal for across-the-board tax cuts—smaller than those proposed by Reagan twenty years earlier and with features to benefit lower income groups—came amid huge surpluses in the federal budget and some postelection concern that an economic slowdown could lead to a recession. On other tax matters, Republicans delivered on their pledge to eliminate the estate and gift tax and to eliminate the so-called marriage penalty; although both had received considerable support from congressional Democrats, Clinton vetoed the separate plans before the election and there were not sufficient votes to override him.

On other issues such as education policy the thin Republican majorities in the House and Senate made it clear that Republican success would require bipartisan cooperation. Seeking to break Washington's gridlock, Bush repeatedly said that he was "a uniter, not a divider." He cited his success as governor in working across the aisle with the Texas legislature.

Notwithstanding his narrow victory, Bush acted as though he had a strong electoral mandate while he prepared to take office. If he succeeds in enacting substantial parts of his legislative agenda, he may break the political rulebook again by showing the benefits of bold self-confidence. Another factor that might work in Bush's favor is that, with the broad consensus in the national political climate, his campaign agenda was not radically different from Gore's. Both candidates discussed, for example, the need to provide prescription drug coverage to seniors, though they differed on the details and on whether to make the benefit part of the Medicare program. So, too, Bush's pledges to improve education standards and restore more accountability to local schools were promises that many Democrats could support.

Even in the most positive political circumstances, legislative success requires skill, timing, and some luck. But the most important lesson of the past forty years may be that presidential agenda setting requires a well-planned and consistent political message. If the national leader wants to change public policy, he must reach out from the start to the lawmakers whose support will be essential.

NOTES

1. Richard E. Cohen, *Rostenkowski* (Chicago: Ivan R. Dee, 1999), 51.
2. Paul A. Gigot, "Now Bush Has to Win on the Issues," *The Wall Street Journal*, 8 September 2000: A18.

6

Presidential Influence on Congress: New Solutions to Old Problems

Nathan Dietz

The literature on interbranch relations often focuses on a single, seemingly simple question: Which branch has more power, the executive or the legislative? Not surprisingly, scholars who study the balance of power between the branches have likened "power" to a number of related concepts, such as a president's "success" or "support" in Congress and the president's "influence" over Congress.[1] Much research in the field focuses on one of the first two concepts, for "success" and "support" are both intuitively appealing and amenable to empirical analysis: Does Congress pass the legislation the president advocates and reject the bills he dislikes? In fact, the excellent survey of the empirical literature by Bond, Fleisher, and Krutz calls the question of why presidents enjoy more or less success in the legislative arena primary in the field.[2] The authors distinguish president-centered studies of executive–legislative interactions from Congress-centered studies by noting that the former approach is dedicated to the search for influence while the latter studies success. Moreover, they argue that because much of the president's legislative environment is beyond his control, "the question of success is broader and more important than the question of presidential influence."[3] Thus, the idea of influence—the ability of the president to get Congress to do what it would not otherwise do—has not received nearly as much attention from empirical scholars as success and support have.

Certainly, influence is difficult to measure, especially compared with success. Presidential influence is extremely difficult to characterize and measure, mainly because it manifests itself in so many different ways.[4] When the president takes a position on a policy proposal, mentions the proposal to the press, or even delivers an address about it to the public, he is unmistakably attempting to influence the legislative process. However, when he dispatches an aide to Capitol Hill to lobby legislators or communicates his policy preferences to his partisan allies behind closed doors, his influence is harder to verify but may in fact be more potent. Most frustratingly for empirically minded scholars, the president frequently influences the legislative process without doing anything at all; the literature on anticipated reactions is based on the idea that presidential influence may be most powerful of all when it is unseen. To the extent that this is true, documenting and measuring presidential influence seem impossible.[5]

In this chapter, I survey recent works in the field that use the logic of formal theory and innovations in quantitative empirical analysis in an attempt to characterize the president's influence on what Congress does. Potentially, the payoffs are huge; a successful characterization of influence would satisfy presidential scholars of every methodological persuasion. If the concern of scholars who study presidential success is to characterize "governmental responsiveness,"[6] a better understanding of the things to which the government and the actors within it respond certainly furthers this goal. Moreover, the ability to measure influence is more important, not less, because much of the apparatus of government is beyond the president's control. If, today, the president is less capable of utilizing established means of influence to achieve his goals—because of declining partisan affiliation in the electorate, the electoral security of legislators, and the limitations of plebiscitary government[7]—then presidents who are adept at using other means of influence will enjoy much more legislative success than less skilled presidents. Far from being an outmoded concept in today's national political environment, influence is still a key theoretical concept.

However, as is the case in other fields in political science, the impact of much current research is tempered by its technical complexity. Many scholars, not to mention practitioners, in the field are unaware of the vast progress that has been made in recent years in studying presidential influence, as opposed to success. In this chapter, I survey a wide range of recent work that attempts to untie the knotty problem of characterizing and measuring presidential influence. Several excellent surveys review the research designs used by empirical scholars of presidential success in the legislative arena, but to date only one survey of the literature related to influence is available.[8]

The focus of this chapter is a basic model of interbranch activity in the policy-making process, in which inactivity, or "gridlock," is caused by the resistance of those actors who possess veto power over certain proposed policy changes. Following this discussion, I turn to the role of parties and elections as possible antidotes to gridlock; later, I discuss models in which both legislators and presidents can exploit private information about their own preferences to gain bargaining advantages over their adversaries. The need is greater than ever for suitably sophisticated theories of the strategic interaction between the president and Congress, especially after the 2000 elections, when President Bush confronts a Congress in which the parties are closer to equal strength than they have ever been in the postwar era. Without a clear mandate from the electorate, whatever success he enjoys will be due chiefly to his "skill and will," to quote Richard Neustadt[9]; now more than ever, scholars of interbranch politics are able to explain what that means and how important it is.

INTERBRANCH RELATIONS AND THE LEGISLATIVE PROCESS: THE BASIC GRIDLOCK MODEL

To begin, consider figure 6.1, which illustrates the essential features of the interaction that could occur between the president and Congress when a policy is proposed.[10]

Assumptions

The straight line in figure 6.1 represents the *policy space* or range of possible policy alternatives within a given issue area. Most models assume that the policy space is *unidimensional* or that the primary differences of opinion among political actors can be reduced to a single dimension. This is true, for instance, of the many issue areas in which the policy proposals could be extremely liberal, extremely conservative, or anywhere in between, with subtle but discernible differences among all the policy alternatives. All "players" in the model are assumed to be self-interested in the sense that they derive benefits, or *utility*, from any proposal that becomes law. Every player's preferences over the range of possible alternatives are *single peaked*. That is, of all the possible alternatives, exactly one—one's *ideal point*—gives the player maximum utility, and each player gains progressively less utility from proposals that are located farther away from that ideal point. A convenient assumption is that the preferences of each player are both single peaked and *symmet-*

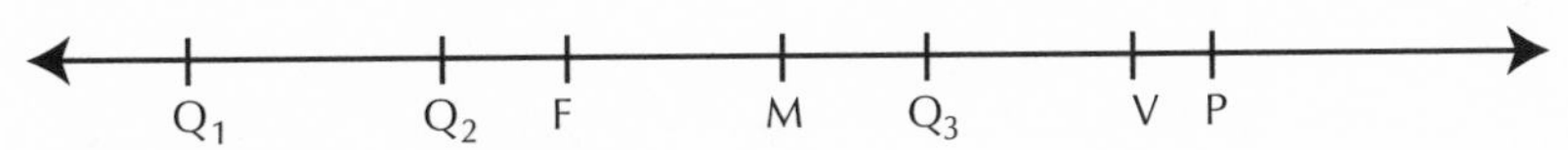

Figure 6.1 The Basic Gridlock Model

ric: a policy that is one unit to the left of one's ideal point yields as much utility as a policy that is one unit to the right, however units are measured.

Notation

The letters on the line in figure 6.1 denote the ideal points of the most important players; for simplicity, assume that the players with ideal points on the far left are liberals and those with ideal points on the far right are conservatives. M is the ideal point of the median member of the House, the 218th most liberal (or 218th most conservative) member; for simplicity, suppose that M is also the ideal point of the median member of the Senate.[11] Suppose that the president is a conservative; in that case, his ideal point *P* is located to the right of both medians. The remaining ideal points belong to members who play crucial roles in the legislative process. The first, the *veto pivot* in the House, has an ideal point denoted by *V*. The veto pivot is the 146th most conservative House member, and he or she plays a crucial role should the president veto a policy proposal. If the House were to attempt to override the veto of a bill that the president considers too liberal, the veto pivot and the 145 members more conservative than the pivot would vote to sustain the president's veto, thus preventing the policy proposal from becoming law. The remaining ideal point, *F*, belongs to the *filibuster pivot*, who plays a similar role in blocking legislation. The filibuster pivot, the forty-first most liberal senator in this context, will vote with the forty more liberal senators against cloture, which would enable any of them to filibuster an unacceptable policy proposal, thus preventing it from becoming law.

Sequence of Play

Any policy proposal must pass through four stages before becoming law:

1. The House passes a bill.
2. The Senate passes a bill, which, if different from the House bill, results in a compromise forged by a conference committee.
3. The president signs the bill, ending the game, or vetoes it, sending the bill to stage 4.
4. Both houses decide whether to override the president's veto, after which the bill becomes law if a two-thirds supermajority in both houses votes to override the veto.

All legislators and the president have perfect knowledge of the preferences—that is, the ideal points—of all other players in the model. Everyone knows, for instance, the president's *veto strategy*: his plan that dictates whether he will veto any proposal that Congress sends up to Capitol Hill. Moreover, everyone knows that each House member has a *voting strategy* and an *override strategy* that dictates how each will vote on final passage and on an override, if one occurs. Finally, everyone knows what the *voting strategy* and the *cloture strategy* are for each senator. Armed with this *perfect information* about the ideal points and strategies for each player, everyone is able not only to foresee the eventual fate of any proposal but also to anticipate the reactions to any move he or she makes. A member who wants to change the status quo knows, for instance, whether a proposal for change will pass the House and survive the Senate without getting filibustered, whether the president will veto the final bill, and whether or not the veto will be overridden. Everyone chooses a strategy that is poised to deliver the most utility, given the preferences and strategies of the other players. When everyone has chosen a strategy that is *optimal* given the strategies of the other players, the game is said to be in *equilibrium*; the outcome that results—with or without a bill becoming law—is the *equilibrium outcome*.

Equilibrium Outcomes and Gridlock

It is clear from the model that the structure of the policy-making process allows for change only under certain circumstances.[12] The locations of the *status quo policies* Q_1, Q_2, and Q_3 in figure 6.1 illustrate the various ways in which legislation can change the law or the various equilibrium outcomes the model predicts. First, a relatively unpopular status quo policy like Q_1, which the president probably promised to correct in his winning campaign, is a sitting duck. Everyone but the most liberal members of Congress would prefer a less liberal policy; assuming (again, for simplicity) that the initial proposal is made in the House under an open rule, the bill will be amended until its location is exactly at M, the House median.[13] Since, by definition, the median and at least half the House prefer M to Q_1, the bill will pass. In the Senate, even if some liberal senator threatens to filibuster the bill, there are certainly enough votes to invoke cloture; because the House bill is also located at the Senate median, the Senate also will pass it.[14] The president also prefers M to Q_1, so he will sign the bill. Thus, the effect is *full convergence* to the median, the same prediction that we would make if the lawmaking process involved a unicameral legislature and no presidential involvement at all.[15]

For a status quo policy like Q_2, change is possible, but moderate lawmakers will likely feel unsatisfied with the amount of change that can be attained. The House would like to pass M again and send it to the Senate, but liberal senators who threaten to filibuster it have enough support to make their threat credible. Judging from the location of the filibuster pivot *F*, at least forty senators will vote against cloture because they prefer Q_2 to M, so that M would never become law. Either because the House realizes this and offers a more liberal proposal or because a compromise forged in conference committee would likely make the bill more liberal than M, the bill sent to the White House is located between *F* and M, exactly as far to the right of *F* as Q_2 is to *F*'s left. Thus, the filibuster pivot *F* is satisfied; the president signs the bill, however grudgingly given his preferences for a truly conservative policy; and the equilibrium outcome is *partial convergence* to the median.

Finally, for a status quo policy like Q_3, no bill will become law even though a majority of both members would prefer at least some change. Liberals in either house cannot propose a more liberal policy because the president will veto the bill, and his veto will be upheld, because *V* and the 145 House members more conservative than *V* will vote to sustain it.[16] Conservatives in the House cannot propose anything more conservative than Q_3 because, as the location of M illustrates, a majority of at least one house will vote against this proposal. Thus, the equilibrium outcome in this situation is *gridlock*: no policy change occurs. In this case, the president's influence is present but only as a negative force; he can credibly threaten to veto an unacceptably liberal policy proposal because, as everyone realizes, his allies in the House have the votes to thwart an override attempt.

The model is thus capable of predicting policy changes that are acceptable to moderate members; policy changes that are not as moderate as these members would prefer because of obstructionist tactics, or threats thereto, from pivotal legislators; and gridlock, whereby nothing seems to be happening although many people want change. Furthermore, it is easy to generalize: if the president is liberal, his ideal point simply shifts to the left of the median. His vetoes are then upheld by *V*, the 145th most liberal House member (or the thirty-fourth most liberal senator), and the forty-first most conservative senator acts as the filibuster pivot, representing the senator who must be pacified if a filibuster is to be prevented. If the president is more conservative (or liberal) than the median in both houses, but less conservative (or liberal) than the veto pivot *V*, then his ideal point *P* and not *V* acts as the constraint on policy proposals by liberals (or conservatives). Finally, the degree of convergence toward the median by a policy that becomes law depends on how far the status quo policy is from the median of each house. If the status quo lies within the interval bracketed by *F* and *V* in figure 6.1, for instance, no policy change at all can occur; thus, this range is known as the *gridlock region*.

ELABORATIONS ON THE BASIC GRIDLOCK MODEL

The Electoral Connection

Skeptics may immediately respond that the gridlock model in its simplest form abstracts far too much away from real U.S. politics. First, it seems to leave the role of constituents, interest groups, campaign contributors, and the like completely unspecified. Second, it predicts that very little change will occur, except under special circumstances. One important and timely question is, What happens when a national election occurs that sweeps in a new president, new members of Congress, and at least one new set of campaign promises? The winning candidates argue they have a mandate to fulfill, especially if their party controls not only the presidency but also both houses of Congress. Does the model predict that such change seldom occurs, even under unified government? The important and provocative answer to that question, in the context of the model, is best elucidated by Krehbiel and by Brady and Volden.[17]

Exponents of models like the one illustrated above argue that the ideal points of legislators and presidents are determined, in part, by the influence of constituents, interest groups, media coverage, and party loyalty.[18] Because the model is only designed to explain policy making at a particular moment in time, it is possible in principle to develop a model of how these factors determine the ideal points of all players in the model for the issue area in question at any given moment. In practice, formal theories of lawmaking treat political preferences as products of some unspecified mechanism that translates external influences, "inside-the-Beltway" influences like cues from trusted colleagues,[19] and personal policy preferences into induced preferences over policy alternatives that can be located on a single policy dimension, such as the one depicted in figure 6.1.

Normative critics of gridlock in government often lament that positive theories such as this are silent about the real problem: When the public elects a president and a Congress, they want results. When instead they get gridlock, whether because of interparty conflict or the necessity of forming supermajority coalitions, their expressed will is subverted. Thus, a particularly provocative question is whether the origins of divided government can be found in the electorate. Much empirical literature has focused on the fact that congressional and presidential election results are only tenuously connected, if at all, not only because they take place at different times but also because voters may have different reasons to vote for a president and for their representatives in Congress.[20] Might voters actually prefer divided government, and perhaps gridlock, to unified government that attempts vigorously to fulfill its perceived mandate?

Political economists Alberto Alesina and Howard Rosenthal, with various other authors,[21] have developed a model in which voters purposely split their tickets: they coordinate their votes in presidential and congressional elections because they prefer divided government. They split their tickets purposely to achieve a balance between two ideologically motivated parties. Because broader programmatic change than they would prefer occurs under unified government, and divided government yields more moderate policies, voters are satisfied in equilibrium. In their model, because voters cast their ballots under considerable uncertainty over how the parties will translate their platforms into policy change, some voters withdraw their support of the president's party in midterm elections after learning how his party actually governs. The model assumes that voters are sophisticated enough to revise their assessments of the president's party, if necessary, after the first two years. Thus, unified control of the government can be a mixed blessing; the price of control over both lawmaking branches for the majority party is increased accountability to an often unforgiving electorate. Ingberman and Villani make this assumption explicit by stating that parties receive diminishing returns from holding "too many" offices; all else being equal, they would prefer to control Congress and the presidency, but the utility that they gain from controlling both branches is less than the sum of its parts.[22]

Although these models predict that policy change does occur after elections, and the assumptions about voter behavior have been empirically tested and often verified,[23] the lawmaking models focus on the conditions under which elections relieve the pressure of policy gridlock, not on the motivations of voters. Rather than incorporate elections into the model explicitly, the exponents of the gridlock model discuss how elections cause sudden change in the types of policy change that can occur. What is remarkable, given the role of elections in these theories as the primary means of relieving policy gridlock, is how limited their effects often are. Figure 6.2, from Krehbiel, illustrates the effect of elections on the size of the gridlock region from the Carter presidency through the first two years of Clinton's first term.[24] Because Democrats controlled Congress throughout this period, and because of the tremendous advantage that congressional incumbents held during this period, the chief effect of these elections was to change the president's ideology. When this happened—in 1980 and 1992—a small range of policies on the Right and Left were "released" from the gridlock region. When this happens, a skilled president can enjoy substantial success by changing status quo policies that had not been changed in at least four years. It is clear from figure 6.2, though, that many moderate status quo policies remain in the

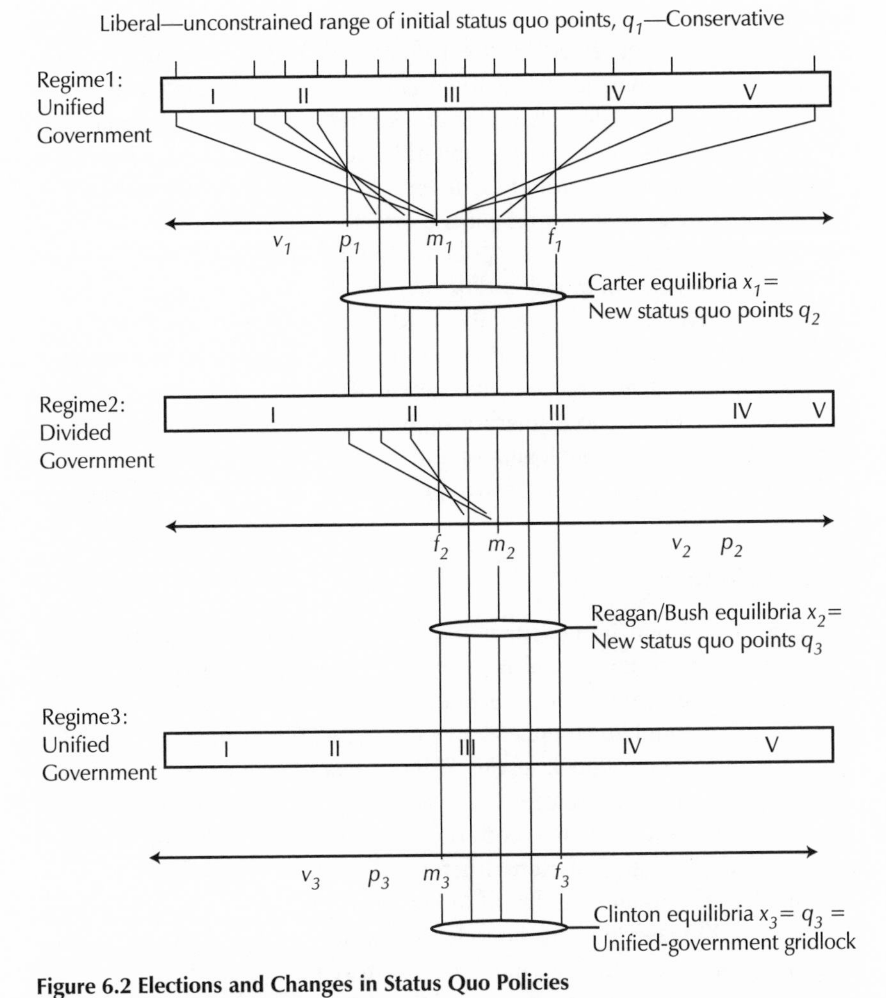

Figure 6.2 Elections and Changes in Status Quo Policies

Source: From Keith Krehbiel, *Pivotal Politics: A Theory of U.S. Lawmaking* (Chicago: University of Chicago Press, 1998), p. 41. Reprinted with permission.

gridlock region and cannot be changed; moreover, the model implies that the administration gets exactly *one* chance to address the major issues of its first term before gridlock again ensues.[25]

The implications of this are profound for students of presidential influence. Krehbiel argues that this figure explains the existence of "honeymoon" periods of extreme legislative productivity for newly elected presidents, as well as the disappointment that many observers felt when Clinton's election led largely to "unified gridlock" and not to the broad programmatic overhaul of the status quo suggested by the Democrats' 1992 platform.[26] In fact, extending this rationale leads one to question even more of the received wisdom about elections. The only way gridlock is reduced by congressional elections is if the locations of the veto and filibuster pivots change considerably. A change in partisan control of Congress, as occurred in 1994, may change the type of policies that can pass if the preferences of the median member change. But the range of existing policies that *can* be changed is still defined by the size and location of the gridlock region. Thus, for instance, if liberals and conservatives each compose about 40 percent of the Senate and one-third of the House, even constant turnover among moderates near the middle of the line in figure 6.1 in national elections may not reduce gridlock appreciably.[27] One of the primary insights of the simple gridlock model is that the "hard core" of ideologues on either side of the spectrum can always exploit the structure of the legislative process to keep laws from passing.

The Party in Government

Another obvious omission of these gridlock models is political parties. Considering that the congressional literature has long been engaged in a lively debate about the strength of congressional parties and the reasons for their strength, their complete absence as an explanatory factor in gridlock models seems glaring.[28] The gridlock model seems at first glance to be better suited to eras during which the parties were seen as weak because they were less polarized, as in the 1950s when both the Democrats and the Republicans had liberal and conservative factions. In today's political atmosphere, with far fewer moderate legislators and with interparty hostilities at a fever pitch following the 2000 election, can a model of lawmaking that does not afford a prominent role to parties have much explanatory power?

One obvious answer to the basic model is that a strong party, especially in the House, controls the Rules Committee and can prevent the moderation of party leaders' proposals via floor amendments by using restrictive rules.[29] Thus, the majority party's agenda control does, in fact, matter; the policies that emerge from the House can reflect more of the will of the party leadership than would be the case if parties were weaker. However, assuming that majority party leaders in the House are confident enough in the cohesion of their partisans to propose relatively extreme change, the bills still have to pass the Senate, in which the filibuster pivot may still credibly threaten to invoke Rule 22 against insufficiently moderate bills. Finally, as House Republicans discovered in 1995 and 1996, the president can credibly threaten to veto key planks of the majority party's platform, forcing either compromise or a virtual collapse of the lawmaking process.

The assumption of complete information among all members is the reason why party leadership does not play a more significant role in gridlock models. The only effect that polarization of the parties has is on the size of the gridlock region; if every Democrat is a confirmed liberal, and every Republican is a staunch conservative, then the gridlock region, as defined by the veto and filibuster pivots, will be quite wide and little change will happen. Given that everyone knows the strategy that every other player is prepared to employ, the hands of any policy proposer are tied. Coalition leaders, for instance, never need to twist arms or make concessions to individual members to gain their support because they know with certainty where every legislator stands and must act accordingly. Because, in equilibrium, deviations from this pattern are unexpected, analyses like Krehbiel's of presidential power are not consistent with the basic gridlock model. Although Krehbiel develops a quantifiable measure of presidential power and draws many interesting conclusions, the fact remains that vetoes never should occur in equilibrium in the basic model, nor should members switch their positions in equilibrium, given the assumption of complete information.[30]

Multidimensionality

One of the more esoteric objections to the basic model, but nonetheless an important one, is the assumption that all the differences of opinion that matter in an issue area can be reduced to a single dimension. Even if most of the time members vote according to their ideological stances, what guarantees that this is the case in all issue areas of interest? To take one recent example, the issues involved in the spring 2000 negotiation over granting China permanent most-favored-nation status as a trading partner separated legislators along many dimensions: the likelihood that district businesses would prosper or suffer, objections to the Chinese government's substandard record on human rights issues, and concerns about the globalization of U.S. industry, certainly among others. In general, negotiations over the budget often break down as members seek to add riders to appropriations bills to help their own districts. Especially given the fact that the unidimensionality assumption is least likely to hold for important issues like this, is the basic model really useful in most circumstances?

One answer to the question has to do with tractability. Positive political theorists have long recognized that even when there are only two dimensions to a policy issue, virtually any outcome can occur; because the model is unable to advance concrete predictions even in this case without assuming some constraints on the agenda-setting process, its real world applicability is minimal.[31] Even though the legislative process in the basic gridlock model explicitly incorporates realistic constraints on the behavior of the players, extending the model to a multidimensional policy space would be difficult. For this reason, many authors argue that there are justifiable reasons to assume that the wide ranges of differences of opinion on most, if not necessarily all, issues reduce to differences along a single dimension: the liberal–conservative dimension. Voters, no less than legislators, often employ the cognitive shortcut of reducing most issues to the simple liberal–conservative question when forming their attitudes about politics.[32] Poole and Rosenthal summarize their analyses of roll-call voting in every session of Congress by noting that the liberal–conservative dimension, however liberals and conservatives are defined in the parlance of the times, explains around 80 percent of the variance among legislators in an average legislative session.[33] They do find evidence that a second dimension occasionally influences roll-call voting, as in the 1950s and 1960s when racial politics became salient as a dimension that divided not only economic conservatives but also economic liberals. However, as Carmines and Stimson illustrate,[34] over time liberals and conservatives began to adopt distinctive stances on racial issues as well as economic issues, so that this second dimension slowly became indistinguishable from the primary liberal–conservative dimension.

In terms of the model, if it were feasible to consider a multidimensional choice space, it would certainly be more possible to imagine a more influential president and more policy change in general. Even though the preferences of all actors would still be common knowledge, a skilled proposer would still be able to add seemingly unrelated riders to any bill, forcing would-be opponents to decide whether the amended bill is basically a liberal–conservative issue or something else. The president, meanwhile, would be able to induce more concessions toward his position by threatening vetoes, even though his rationale for issuing the veto would seem to be unrelated to the "real" issue at hand.

In practice, the legislative process sometimes takes "wrong turns" that would never be predicted by the basic gridlock model: although the basic model predicts that these events never occur, we occasionally see presidential vetoes, filibusters, and policy proposals that pass even though they are far from the preferred policies of moderate members. Luckily, there is no need to stipulate that the policy space is multidimensional to explain these phenomena; all we need to do is relax the assumption of complete information for players in the model.

RELAXING THE COMPLETE INFORMATION ASSUMPTION: UNCERTAINTY ABOUT LEGISLATIVE PREFERENCES

To many observers, the logic of the gridlock model is intuitive and its predictions seem generally accurate. It predicts that the president and Congress will occasionally agree on policy change, depending on the array of preferences among the players; that many, if not most, bills will pass by supermajorities, whether because the status quo has few defenders or because of the need to neutralize the threat of filibusters and presidential vetoes[35]; and that the president very often exercises his influence silently, by making legislators gather enough support for a bill to override a veto if necessary. However, vetoes, filibusters, and other characteristics of the political process are very often absent, as are more traditional presidential activities, such as lobbying legislators, taking positions on upcoming legislation, and "going public" with direct appeals to voters to support favored legislation. As these activities do not occur in the basic model because of the assumption of complete information, it is necessary to relax this assumption. The following two sections discuss studies that have done just that, which allows for richer theories of presidential influence.

Persuasion and Conversion of Legislators

These terms have similar, but not identical, meanings for congressional and presidential scholars. *Persuasion* tends to refer to targeted arguments that sway a legislator's mind on an issue, while *conversion* tends to refer to changes of one's mind that persist beyond the vote in question.[36] *Persuasion*, as described in the literature, typically involves convincing a legislator that his or her constituents will not object to his or her vote on a bill, while *conversion* usually refers to a legislator changing his or her preferences for change in an entire issue area.[37] Each term is usually distinguished from tangible short-term inducements, such as favor trading, and from bargaining, which can mean either the granting of favors or particularized benefits or the alteration of a policy proposal to win additional support. All these concepts have one thing in common: the president must use them if he either is uncertain about the level of support for a preferred policy or thinks that he can attract more support with positive inducements of some kind.

The chief difficulty in determining the impact of presidential persuasion is that it is very often unobservable. Generally, this problem can be resolved if the analyst has a way of knowing, or estimating, what voting on a bill was expected to be, given all the factors that enter into a legislator's voting decision. Calvin Mouw and Michael MacKuen use *cutpoint analysis* to determine the extent to which members are voting differently than would be predicted by a simple liberalism–conservatism measure.[38] Using roll-call voting data, they use an algebraic trick to determine the location of the "cutpoint," the most likely point on the liberal–conservative dimension that separates bill supporters from bill opponents, on bills on which the president takes a position. Using these cutpoints, they classify members according to whether they are more or less liberal than the cutpoint and use this classification as a baseline prediction about the vote tally. Finally, they infer presidential influence from the difference between the normal vote prediction and the observed vote tally.

The Mouw–MacKuen baseline model is cleverly simple and easy to apply to other types of influence. The authors also use the approach to measure the influence of congressional party leaders, where the analogue to a presidential position is a unified voting stand by the party's two top leaders. However, their method only works for issues for which the liberal–conservative dimension is a good indicator of member preferences. By purging their sample of votes of all bills that divide members along other dimensions, they lose the ability to identify presidential influence over issues that tend to split well-established coalitions of members.

In a series of papers,[39] Terry Sullivan uses *headcount analysis* to study presidential influence, most often in Lyndon Johnson's administration. His data, perhaps the most unique data set in the field of presidential–congressional relations, come from private records from White House congressional liaisons, who had the responsibility of conducting "headcounts" or polling legislators to find out how they would vote on administration proposals. These studies generally uncover evidence that these presidential lobbying initiatives coincided with considerable change between the initial stated positions of members and their final voting decisions. In certain studies, Sullivan also uses a baseline model to predict member support before the first headcount is taken.[40] As with cutpoint analysis, Sullivan builds a multivariate model that incorporates most of the key influences on legislative decision making to estimate likely voting behavior before the president begins lobbying for votes. Any change that occurs is presumed to have occurred because of presidential contact, a conclusion that is quite powerful because the analysis takes place prior to the roll-call vote.

The chief drawback of headcount analysis is that the data are generally difficult and costly to obtain.[41] Reliable data on presidential liaison activities are available only for a few presidents, and generally speaking, these data are hard to gather until a presidential library opens. Moreover, the fact that

Sullivan's studies typically center around the Johnson administration opens the question of how generalizable his results are to other, less Congress-oriented presidents. Finally, as George Edwards notes,[42] headcount data are often taken hastily and reflect the fact that certain opponents are probably not worth calling on, even for a president as ambitious and persuasive as Lyndon Johnson. Still, despite their flaws, these data give Sullivan the enviable ability to measure the effects of presidential lobbying before floor activity began, which is key to headcount analysis.

Finally, Keith Krehbiel as well as Brady and Volden employ *switcher analysis* to determine which legislators changed positions over two or more related votes.[43] Although the gridlock model they employ does not predict that any member will switch his or her vote, these authors leave open the possibility that someone or something might convince a member to change his or her vote or that switching occurs primarily among members who are close to indifferent between voting for and against a motion—that is, among members closest to pivotal members. They conclude that the instances of switching they observe occur most frequently among members either close to the median (Brady and Volden) or close to the veto or filibuster pivots (Krehbiel). The only drawback to switcher analysis is that two or more votes are required, and the votes must be "clean," in that the bill in question must not be altered substantially between the motions under consideration.[44] Also, the likelihood that these bills or issues are qualitatively different from those bills that sail through the legislative process, as predicted by the model, makes it difficult to use switcher analysis to explain position switching in general.

How successful is persuasion as a means of influencing Congress? The president tends to recall previous attempts at persuasion when trying to change the minds of legislators, realizing the dangers of "going to the well" too often with personal appeals.[45] Additionally, members who seem to be easily persuaded by the president often suffer a lack of respect from other legislators, who view members who blindly follow the president's advice on all issues as "water carriers."[46] Thus, some scholars have posited that the returns from trying to persuade members too often diminish rapidly over time. However, studies that test this notion have found that this generalization is not true in the aggregate.[47] In fact, Sullivan infers from the notion that initial support for the president's position declines over time, while the percentage of "persuadable" legislators who change their minds remains constant, that Johnson's influence—defined here as the ability to cause members to vote for a bill that they had earlier expressed a reluctance to support—may actually have *increased* over time. Still, a popular president probably needs to worry less about wearing out his welcome. To the extent that legislators and presidents share a "common electoral fate,"[48] members are leery of following the policy advice of an unpopular president but may be more likely to follow a popular president's lead, especially a newly elected president.[49]

Vote Trading

When might a president enter into a quid pro quo arrangement with a legislator, given the other, lower cost means of influence he could use instead? Vote trading occurs when a policy is so important that failure could hamper the president's effectiveness in the future.[50] In rare cases, a president may implement the "full-court press," combining scores of personal appeals and full attention by the liaison staff with offers of particularized benefits for members who support his proposal. Generally, however, staffers from the liaison office guard the president's time jealously, preferring instead to lobby members of Congress themselves.[51]

As with persuasion, there are good reasons why presidents cannot make a habit of trading for legislators' votes. Some members' votes are simply impossible to procure because there is little they need. Edwards characterizes southern Democrats of the 1960s, with their near invulnerability in the one-party South and their independent sources of campaign support, in this way; the president could offer them nothing that could change their minds about policies they opposed.[52] Another constraint on the president's ability to bargain with members over time is outlined by Sullivan.[53] He notes that when the president possesses imperfect knowledge about the preferences of legislators, he cannot interpret the legislator's reluctance to take a position as true indifference on the issue. Because the member may be misrepresenting his or her preferences to gain additional benefits from the president, the president must have some doubt that the member is bargaining in good faith. However, to counteract this doubt, the member occasionally finds it worthwhile to take clear positions even when he or she is truly unsure or ambivalent about supporting the policy. In some cases, for some members of Congress, the short-term gains from misrepresenting one's preferences to the president may not outweigh the loss in credibility and the subsequent loss in bargaining position resulting from this misrepresentation.

Legislators trade votes with each other in much the same way as the president trades for members' votes. Diana Evans discusses the long-term impacts of the vote-trading practices of committee chairs who control the allocation of public works projects.[54] The main options from which the chairs must choose include giving projects to supporters of the bill, buying the votes of a minimal winning coalition at the lowest possible cost, or giving projects to anyone who asks for one. The first option seems wasteful, at least in the short run, but may be necessary to fend off a possible veto or a parliamentary challenge. The second option is the most efficient from the chair's point of view, for one's supply of favors to trade is limited, but it is also the option that places the passage of the allocation plan in the most jeopardy. The third option seems foolish, indeed, but may make it easier for the chair to craft similar proposals in the future. Thus, it may actually be cheaper in the long run.[55]

In theory, vote trading could occur in complete information models like the simple gridlock model, if the president decides that he can trade for the votes of members who would certainly oppose him in the absence of favor trading. When the president faces a rival coalition leader, who also has favors to trade for votes *against* the president's bill, he is often faced with a bidding war; as a result, he has to construct a coalition of supporters that is greater than a minimal winning vote to ensure that his rival coalition builder does not cut too deeply into his margin of victory.[56] In the absence of such a rival, the president, at least as much as political action committees are in James Snyder's model,[57] is able to act as a clearinghouse, releasing members to "vote their districts" and debiting their accounts so that the defecting legislator "owes him one."[58]

In short, vote-trading initiatives are uncommon among both presidents and congressional leaders, except in special circumstances. When they do occur, however, they do not always take the expected form; sometimes the president offers favors not to the members who are ideologically most predisposed to supporting the bill but, rather, to potentially supportive members who have not already taken a position or who do not have overwhelming constituent interests that effectively determine their voting decisions.[59] In the case of the North American Free Trade Agreement (NAFTA), for instance, after controlling for constituency interests and campaign contributions, the likelihood that President Clinton offered a legislator a benefit in exchange for his or her support of NAFTA does not depend on the member's economic philosophy.[60] Tests of the impact of vote trading, then, when researchers are lucky enough to have data on who bargained with the president, should include measures of constituency influence to make sure that the true impact of presidential influence is not overstated.[61]

UNCERTAINTY ABOUT THE PRESIDENT'S PREFERENCES: VETO THREATS, PUBLIC STATEMENTS, AND THE PRESIDENT'S REPUTATION

Even though "everyone knows" that vote trading and presidential persuasion affect the way legislators vote, empirical evidence of their impact is difficult to find, perhaps because theory has only recently begun to tell researchers where to look for it. Much the same can be said for the president's reputation and prestige, two concepts that are central to Richard Neustadt's classic work on the modern presidency.[62] As Charles Cameron points out, these ideas also remained indistinct to empirically minded presidential scholars for too long; not only were they theoretically indistinct, but they were difficult to measure. To paraphrase Cameron, who borrows from the language of Bachrach and Baratz and others, presidential power or influence appears in three forms or "faces."[63] The first, outright compulsion, rarely occurs in the legislative arena, although Terry Moe and his coauthors argue that it structures interaction between the branches.[64] The second, anticipated reactions, is present in the gridlock model through the implicit threat of the president and ideologically extreme members of Congress to derail the legislative process. The third, the ability to use one's reputation to manipulate the beliefs of others, has remained elusive. As Cameron points out, although the concept has been right there in Neustadt for forty years, only now are theorists able to develop models that characterize the third face of power and illustrate its effects.

Sequential Veto Bargaining

Cameron begins by noting that complete information models, like the simple gridlock model analyzed above, never predict that the president uses anything but the second face of power to influence the legislative process, for he never actually vetoes any bills in equilibrium but undoubtedly induces changes in the bills that Congress considers.[65] Thus, Cameron begins his explication of the *veto-override model* by relaxing the assumption in the unidimensional model that everyone knows with certainty whom the veto pivot is. Such uncertainty about this member's identity makes the president, as well as the proposer, less certain about the outcome of an override attempt, but everyone is able to narrow down the possible veto pivots to members whose ideal points fall within a given interval. This is illustrated in figure 6.3, where for simplicity the location of the filibuster pivot is not specified,

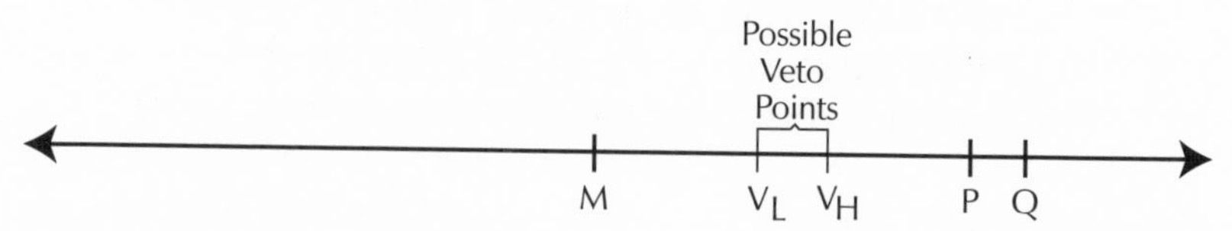

Figure 6.3 The Veto-Override Model

the status quo is Q, the president (a conservative) has an ideal point P, the House median is at M, and the range of possible veto pivots is bounded above by V_H and below by V_L.

The game is repeated twice, and there is a chance that bargaining will break down after the first period of play if the president vetoes the first bill because of an insurmountable impasse. However, if a veto occurs, the president has no choice but to adopt the same veto strategy again if Congress overrides his veto and passes another bill, for the veto pivot is randomly selected from the range of possibilities (as far as the president knows). There is a chance that the first bill that Congress presents, which the president will always veto because it will always be in the interval $[V_L, V_H]$,[66] will not be overridden, which preserves the status quo. Thus, the president actually enjoys an advantage in equilibrium that he would not have if he knew the exact preferences of the veto pivot, which is odd considering that this advantage is due to the fact that he is somewhat ignorant about who will support him in an override attempt. Moreover, in equilibrium, Congress never has an incentive to modify a bill the president has vetoed, for the president will adopt the same veto strategy the second time around.[67]

As Cameron points out, the veto-override model cannot explain how the president can exercise the third face of power, for the beliefs of Congress about what he would do in the second period never change after the outcome of the first period. Thus, in Neustadt's sense, the president has no opportunity to establish a reputation; because legislators know the location of his ideal point, they know exactly which bills he would sign and which he would veto. Neustadt argues instead that the source of presidential power within Congress resides in the president's ability to keep Congress unsure about how he will respond to what they do.[68] A president, then, who can manipulate the beliefs of legislators—thus exercising the third face of power—will find that his exercise of the second face of power is more potent.

Thus, Cameron turns to a model in which the location of the veto pivot is known with certainty to all legislators and to the president but the ideal point of the president is not known to Congress.[69] As figure 6.4 illustrates,[70] the president's ideal point can fall into one of three categories, so that the president can be one of three *types*. The friendliest type of president, from the standpoint of Congress, is the *accommodator*, whose preferences for change are so intense that he will approve a bill that the median legislator most prefers. Less friendly but still amenable to bargaining is the *compromiser*, who is willing to sign a bill that the median legislator would prefer to be more liberal, even though the president would prefer a more conservative bill. The worst-case scenario for Congress is the *recalcitrant* president, who

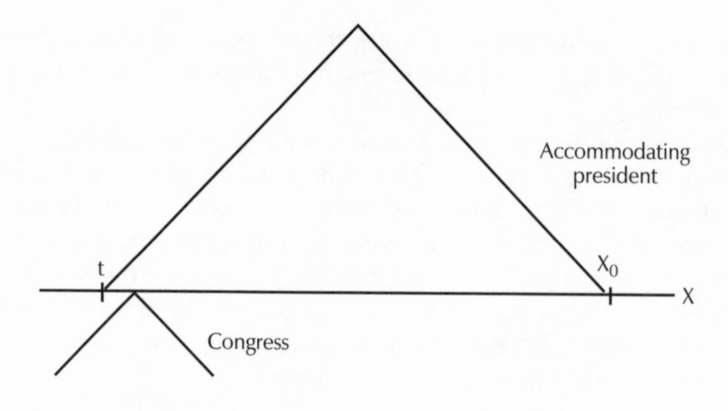

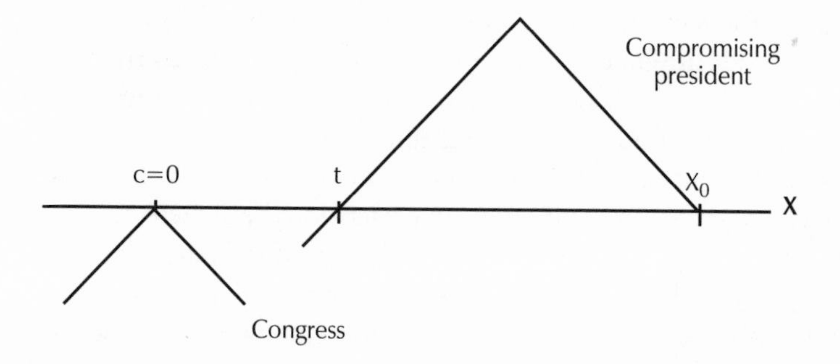

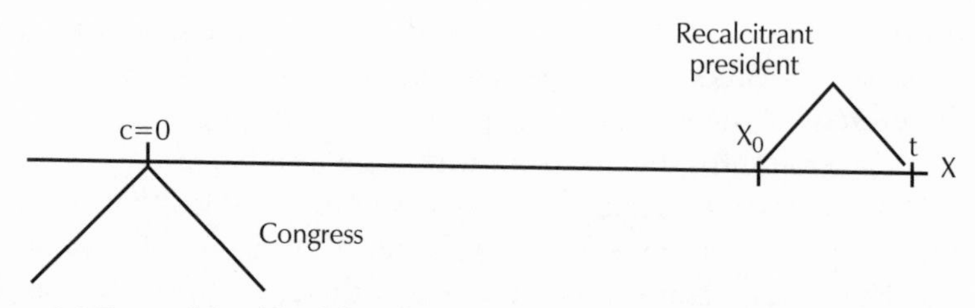

Figure 6.4 Types of Presidential Preferences

Source: From Charles M. Cameron, *Veto Bargaining: Presidents and the Politics of Negative Power* (New York: Cambridge University Press, 2000), p. 93. Reprinted with the permission of Cambridge University Press.

prefers the status quo to anything Congress might propose and will thus veto any proposal.

What happens when Congress is uncertain about the president's type? The same thing as Neustadt would predict: the president is occasionally able to win concessions from Congress the second time around if he vetoes the first bill—assuming that bargaining does not break down. A veto quickly informs Congress that the president is not accommodating, so members present a second bill that resembles the second offer in the veto-override model that is frequently intended to be veto proof. Depending on whether the president is compromising or accommodating, he either signs the bill or "revetoes" it despite the fact that Congress has made policy concessions to him. Because the policy-making process in this model may involve several sequences of bill passage, veto, bill repassage, reveto, and so on, Cameron calls the model the *sequential veto bargaining*, or *SVB*, *model*.[71]

Later, Cameron verifies the model's predictions by cutpoint analysis, to determine the extent to which Congress made policy concessions on bills that were repassed following a presidential veto.[72] His rationale is that because the preferences of members did not change, and because the status quo is still current policy, any change in the likely dividing line between supporters and opponents must reflect concessions that the legislators made to the president. With few exceptions, Cameron finds that bills presented a second time to the president were supported by more of the president's ideological allies, which Cameron takes as evidence of policy concessions to the president.[73]

Of course, this raises the question of why Congress altered the bill to make it more appealing to the president. When Congress does this voluntarily, it would be because of the president's reputation, to borrow loosely from Neustadt; a president's veto resolves uncertainty about his willingness to act on his principles, which makes his supporters more certain about the (eventual) benefits of supporting the president and his opponents more certain about the (eventual) costs of opposing him.[74] When Congress offers concessions because of public pressure instigated by the president, the president is influential because of his prestige. The following section investigates what may be called models of presidential prestige; they explain how the president can use public statements to influence Congress.

Veto Threats and Presidential Prestige

The lesson from the SVB model is that the president has more influence over Congress if he is willing to be a tough negotiator, though not too tough. Game theorists in other fields have posited that self-interested players in games like this sometimes have incentives to cultivate reputations as utterly recalcitrant, perhaps unreasonable, negotiators to extract maximum concessions. But even if the political world is as resistant to change as the gridlock model describes, Congress can always pass policies via veto override if the president successfully convinces them that he is never willing to compromise.[75] Although the gridlock model does not incorporate this explicitly, one can imagine that the preferences of legislators for policy change might be altered in such a case, perhaps because of public frustration with the president's intransigence. Thus, a president wants to establish a reputation for toughness but also must develop a habit of compromising when he and his allies have "wrung every concession possible from their counterparts."[76]

Costly Veto Threats and Presidential Commitments

What the president says after a veto can go a long way toward clarifying for Congress that he is willing to sign *a* bill but not until Congress allays a few more of his concerns.[77] However, before issuing a veto, the president often has incentives to make public statements that convey the message that he is unwilling to sign anything that Congress presents to him. Because actions speak louder than words, the president can build this reputation most effectively by vetoing bills on occasion. Yet public statements can also establish that the president is committed to a certain type of policy change and will veto anything that does not meet his minimal standard for change. Canes develops a model in which the president assumes some risk by issuing a public statement of support for a policy outcome, where the risk takes the form of lost utility to the president for making the commitment itself.[78] Ingberman and Yao describe a case in which the president can pay a cost and publicizes his willingness to veto an unacceptable bill, with the added twist that he loses utility if he breaks his commitment to veto a bill.[79]

Although these models suggest that the president often has the strict incentive to publicize his veto threat, incurring a certain opportunity cost or potential blow to his credibility, the fact remains that "going public" produces diminishing returns. As Kernell argues,[80] a president who goes public too often taxes the patience of the news media and the public, and too much publicity can poison an interbranch bargaining process that is most effective when it takes place behind closed doors.[81] This rationale may explain Lyndon Johnson's legislative lobbying strategy, whereby he often preferred to "stay private" rather than incur the potential costs to his reputation of going public.[82] What these commitment models illustrate is that the costs of going public are frequently worthwhile for presidents, increasing their influence and justifying the risk to their reputations.

Cheap Talk Models: Costless Veto Threats and the President's Reputation

What may be more surprising is that presidents frequently derive benefits from public announcements of their policy preferences even when such announcements are costless. That is, the president can build his reputation for toughness even when he cannot "put his money where his mouth is" and incur immediate or potential costs to his reputation through his public statements. Such models of cheap talk add a wrinkle to Cameron's SVB model: before a bill is proposed, the president may issue a veto threat or a conciliatory message that he will sign anything Congress sends to him. Given common knowledge within Congress of the types of messages the president can send, the president can achieve more utility by sending costless messages than he would achieve without this ability.[83]

As Steven Matthews argues,[84] the type of president who would benefit the most is an accommodating president who would nonetheless prefer more change than Congress would propose if members knew exactly how eager the president was to change the status quo. Not all accommodating presidents would want to send veto threats; some would prefer to give Congress the "green light" to propose the policy that the median legislator prefers, and Congress is all too happy to oblige. The kind of accommodating president who benefits from a veto threat is the kind who actually would sign anything Congress proposes but is less unhappy with the status quo than those who would tell Congress explicitly how eager they are to sign a bill.[85] These presidents benefit because, to legislators, they look like compromisers—presidents who might conceivably veto the bill Congress most prefers—and are treated as if they are by members of Congress, who make policy concessions after hearing the president issue a veto threat. Thus, these accommodators get the same proposals that compromisers do; in the language of these models, they are able to "pool" with them and induce a better outcome than they would receive if Congress knew more about their true preferences. Recalcitrant presidents in this model veto any proposal that Congress makes because they are so committed to the status quo.

Blame Game Politics

Finally, a model by Tim Groseclose and Nolan McCarty discusses the reasons why both the president and Congress may have electoral incentives to contribute to gridlock rather than accept a negotiated compromise simply to forestall conflict.[86] The innovation here is that the president and members of Congress are perfectly informed about every actor's preferences except those of the public, which registers opinions of the president after he signs or vetoes a bill. Legislators and the president all derive utility both from the public's opinion of the president and from any policy change, and the public learns more about the president's preferences after every outcome. Thus, the policy makers in this model care about the president's prestige as well as his reputation, and inactivity may be preferable to the "wrong" action, especially for the president, who operates under a severe disadvantage when bargaining with a hostile Congress.[87] However, the bills that are vetoed in equilibrium are often crafted by legislators to force a veto so that the public is alerted to the possibility that the president may have unacceptable preferences.

EMPIRICAL IMPLICATIONS AND THE 2000 ELECTIONS

Whether publicizing their preferences is costly or not for presidents, they benefit on average from every type of public pronouncement. When they take positions, they are more likely to get the type of policies they prefer from Congress,[88] which is not surprising given that the president probably decides whether to announce his preferences wisely, with his reputation in mind. This also seems obvious given the traditional perception of the president as an influential figure who uses the "bully pulpit" to rally public support to create change that not everyone in Congress is eager to enact. However, traditional studies of presidential success in the legislative arena are incapable of confirming that the president has been influential; members of Congress may support a policy on which the president has taken a position because they have watered his proposal down until they find it satisfactory, because they were going to pass the proposal anyway, or because the president voiced his support for the proposal after Congress had already begun work on the bill. To measure the president's legislative influence, it is necessary to move beyond "scorecard" or "batting average" measures of his legislative success, which treat all these scenarios as "wins" for the president.

Previous research has shown that the more successful the president is in the legislative arena, the more popular he gets, which in turn allows him to successfully prosecute the case for more policy change.[89] However, he is most successful at the beginning of his term, during the so-called honeymoon period, whether this is because of all the status quo policies that have been "released" from the gridlock interval following the election or because the president is able to exploit fully legislative uncertainty about his true preferences.[90] Both the gridlock models and the reputation-building models suggest that the president is best able to achieve legislative success early in his term, and that his fortunes take a turn for the worse following the honeymoon, because of a variety of factors: the well-known "coalition of minorities" effect, in which one-time supporters all seem to find different reasons to dislike the president[91]; broken commitments, such as George H. W. Bush's "no new taxes" pledge and Bill Clinton's pledge to reform health care[92]; or a natural overloading of the congressional or public agenda.[93]

The striking thing about these models, all of which were derived from techniques popularized by economics, "the dismal science," is how well they illustrate the ways in which the president and Congress can interact, maybe even successfully, even after an election as tumultuous and divisive as the 2000 election. Because of the polarization of both houses of Congress, there may certainly be gridlock, especially because the locations of the veto pivots are unlikely to change. As figure 6.2 illustrates, because George W. Bush won the election, a number of status quo points on the left will be released from the gridlock region, and subject to replacement by conservative proposals, because of the fact that Bush must only forestall a filibuster by Senate liberals. If Gore had won, the array of preferences for the pivotal actors probably would not have changed much—any change that would have been possible under Clinton would have been possible under Gore.

No matter who the president is, figure 6.2 illustrates the salient question: How many noncentrist status quo policies existed in late 2000, after eight years of winnowing by a moderate-left Clinton administration and almost twenty years of divided government? If there were few, then not much will happen regardless of who is president, despite the fact that liberals and conservatives may rattle their sabers continuously in an attempt to claim legitimacy for their parties for the 2002 and 2004 elections. As the "blame game" model of Groseclose and McCarty suggests, gridlock can occur not because of the veto power of Washington actors but because of the tendency of these actors to focus more on the public's response to politics than the response to policy change. Thus, the gridlock that we observe may be exacerbated, or even caused, by the political benefits that could accrue to whichever of the major parties succeeds in characterizing the other as the cause of the government's ineffectiveness.

Generally speaking, the models surveyed here indicate that policy change may occur through two routes. First, if members from both sides of the aisle decide to work together, the preferences of all pivotal actors will effectively all converge at some point on the line in figure 6.1. Only this sort of preference consensus on key policy issues, and not simply unified partisan control of the government, separates an effective Congress from an ineffective one. Second, like Gore, Bush campaigned as a moderate, which should have increased his influence over Congress at least momentarily, as long as uncertainty about his preferences prevailed among voters and legislators. As the first year of the Bush administration concludes, the challenge for the president will be to harness the support of the public and to lead legislators down paths that they would not otherwise travel.

NOTES

1. Steven Shull and Thomas Shaw provide an excellent survey of the various operational definitions of presidential power in recent empirical work. See Steven A. Shull and Thomas C. Shaw, *Explaining Congressional–Presidential Relations: A Multiple Perspective Approach* (Albany: State University of New York Press, 1999), 34–35.

2. Jon R. Bond, Richard Fleisher, and Glen A. Krutz, "An Overview of the Empirical Findings on Presidential–Congressional Relations," in *Rivals for Power: Presidential–Congressional Relations*, ed. James A. Thurber (Washington, D.C.: CQ Press, 1996), 103–39.

3. Bond, Fleisher, and Krutz, "An Overview of the Empirical Findings on Presidential–Congressional Relations," 105.

4. Robert Dahl uses presidential–congressional relations to illustrate his contention that "a straightforward presentation of an empirical theory of power relations in political systems is a rarity." See Robert A. Dahl, "Power," in *The Presidency*, ed. Aaron Wildavsky (Boston: Little, Brown and Co., 1969), 151–68.

5. As Charles Cameron points out, even when an event occurs that indicates policy disagreement between Congress and the president, such as a veto or a closely fought battle to confirm a president's nominee for appointed office, the inference that the president was influential is still difficult to characterize. See Charles M. Cameron, "Bargaining and Presidential Power," in *Presidential Power: Forging the Presidency for the Twenty-first Century*, ed. Robert Y. Shapiro, Martha Joynt Kumar, and Lawrence R. Jacobs (New York: Columbia University Press, 2000), 56–57.

6. Bond, Fleisher, and Krutz, "An Overview of the Empirical Findings on Presidential–Congressional Relations," 106.

7. Theodore W. Lowi, *The Personal President* (Ithaca: Cornell University Press, 1985).

8. Bond, Fleisher, and Krutz and Shull and Shaw provide the best recent surveys of the empirical, primarily success-oriented, literature; Cameron surveys the recent literature on interbranch bargaining. See Bond, Fleisher, and Krutz, "An Overview of the Empirical Findings on Presidential–Congressional Relations"; Shull and Shaw, *Explaining Congressional–Presidential Relations*; and Cameron, "Bargaining and Presidential Power."

9. Richard E. Neustadt, *Presidential Power and the Modern Presidents: The Politics of Leadership from Roosevelt to Reagan* (New York: Free Press, 1990).

10. This discussion draws most heavily on the discussion in Keith Krehbiel, *Pivotal Politics: A Theory of U.S. Lawmaking* (Chicago: University of Chicago Press, 1998), 20–26. However, the main ideas occur in many other like-minded works, especially David W. Brady and Craig Volden, *Revolving Gridlock: Politics and Policy from Carter to Clinton*

(Boulder: Westview Press, 1998); and Charles M. Cameron, *Veto Bargaining: Presidents and the Politics of Negative Power* (New York: Cambridge University Press, 2000).

11. Technically, the location of the Senate median is halfway between the ideal points of the fiftieth most liberal senator and the fifty-first most liberal senator, so that exactly fifty senators are more liberal and exactly fifty are less liberal.

12. This discussion draws heavily from Krehbiel, *Pivotal Politics*, 34–40.

13. This assumption is justified as follows: If the median member proposes the bill, he or she will propose M, his or her ideal policy. If, for instance, a more conservative member proposes a bill, someone—not necessarily the median member—offers amendments making it more liberal, and at least a majority of members votes for the amendments as long as the amendments do not make the bill more liberal than M. The final amendment offered moves the policy proposal to M, and it is also accepted. Thus, the final vote is between the bill as amended into M or the status quo Q_1—and the bill passes, probably by a wide margin. See Krehbiel, *Pivotal Politics*, 83–84.

14. If we assume instead that the House and Senate medians are located at different points, a conference committee resolves any differences. The models surveyed here typically abstract away from this consideration. For formal models of the House–Senate conference process, see Kenneth A. Shepsle and Barry R. Weingast, "The Institutional Foundations of Committee Power," *American Political Science Review* 81, no. 1 (March 1987): 85–104; Keith Krehbiel, "Why Are Congressional Committees Powerful?" *American Political Science Review* 81, no. 3 (September 1987): 929–35; and Douglas Dion and John Huber, "The Sound of Silence: Anticipated Reactions and the Discharge Petition in the United States House," unpublished MS, University of Michigan, December 1993.

15. This is what the classic median voter theory, most often associated with Duncan Black, would predict. See Duncan Black, *The Theory of Committees and Elections* (London: Cambridge University Press, 1958).

16. Of course, nothing prevents the relevant veto pivot from being a senator. Because veto overrides have to pass both houses of Congress, if the thirty-fourth most conservative senator is more conservative than the 146th most conservative House member, V is that senator, and the veto pivot in the House is satisfied whenever V is satisfied.

17. Krehbiel, *Pivotal Politics*, 39–48; Brady and Volden, *Revolving Gridlock*, chapter 2.

18. Brady and Volden state this view most simply: "A key reason to focus on preferences and supermajority institutions, rather than on special interests, parties, the media, and so on, is that in an important sense these latter variables are subsumed in the election results and the winning members' preferences" (*Revolving Gridlock*, 4). Similar sentiments are found in Cameron, *Veto Bargaining*, 86–88; and in Krehbiel, *Pivotal Politics*, 55–57, although here Krehbiel is critical of the attempt by Mayhew to include the "public mood" as a predictor of the number of "important laws" that are passed in a legislative session. See David R. Mayhew, *Divided We Govern: Party Control, Lawmaking, and Investigations* (New Haven: Yale University Press, 1991).

19. For treatment of these issues, see John W. Kingdon, *Congressmen's Voting Decisions*, 3d edition (Ann Arbor: University of Michigan Press, 1989); and John L. Sullivan, L. Earl Shaw, Gregory E. McAvoy, and David G. Barnum, "The Dimensions of Cue-Taking in the House of Representatives: Variation in Issue Area," *Journal of Politics* 55, no. 4 (December 1993): 975–97.

20. Among the many articles that examine the relationship between presidential and

midterm congressional elections, see especially Dennis M. Simon, Charles W. Ostrom Jr., and Robin F. Marra, "The President, Referendum Voting, and Subnational Elections in the United States," *American Political Science Review* 85, no. 4 (December 1991): 1177–92; James E. Campbell, "The Revised Theory of Surge and Decline," *American Journal of Political Science* 31 (December 1987): 965–79; Robert S. Erikson, "The Puzzle of Midterm Loss," *Journal of Politics* 50, no. 4 (December 1988): 1012–29; and Richard Born, "Surge and Decline, Negative Voting, and the Midterm Loss Phenomenon: A Simultaneous Choice Analysis," *American Journal of Political Science* 34 (August 1990): 615–45. A valuable overview of empirical evidence that voters tend to vote for different reasons in presidential and congressional elections is Gary W. Cox and Samuel Kernell, *Divided Government* (Boulder: Westview Press, 1991).

21. These works are summarized in Alberto Alesina and Howard Rosenthal, *Partisan Politics, Divided Government, and the Economy* (New York: Cambridge University Press, 1995).

22. Daniel E. Ingberman and John J. Villani, "An Institutional Theory of Divided Government and Party Polarization," *American Journal of Political Science* 37, no. 2 (May 1993): 429–71. By making this risk-aversion assumption explicit—and assuming that parties care about nothing but holding office—Ingberman and Villani are able to relax the Alesina–Rosenthal assumption that parties differ discernibly in their positions on major issues, as well as the assumption that all voters must be as farsighted as Alesina and Rosenthal assume. The Ingberman–Villani model explains the conditions under which the two major parties might adopt similar or distinct platforms, as well as why, for instance, voters might prefer a Republican president and a Democratic Congress when government expenditures are the salient electoral motivation.

23. Tests of a model developed by Morris Fiorina that is similar to Alesina and Rosenthal's in its prediction that voters balance their votes to gain the moderate platform they cannot achieve by granting one party unified control have often borne out this prediction. Walter Mebane demonstrates that voters actually do vote as if they care about the expected relationship between the president and Congress, just as Alesina and Rosenthal predict. For example, in 1996 support for Bob Dole was noticeably dampened by the perception that he would not sufficiently check the ideological agenda of Newt Gingrich and the Republican "Class of 1994." See, among others, Morris P. Fiorina, "The Reagan Years: Turning to the Right or Groping toward the Middle," in *The Resurgence of Conservatism in Anglo-American Democracies*, ed. Barry Cooper, Allan Kornberg, and William Mishler (Durham: Duke University Press, 1988): 430–59; Fiorina, *Divided Government* (New York: Macmillan, 1992); Richard Born, "Split-Ticket Voters, Divided Government and Fiorina's Ticket-Balancing Model," *Legislative Studies Quarterly* 19, no. 1 (March 1994): 95–115, and the accompanying discussion between Fiorina and Born—Fiorina, "Response to Born," *Legislative Studies Quarterly* 19, no. 1 (March 1994): 117–25, and Born, "Rejoinder," *Legislative Studies Quarterly* 19, no. 1 (March 1994), 126–29; and Walter R. Mebane Jr., "Coordination, Moderation, and Institutional Balancing in American Presidential and House Elections," *American Political Science Review* 94, no. 1 (March 2000): 37–57.

24. Krehbiel, *Pivotal Politics*, 41, figure 2.8.

25. Krehbiel, *Pivotal Politics*, 42. This happens, of course, because policies that are proposed by the president or anyone else are moderated as much as possible, as is argued in

the previous section. After this has occurred, further change can be blocked by one of the two pivotal legislators whose ideal points define the gridlock interval.

26. Krehbiel, *Pivotal Politics*, 42–47; Brady and Volden, *Revolving Gridlock*, 26–27.

27. This conclusion is rarely challenged by scholars who rely on gridlock models and discuss the disruptions that elections can cause. For instance, Brady and Volden seem to illustrate that the 1994 House elections shifted the location of the veto pivot to the right, but this seems unlikely. It is true, as Krehbiel argues, that moderate Democrats who strongly supported President Clinton against their constituents' wishes were most likely to lose their seats to Republicans. However, the assertion that this reduced the number of committed liberals in the House to below one-third of the membership remains unproven. Also, if this were true, Clinton would not have been able to combat House Republicans so successfully with vetoes and veto threats. Finally, even if most retirees recently have been moderates, as noted by Krehbiel (in *Pivotal Politics*, note 33), the gridlock region would only move if the members were replaced by staunch ideologues. Many were, but many others were replaced by like-minded partisan allies, and this would not necessarily change the size of the gridlock region. Empirical clarification of exactly how the gridlock region changed after these elections would address this important and outstanding question. Finally, if moderates do retire more often than liberals or conservatives because they are frustrated by gridlock, then elections are not the "exogenous shocks" that gridlock theorists treat them as but, rather, endogenous products of a lawmaking process that suppresses change and causes legislative turnover. See Brady and Volden, *Revolving Gridlock*, 141, 146–47; and Krehbiel, *Pivotal Politics*, 44–47, 220–24.

28. The weak party argument is often associated with the individualistic, reelection-driven archetypical representative portrayed by David Mayhew, but as Krehbiel points out, the argument that congressional parties are too weak is a very old one. See David R. Mayhew, *Congress: The Electoral Connection* (New Haven: Yale University Press, 1974); and the quotations in Krehbiel, *Pivotal Politics*, 26–28, especially 27, note 9. The most prominent recent arguments that parties in Congress are strong are made by Gary Cox and Mathew McCubbins, David Rohde, and John Aldrich; the most consistent critic of these arguments has been Krehbiel himself. See Gary W. Cox and Mathew D. McCubbins, *Legislative Leviathan: Party Government in the House* (Berkeley: University of California Press, 1993); David W. Rohde, *Parties and Leaders in the Postreform House* (Chicago: University of Chicago Press, 1991); and John H. Aldrich, *Why Parties? The Origin and Transformation of Party Politics in America* (Chicago: University of Chicago Press, 1995). For Krehbiel's criticisms, see especially *Pivotal Politics*, chapters 8–9; and Keith Krehbiel, "Where's the Party?" *British Journal of Political Science* 23, no. 2 (April 1993): 235–66. For a targeted response, see John H. Aldrich and David W. Rohde, "The Consequences of Party Organization in the House: The Role of the Majority and Minority Parties in Conditional Party Government," in *Polarized Politics: Congress and the President in a Partisan Era*, ed. Jon R. Bond and Richard Fleisher (Washington, D.C.: CQ Press, 2000), 31–72.

29. The (momentary) defeat of campaign finance reform legislation in July 2001 illustrates that the most important interparty conflict often centers on whether to grant a restrictive rule to major legislation. See Douglas Dion and John Huber, "Procedural Choice and the House Committee on Rules," *Journal of Politics* 58, no. 1 (February 1996): 25–53; Keith Krehbiel, "Restrictive Rules Reconsidered," *American Journal of Political Science* 41, no. 3 (July 1997): 919–44; and the exchange between Dion and Huber and Kreh-

biel that follows—Dion and Huber, "Sense and Sensibility: The Role of Rules," *American Journal of Political Science* 41, no. 3 (July 1997): 945–57, and Keith Krehbiel, "Rejoinder to 'Sense and Sensibility,' " *American Journal of Political Science* 41, no. 3 (July 1997): 958–64.

30. Krehbiel does offer a measure of presidential power, which is based on pairs of votes on bills that the president vetoes and on which Congress attempts to override his vetoes. Power, as measured by Krehbiel, is based on the success the president has in attracting opponents of the bill's final passage during the vote to override his veto and on his success in retaining the support of those who supported him on the final-passage vote during the override attempt. See Krehbiel, *Pivotal Politics*, chapter 7.

31. The classic reference is Richard D. McKelvey, "Intransitivities in Multidimensional Voting Models and Some Implications for Agenda Control," *Journal of Economic Theory* 12 (July 1976): 471–82. See David Austen-Smith and Jeffrey Banks, *Positive Political Theory I: Collective Preference* (Ann Arbor: University of Michigan Press, 1998), 52–54, however, for a defense of the model as a theoretical baseline.

32. Most of the literature refers to the liberal–conservative dimension as the single dimension in question. See, for example, the arguments in Melvin J. Hinich and Michael Munger, *Ideology and the Theory of Political Choice* (Ann Arbor: University of Michigan Press, 1984), chapters 1–4. This view is not inconsistent with theories of party realignment, in which the parties come to be distinguished by new stances they have taken on key issues or stances on newly emerged issues. Such realignments certainly would change the positioning of players in the one-dimensional policy space, due to changes in membership caused by "critical elections" such as the 1932 election, and, at least as importantly in the context of the gridlock model, would also change the perceived location of the status quo for many issues. For a discussion of these effects, see especially Brady and Volden, *Revolving Gridlock*, 27–30.

33. Keith T. Poole and Howard Rosenthal's book *Congress: A Political Economic History of Roll Call Voting* (New York: Oxford University Press, 1997) uses NOMINATE scores, estimated ideal points for every member who has ever served in Congress for an appreciable length of time, to support their conclusions. Thanks to their reliability and availability, the latter being due to the generosity of Keith Poole in making them freely available on his website, these scores are widely used in the quantitative study of Congress. In fact, by treating presidents as legislators who do not cast roll-call votes but do take positions on key issues, Poole and Rosenthal are able to estimate ideal points for presidents as well as legislators.

34. Edward G. Carmines and James A. Stimson, *Issue Evolution: Race and the Transformation of American Politics* (Princeton: Princeton University Press, 1989).

35. On the issue of coalition size, see Krehbiel, *Pivotal Politics*, chapter 3.

36. One prominent exception in the use of *conversion* as meaning long-term attitudinal change is Terry Sullivan, "The Bank Account Presidency: A New Measure and Evidence on the Temporal Path of Presidential Influence," *American Journal of Political Science* 32 (August 1991): 567–89.

37. Most authors agree that conversion in the sense of profound and lasting changes in policy preferences rarely occurs among legislators. The reported metamorphosis of Arizona Senator John McCain from a staunchly conservative Republican to a moderate or even liberal Republican has few precedents in U.S. history. The phenomenon of party

switching is relatively much more common, but even in the celebrated example of Vermont Senator Jim Jeffords's decision to leave the Republican Party, most observers felt that Jeffords's preferences changed far less than did the orientation of the Republican leadership. The notion that President Bush's lobbying tactics influenced Jeffords's decision is difficult to verify; in general, because of constituency pressures and the stability of political attitudes, presidential influence or any other factor is unlikely to induce conversion of legislative preferences. See John Hibbing, *Congressional Careers: Contours of Life in the U.S. House of Representatives* (Chapel Hill: University of North Carolina Press, 1991); Keith Poole, "Changing Minds? Not in Congress!" unpublished MS, Carnegie-Mellon University, 1998.

38. Calvin Mouw and Michael MacKuen, "The Strategic Configuration, Personal Influence, and Presidential Power in Congress," *Western Political Quarterly* 60 (September 1993): 579–608.

39. See the following articles by Terry Sullivan: "Presidential Leadership in Congress: Securing Commitments," in *Congress: Structure and Policy*, ed. Mathew D. McCubbins and Terry Sullivan (New York: Cambridge University Press, 1987), 286–308; "Headcounts, Expectations, and Presidential Coalitions in Congress," *American Journal of Political Science* 32 (August 1988): 567–89; "Bargaining with the President: A Simple Game and New Evidence," *American Political Science Review* 84 (December 1990): 1167–95; "Explaining Why Presidents Count: Signaling and Information," *Journal of Politics* 52 (August 1990): 939–62; and "The Bank Account Presidency."

40. Sullivan, "Headcounts, Expectations, and Presidential Coalitions in Congress"; Sullivan, "Bargaining with the President."

41. In the Information Age, however, the availability of on-line daily digests of legislative activity may yield headcount data more often and more quickly. For instance, before the 1997 vote to reauthorize the fast-track policy-making procedure in the House and again before the vote on most-favored-nation status for China, *CongressDaily* conducted a series of headcount polls to determine the likelihood of each bill's success. The fast-track headcount data are analyzed in Nathan Dietz, "Presidential Credibility, Repeated Bargaining, and the Renewal of the Fast Track Policymaking Process," paper presented at the Annual Meeting of the American Political Science Association, Atlanta, September 1999.

42. George C. Edwards III, "Presidential Influence in Congress: If We Ask the Wrong Questions, We Get the Wrong Answers," *American Journal of Political Science* 35 (August 1991): 724–29.

43. Krehbiel, *Pivotal Politics*, chapters 5–7; Brady and Volden, *Revolving Gridlock*, 113–33.

44. Krehbiel, *Pivotal Politics*, 124–26.

45. George C. Edwards III, *At the Margins: Presidential Leadership of Congress* (New Haven: Yale University Press, 1989), 193.

46. Richard L. Hall, *Participation in Congress* (New Haven: Yale University Press, 1996).

47. See Mouw and MacKuen, "The Strategic Configuration, Personal Influence, and Presidential Power in Congress"; and Sullivan, "Bargaining with the President." These studies, however, do not differentiate between vote trading and persuasion. It may be the case, then, that members who would have been persuadable had the president not "gone

to the well" too often previously eventually require more tangible benefits before they change their votes.

48. Douglas Rivers and Nancy L. Rose, "Passing the President's Program: Presidential Influence in Congress," *American Journal of Political Science* 29, no. 1 (February 1985): 183–96.

49. Edwards, *At the Margins*, 38, 46–47.

50. Edwards, *At the Margins*, 72.

51. Not surprisingly, given his reputation as a master bargainer, Lyndon Johnson had a reputation for boundless energy when it came to lobbying legislators. See, among others, Mark Peterson, *Legislating Together: The White House and Capitol Hill from Eisenhower to Reagan* (Cambridge, Mass.: Harvard University Press, 1990), 67–70, 167–69.

52. Edwards, *At the Margins*, 86.

53. Sullivan, "Bargaining with the President," 1169–70.

54. Diana Evans, "Promises and Pork: The Distribution of Pork Barrel Projects and Vote-Buying in Congress," unpublished MS, Trinity College, 1997.

55. In a related work, I test and find support for the hypothesis that after President Clinton revealed to members that he was willing to trade favors to gain support for NAFTA, members withheld prior support from fast track in 1997 in the hope that he would bargain with them again. See Dietz, "Presidential Credibility, Repeated Bargaining, and the Renewal of the Fast Track Policymaking Process."

56. Tim Groseclose and James M. Snyder Jr., "Buying Supermajorities," *American Political Science Review* 90, no. 2 (June 1996): 303–16.

57. James Snyder, "On Buying Legislatures," *Economics and Politics* (July 1991): 93–109.

58. Nolan McCarty argues that in distributive politics, commonly known as "pork-barrel politics," the president is frequently able to influence policies proposed by other legislators. In McCarty's model, the president gains more utility when his partisan allies receive shares of the "pie" than when members of the opposition do. The president prefers that pork-barrel politics be kept to a minimum but wants his copartisans to receive more benefits than his opponents on distributive bills. Thus, by using or threatening his veto power, the president is frequently able to slow, but not stop, inefficiency in federal spending, even under a line-item veto. See Nolan M. McCarty, "Presidential Pork: Executive Veto Power and Distributive Politics," *American Political Science Review* 94, no. 1 (March 2000): 117–29.

59. This is the prediction of both Krehbiel and Brady and Volden. See Krehbiel, *Pivotal Politics*, 97–101; and Brady and Volden, *Revolving Gridlock*, 113.

60. Nathan Dietz, "Presidential Influence on Legislative Behavior in the U.S. House of Representatives," Ph.D. dissertation, University of Rochester, 1998, 243–62. In theory, this leaves presidential scholars more optimistic than Groseclose about the likelihood of determining whether vote trading took place on a given bill. Increasingly, vote-trading initiatives are not only mentioned in the press but, as noted in note 36 above, detailed in on-line journals of legislative news. See Tim Groseclose, "An Examination of the Market for Favors and Votes in Congress," *Economic Inquiry* 34, no. 2 (April 1996): 320–40.

61. Besides the analysis in Dietz, "Presidential Influence on Legislative Behavior in the U.S. House of Representatives," Eric Uslaner draws much the same conclusion in "Let the Chits Fall Where They May? Executive and Constituency Influences on Congressional Voting on NAFTA," *Legislative Studies Quarterly* 23, no. 3 (August 1998): 347–71.

62. Neustadt, *Presidential Power and the Modern Presidents*, chapters 3–4.

63. Cameron, *Veto Bargaining*, 18–19, 107–08; Peter Bachrach and Morton Baratz, "The Two Faces of Power," *American Political Science Review* 56 (June 1962): 947–52.

64. Terry Moe and his coauthors have sketched what may be called a theory of the "first face of power": the power to take unilateral actions, such as structuring the executive branch and issuing executive orders. They argue that this type of power allows the president to gain crucial advantages over the legislative branch, which tips the balance of interbranch power toward the executive branch. See Terry M. Moe and Scott A. Wilson, "Presidents and the Politics of Structure," *Law and Contemporary Problems* 57, no. 2 (spring 1994): 1–44; and Terry M. Moe and William G. Howell, "Unilateral Action and Presidential Power: A Theory," *Presidential Studies Quarterly* 29, no. 4 (December 1999): 850–69.

65. This discussion draws heavily from Cameron, *Veto Bargaining*, chapter 4, 83–116.

66. This is because the president will certainly veto anything more liberal than V_L, and Congress, not wanting to concede too much ground to the president, would never proposing anything more conservative than V_H, which the president knows is veto proof because even his staunchest ally among the possible veto pivots would be willing to support the bill in an override attempt. In equilibrium, Congress will propose a bill that the president may veto some of the time (technically, if this is more liberal than V_H) and a veto-proof bill (V_H) otherwise, which will become law via veto override if the president vetoes it. See Cameron, *Veto Bargaining*, 117–20.

67. Recall that the possibility of an impasse between Congress and the president allows for the far more common equilibrium outcome: after a veto, Congress concludes that support for the bill is insufficient.

68. Neustadt, *Presidential Power and the Modern Presidents*, chapter 4.

69. Nolan McCarty develops a similar model in "Presidential Reputation and the Veto," *Economics and Politics* 9, no. 1 (March 1997): 1–26.

70. Following Steven Matthews's model design and terminology, the triangles in figure 6.4 represent the *tent utility functions* for the president and the median legislator. With a tent function, the ideal point is at the "peak" of the tent, and the point *t* represents the *utility-equivalent point* for the status quo policy Q. That is, the president is indifferent between retaining a policy as conservative as Q and approving a policy as liberal as *t* because he gets equal utility from either change. Thus, any policy proposal "under the tent" will not be vetoed by the president. The benefit of this representation of the president's utility is that the president's type can be cast in terms of *t*, and it is convenient to specify legislators' beliefs about the actual location of *t* by describing the probability—given everything that may have happened over the course of the administration—that the president's type *t* lies within a certain interval or takes on a given value. See Cameron, *Veto Bargaining*, 88–90; and Steven Matthews, "Veto Threats: Rhetoric in a Bargaining Game," *Quarterly Journal of Economics* 103 (June 1989): 347–69.

71. Cameron and his coauthors have generalized the SVB model to situations in which the lawmaking process can complete more than two rounds. Because only thirteen "veto chains" empirically have lasted as long as three rounds from 1945 to 1994, this generalization is mostly for theoretical purposes, but Cameron does consider the question of what happens after the president "revetoes" a bill. In only one case—a proposed tax cut in 1947–48 that Harry Truman vetoed three times and which was enacted on the third try

via override—did the president not sign the third bill in the chain. See Cameron, *Veto Bargaining*, 147, 212–14.

72. Cameron, *Veto Bargaining*, 154–61.

73. Cameron measures cutpoints like Mouw and MacKuen do, using NOMINATE scores as measures of member ideal points. Changes in cutpoint location between the first and second bills reflect the fact that, in all likelihood, the bill is now closer to the president's ideal point than it was, and more legislators with ideal points closer to the president's are now supporting it. See Cameron, *Veto Bargaining*, 154–60.

74. Neustadt, *Presidential Power and the Modern Presidents*.

75. Models of costless communication, or cheap talk models, would predict in this case that Congress does not respond to the president at all. All cheap talk models have as equilibria "babbling equilibria," whereby Congress does not change its course of action no matter what message the president sends. Unfortunately, it is misleading to say that the model would predict this type of outcome, for both types of equilibria exist, and there is little reason within the model to expect one type of equilibrium rather than another.

76. Cameron, *Veto Bargaining*, 236.

77. As Cameron quotes Gerald Ford, "The veto is not a negative, dead-end device. In most cases, it is a positive means of achieving legislative compromise and improvement—better legislation, in other words" (Cameron, *Veto Bargaining*, 230).

78. Brandice J. Canes, "The President's Influence from Going Public: A Formal and Empirical Analysis," paper presented at the Annual Meeting of the Midwest Political Science Association, Chicago, April 1997.

79. Daniel E. Ingberman and Dennis A. Yao, "Presidential Commitment and the Veto," *American Journal of Political Science* 35, no. 2 (May 1991): 357–89.

80. Samuel Kernell, *Going Public: New Strategies of Political Leadership*, 3d edition (Washington, D.C.: CQ Press, 1997).

81. See Canes, "The President's Influence from Going Public." Although Canes disagrees, arguing instead that going public always produces a net bargaining advantage to the president, I conjecture that this is an artifact of her assumption of the determinants of the costs of going public. She argues that these costs represent opportunity costs, among other things, of not talking about other policies and events. This undoubtedly helps explain why these costs differ at different times, but a president with a history of going public should certainly expect the costs to be higher the more frequently he exercises that option. Because Canes assumes that the president can go public only once per round of her two-period model, her model does not reflect these reputation-building considerations.

82. Cary R. Covington, "Staying Private: Gaining Congressional Support for Unpublicized Presidential Preferences on Roll Call Votes," *Journal of Politics* 49, no. 3 (August 1986): 737–55.

83. Again, babbling equilibria, whereby Congress never responds to the president's statements, always exist. See note 75.

84. Matthews, "Veto Threats."

85. As John Gilmour argues, this type of president has the most favorable "BATNA"—best alternative to a negotiated agreement—among accommodating presidents. See John B. Gilmour, *Strategic Disagreement: Stalemate in American Politics* (Pittsburgh: University of Pittsburgh Press, 1995), 9–10.

86. Tim Groseclose and Nolan McCarty, "The Politics of Blame: Bargaining before an Audience," *American Journal of Political Science* 45, no. 1 (January 2001): 100–19.

87. Groseclose and McCarty develop the model for the "interesting" case of divided government, wherein the president is more liberal than the median legislator, although parties do not play an explicit role. See Groseclose and McCarty, "The Politics of Blame."

88. Cary R. Covington, J. Mark Wrighton, and Rhonda Kinney, "A 'Presidency-Augmented' Model of Presidential Success on Roll Call Votes," *American Journal of Political Science* 39, no. 4 (November 1995): 1001–24; Nathan Dietz, "Presidential Position Taking and Legislative Success: Insights from the Spatial Model," unpublished MS, American University, 2000.

89. Rivers and Rose, "Passing the President's Program"; Charles W. Ostrom Jr. and Dennis M. Simon, "Promise and Performance: A Dynamic Model of Presidential Popularity," *American Political Science Review* 79, no. 2 (June 1985): 334–58.

90. See Krehbiel, *Pivotal Politics*; Brady and Volden, *Revolving Gridlock*. See also McCarty, "Presidential Reputation and the Veto," 13–17.

91. John E. Mueller, "Presidential Popularity from Truman to Johnson," *American Political Science Review* 64, no. 1 (March 1970): 18–34.

92. Ingberman and Yao, "Presidential Commitment and the Veto"; Cameron, *Veto Bargaining*, 196–97.

93. Ostrom and Simon, "Promise and Performance"; Rivers and Rose, "Passing the President's Program."

7

Successful Influence: Managing Legislative Affairs in the Twenty-first Century

Gary Andres and Patrick J. Griffin

During the first two years of the George H. W. Bush administration (1989–90), Congressman John Dingell (D-Mich.) championed one of the White House's most important domestic policy initiatives: the Clean Air Act Amendments of 1990. While leading the effort, Dingell engaged in numerous White House meetings, visits with the president, a trip aboard Air Force One, and almost daily access to senior White House staff. On this issue, the White House tried to influence and cajole Dingell. In response, the congressman from Michigan delivered for Bush.

Yet, while extremely helpful on this issue, overall Dingell rated among the lowest in presidential support on House roll-call votes and later led the fight to override Bush the only time Congress failed to sustain one of his forty-six vetoes. Did the president enjoy "success" in his relations with Congressman Dingell? Did the White House "influence" the congressman through lavishing him with attention, or did these efforts fail because he ultimately showed little support on roll-call votes and supported veto overrides?

Few relationships endure more hardships, handshakes, fallings-out, forced reconciliations, screaming, shared accomplishments, deliberate deception, finger-pointing, and honeymoons than that between the American president and the U.S. Congress. How these two institutions "get along"—whether they dance smoothly or step on each other's toes—has broad implications for U.S. public policy making. The above example also demonstrates why understanding concepts like presidential "success" or "influences" is much more complicated than it appears on the surface.

CONGRESSPEOPLE ARE FROM MARS, PRESIDENTS ARE FROM VENUS: A MISUNDERSTOOD RELATIONSHIP

Despite deep Constitutional linkages binding these two institutions and the critical role this relationship plays in American public policy, presidential–congressional relations are also widely misunderstood by the press, pundits, and the public.[1] This chapter helps foster a better understanding of how the relationship works, including its possibilities and limitations. It also makes positive suggestions about how to improve White House relations with Congress in the future.

A BROADER PERSPECTIVE ON PRESIDENTIAL–CONGRESSIONAL RELATIONS

Many colloquialisms like "the president proposes and Congress disposes" simply do not capture the complexities, nuances, and contours that define presidential–congressional relations. Moreover, while there are ways to improve presidential–congressional relations, a deeper understanding of the relationship also suggests that there are a separateness and level of competition that must be maintained along Pennsylvania Avenue. As Richard Cook, a former Nixon legislative affairs aide, says in Kenneth Collier's *Between the Branches*, "A close relationship between the President and Congress is an unnatural thing."[2]

One of the central goals of this chapter is to dispel the common myth that presidents drive the lawmaking process and that "success" and "influence" are based on how much of their agendas the chief executives can get the Congress to accept. We explicitly reject this view, believing that it is both empirically incorrect and damaging to citizens' expectations about the proper role of the various branches of American government institutions. The president and the Congress are truly "separate institutions, sharing power" and, as the title of this volume accurately states, "rivals for power."[3] Keeping this perspective in mind will also help U.S. citizens evaluate successful presidential–congressional relations, creating a new realism about what is possible and what is not under our system of government.

Conventional wisdom suggests that skillful presidents lead and cajole Congress to produce important public policy outcomes. In the twentieth century, the legislative accomplishments of Franklin Roosevelt, Lyndon Johnson, and the first year of the Reagan administration are noted as examples of "success" or "influence" with Congress. Other presidents, such as Truman, Carter, and Bush, had fewer congressional success stories and are often considered less influential—or perhaps even failures—in the legislative arena.

But analyzing how the Congress "processes" presidential initiatives or agendas is only one narrow piece of the puzzle. The roots of the misunderstanding about presidential–congressional relations run deep through America's received conventional wisdom. The "public expectations" systems model illustrated in figure 7.1 underlies the thought process that supports the popular view of presidential–congressional relations.

On the surface, we note several aspects of this model that fail to fit with our experiences and observations about presidential–congressional relations. First, the flow of influence in the real world between the president and Congress is both ways, not unidirectional. Edwards and Woods point out that patterns of influence between the public and the president are interactive.[4] That is, the president influences public attitudes, and the public influences the president. *The same is true between the president and Congress*. It is an interactive relationship with patterns of influence flowing both ways.[5]

In *Legislating Together*, Peterson makes a similar point.[6] He notes that conventional wisdom among the press, public, and scholars about presidential–congressional relations is "president centered." He paints a picture of the president, standing before Congress, giving his State of the Union message with his agenda on the line. If the president can convince Congress to pass it, he wins; if not, he loses. It is all about the president, and it is all about passing his agenda—a one-way set of inputs from the president into the Congress to achieve legislative outputs.

Even some informed political elites, like U.S. senators, also hold this "president-centered" conventional wisdom. During the 1988 presidential campaign, a prominent U.S. senator told the Bush campaign's legislative liaison staff that he would withhold his endorsement of Bush until he heard the candidate's agenda for the first 100 days. According to the senator, the president's "first 100 days" represented his "best and only chance" for great potential legislative accomplishments. In reality, Bush's team spent the first

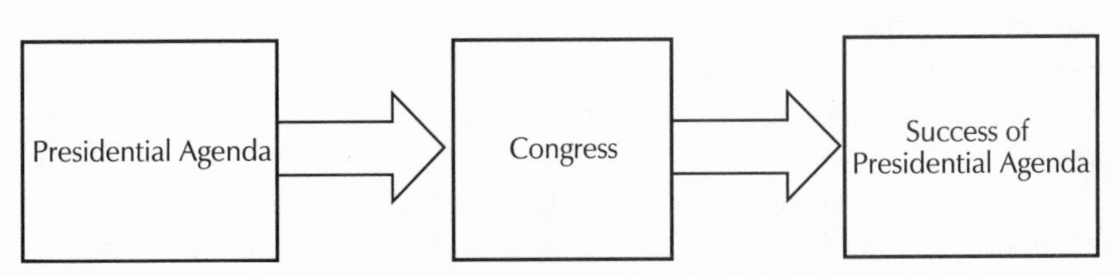

Figure 7.1 Current Public Expectations Model

100 days figuring out where the bathrooms were in the White House and how to respond to a barrage of legislation passed by a Democrat majority over the objections of the Republicans.

This approach views the president as an "input," trying to exert unidirectional influence and gain success in the form of congressional "outputs," much like any other interest group in the legislative policy-making environment. As we note later, this approach is too limited because Congress tries to influence the president as much as the president attempts to wield influence over legislators. *Presidential–congressional relations are best understood as a two-way street with pressure, influence, success, and failure flowing freely in both directions.*

Conceptualizing the president as a unidirectional input to the congressional process leads to a second misunderstanding. This construct views the president as an exogenous force on the lawmaking process. In reality the president can be very much inside the lawmaking process. Recent scholarship demonstrates that incorporating the president's pivotal role through the legislative veto into congressional policy-making models helps explain issues such as gridlock and why most legislation that does pass musters large bipartisan majorities.[7] As we note in more detail later, the role of the president shifts between being an exogenous force on the process to being endogenous within the process, where factors such as personalities, strategic goals, and the type of policy under consideration have major consequences in the public sphere.[8]

Third, models of presidential–congressional relations based on constructs like that in figure 7.1 also tend to view presidential success or influence in "constant" as opposed to "dynamic" terms. Jones, for example, notes this shortcoming in extant scholarship and argues for a dynamic approach. He notes that the "strategies of presidents in dealing with Congress will depend on the advantages they have available at any one time. One cannot employ *a constant model* of activist president leading a party government. Conditions may encourage the president to work at the margins of president–congressional interaction (for example where he judges that he has an advantage, as with foreign and defense issues)."[9]

Finally, conventional wisdom models that view Congress as the "black box" in a systems model also miss the richness of institutional variables that exist in the real world. Factors such as divided government and bicameral variables play a significant role in determining how presidents relate to Congress.

All of Bush's four years and six of Clinton's eight-year term underscore this point. Neither had "bad" relations with Congress. Nor was it the case that they were unskilled in negotiating with legislators. They faced vastly different institutional and political circumstances than, say, Franklin Roosevelt or Lyndon Johnson and could not or did not want to pass major changes in public policy, given the context in which they found themselves. And, as we note later, legislative gridlock also occurs sometimes because of the institutional dynamics of Congress, not just because of a lack of success or influence by the president.[10]

By analyzing presidential–congressional relations using some of the insights suggested above, we gain a deeper, richer, and more realistic understanding of how the system works. Factoring in these variables allows us to analyze presidential–congressional relations from a "pre-outcome" perspective, including the impact of the interactive relationship, institutional and policy variables, and the strategic goals of the actors. The next section of this chapter lays out three "pre-outcome" aspects of presidential–congressional relations that we must appreciate and factor into our models to better understand legislative outputs (or the lack thereof).

Precursors to Outcomes: Three Considerations

Clearly, evaluating success, influence, or leadership from the perspective of votes taken, bills signed, or vetoes sustained is the most traditional and obvious way to gauge who is leading and who is following the dance of legislation between the Congress and the executive branch. While the focus on outcomes is often interesting and relatively easy to measure, it fails to capture the rich and complex dynamics between the branches of government and party leaders that precede each outcome. *In other words, to better understand the final product, one needs to step back and consider the context that shaped these outcomes.*

Outcome measures alone rarely provide any insight into the overall strategic goals and objectives of the president or congressional leaders. Nor do they help in understanding how these sets of goals and objectives relate to each other or to the public. For example, a Democratic president along with his party colleagues in the Congress may embrace an opportunity to show how prodigious their legislative capabilities are. They might welcome a "scorecard" evaluation, laundry listing all the bills they jointly pass and sign into law. In this case, a straight-line evaluation of votes taken, bills passed and signed into law, and vetoes not only would be consistent with the strategic objective of such a presidency but also would likely provide additional perspectives on presidential efforts. However, one could easily imagine a Republican president who campaigned on a platform of a smaller, less active government, who along with his party leaders in the Congress may want to convince their supporters that they are doing more by doing less. With the exception of providing for the national defense and attempting to eliminate Democrat-sponsored programs, their strategic objectives might be to make their role in government as small a target as possible. Outcome measures are likely to still be helpful if they are placed in the context of the larger strategic objectives. These measures reveal more about what one does and less about what one does not do or what one prevents from happening.

Another scenario in which outcome measures produce even less perspective is in divided government. Party control is split between the branches. Each side is openly claiming that its reason for being in office is to thwart the objectives of the other. What did not happen or how a proposal was watered down before it became a law is a better way to define *success* in these cases. An extreme example occurred in 1995 when a Republican majority in Congress fought a Democratic president to a legislative draw. No authorizing legislation and no appropriation bills passed the entire year, shutting down the government three times. In the end, Democrats won a "TKO," apparently convincing most of the public that their effort to stop the Republican agenda was more important than having the GOP stop theirs. The only outcome measure was whose message was more convincing in proving the negative.

Outcome measures also fail to capture the influential role that individual members, committee chairs, and leaders have in promoting, shaping, and even killing policy proposals throughout the entire legislative process. This is typically done by offering and withholding critically needed support at crucial times in the process. It is also accomplished by utilizing parliamentary tactics that obstruct or prohibit the legislative process from progressing. The majority party's leaders at the committee and institutional levels also wield enormous influence by being able to set the schedule, agenda, and conditions for proceeding to specific pieces of legislation.

Individual member motivations vary greatly in their participation in legislative efforts and skirmishes. While members could have considerable impact on specific policies, their positions are typically a reflection of their constituent concerns. On the other hand, committee chairs and party leaders need to factor in not only personal constituent agendas when making decisions that affect legislation but also those of the entire party. Decisions regarding legislative content, when and whether to schedule the legislation, and how and if it might be amended are often worked through as much as possible before the first vote is taken. Outcome measures simply do not begin to reveal the role and influence that the process, context, and strategic goals play in shaping the outcome before the quantification of results.

Process, Context, and Strategic Goals

So let us take a step back from outcomes and investigate process, context, and the participants' strategic goals in evaluating presidential success or influence with Congress. For example, what are the tactics used by successful presidents in producing positive outcomes with Congress? Similarly, how do institutional variables like dealing with mixed versus unified party government, the House versus the Senate, and different types of public policy change the ways in which presidents approach Congress? Finally, how do presidential and congressional strategic goals influence the nature of legislative outcomes and relations? Each of these "precursors" to outcomes is a critical variable in achieving a better understanding of the proper role of the president and Congress in U.S. government.

The balance of this chapter analyzes factors that *shape* outcomes. Focusing on these variables helps explain why some presidents produce prodigious legislative accomplishments and others do not. This approach also suggests how presidents can have "success" or "influence" with Congress in ways not measured by only studying outcomes. Finally, we focus on more than just the president in this dance. A better starting point is one that accepts the reciprocal nature of the relationship: Congress tries to influence the president as much as or more than the president tries to influence Congress. Articulating a broader view of how these two institutions interact, including the challenges, trade-offs, and opportunities, will also lead presidents and their staffs to manage the relationship with more success in the future. We hope that scholars and pundits will use this model to foster a clearer and more realistic understanding of presidential–congressional relations.

PRECEDING OUTCOMES I: PROCESS—A TAPESTRY OF SUCCESS

The "process" of managing White House–congressional relations has many dimensions. "Success" with Congress is an interwoven tapestry of activities rather than a single strand, such as winning roll-call votes. True legislative success builds an active two-way dialogue between the Congress and the president. Bryce Harlow, who adroitly negotiated the shoals of Congress for Presidents Eisenhower and Nixon, has said, "The president's legislative affairs office creates a bridge across a yawning Constitutional chasm, a chasm fashioned by our power-fearing Fathers to keep the Congress and the President at a safe distance from one another in the interest of human liberty."[12] Identifying the tools necessary to build this bridge is the subject of the next section. Most of the recommendations apply to the president and the White House legislative affairs staff.

Active Consultation

Presidents who put a strong emphasis on consultation with Congress, communicating often personally or through the staff with legislators, will get high marks and succeed in influencing the House and the Senate. The Clinton team got high marks early on with the Democratic leadership in Congress for consulting and working in concert on a variety of measures during 1993. Their initiatives included proposals on education and environment, the Family Medical Leave Act, and Motor Voter legislation (two initiatives that President Clinton's predecessor George Bush consistently opposed that now could pass under conditions of unified party government), as well as modest institutional reform proposals regarding campaign finance and lobbying registration. Their agenda also included legislative objectives that began to reposition Democrats as supporting a balanced budget while reducing the size of government and expanding efforts to fight crime.

As is often the case in unified government, the Democrats worked to ensure that their proposals passed without Republican support. The cornerstone of this early agenda was a $500 billion tax increase and spending cut package to reduce the deficit. The measure passed the House by a margin of one, with all Republicans opposing it.

Holding all the Democrats in line on a variety of these initiatives, some of which flew in the face of traditional Democratic rhetoric and interest groups, took many hours of consultation, both by inviting members to the White House and by sending administration personnel to Capitol Hill. Active consultation results in members of Congress believing that someone at the White House is listening and that their views matter. Often just "hearing people out" and attentiveness to their views go a long way toward strengthening and creating positive relations with Congress.

Creating a Capitol Hill Presence

Building successful bridges with legislators requires accessibility on the part of the White House staff on Capitol Hill. The Bush administration legislative affairs team stationed its members in critical places around the Capitol during every roll-call vote in the House and the Senate. This allowed senators and congresspeople to find the staff and vice versa. It helped develop an image of a White House and administration actively engaged with the Congress, listening to members' concerns and complaints, and feeding information back to lawmakers.

Conversely, the Clinton team spent more time early in the administration in internal, policy development meetings in the White House. Soon many on Capitol Hill began to complain that the White House team was "invisible" on the Hill, and complaints about lack of attentiveness began to mount.

Creating a Hill presence is a key ingredient for the White House to engage daily in the ebb and flow of congressional culture. Presidents who dispatch their staff to talk to legislators in this manner will win high marks from Congress. It is a tactic that requires a large time commitment—Bush and Reagan's legislative affairs team was on Capitol Hill whenever Congress was in session. Yet it is also a tactic that will result in major dividends in creating an effective two-way dialogue with Congress.

Engaging the Leadership

Fostering a constructive relationship with the congressional leadership—both the president's party and the opposition—is one of the most important tasks in which the White House can invest time and energy. As we discuss later in this chapter, the nature of the relationship with the leadership changes somewhat when the president's party is in the majority compared with when it is in the minority. For now, it is important to note that the president and his staff must cultivate and forge strong relations with the congressional leadership.

In the Bush administration, the president and his staff worked hard cultivating these relationships, meeting with the congressional leadership nearly every week when Congress was in session during Bush's four-year term. The president and his staff would organize bipartisan, bicameral meetings twice a month, dedicating the other two monthly meetings to only Republicans from the House and the Senate. Bush consciously tried to convey the impression that he was diligently working with the congressional leadership, listening to their views and meeting them halfway on any issue he could.

This strategy had mixed results. Often Bush never moved far enough to accommodate the congressional Democratic leadership, and his Republican allies viewed his actions with suspicion. In the mixed party government environment faced by Bush, engaging the leadership seemed to work best when playing defense. In those cases in which he and his staff could rally the GOP leadership to oppose a Democratic initiative, the combination of the Republican leadership whipping its members and the White House working conservative Democrats did result in a few key legislative wins. House passage of a capital gains tax cut and the first authorization of "fast-track" trade negotiating authority are two primary examples.

Working with congressional leadership emerges as one of the key tasks of White House staff in any review of process and tactics. It is an important ingredient to any successful legislative strategy. Strong relations with the congressional leadership make every other aspect of relating with the House and the Senate operate more smoothly and efficiently. We discuss some of the nuances of relations with a president's own party leadership versus working with the opposition party later in this chapter.

Addressing Needs and Wants

When Trent Lott was minority whip in the House, he used to admonish President Reagan's White House staff, "You've got to take care of members' needs and wants." This is both a big and a small request, but it is important to take care of those needs and wants that can be taken care of. This may involve a letter from the president, a trip on Air Force One back to the district or state, a change in an administration position, or a signing pen from a piece of legislation recently enacted into law. There is no better way to build a reservoir of goodwill and develop a reputation of responsiveness than by attending to member needs and wants.

M. B. Oglesby, legislative affairs chief for President Reagan, told his staff that responsiveness meant that they should never leave the White House at the end of the day without having returned every phone call. A president can vastly improve his relations with Congress by making it clear that he wants to address member needs and wants. Doing so will pay large dividends when it comes time to spend some political capital—even if it fails to produce active support by the opponents, sometimes it can moderate their attacks. In the world of politics, that kind of currency can mean real value.

Access to the President

Effective leadership and influence with Congress includes staff who can speak clearly and authoritatively for the president. In order to do this, White House staff charged with relations with Congress must have unfettered access to the president. One of the biggest mistakes of any White House staff organization is to build too many layers of staff between the president and the personnel that must speak for him on Capitol Hill. A recurrent theme in our own experience and in research by political scientists, such as Ken Collier in his book *Between the Branches*, is that White House staff who lack easy access to the president are diminished in their effectiveness.

When the legislative affairs staff members lack access to the president, they lose stature and ultimately effectiveness in influencing Congress. One of the best examples of this occurred during the Bush administration and the now infamous 1990 budget agreement in which the president broke his "read my lips, no new tax" pledge. Office of Management and Budget Director Richard Darman concocted the 1990 budget strategy with no input from the White House legislative affairs staff. Darman worked closely with the Democratic leadership, sounding them out repeatedly about the outlines of a budget deal, without consulting with the Republican leadership or the White House. The president and Congress reached a final agreement on the budget deal during a morning meeting in the White House that included Bush, Darman, White House Chief of Staff John Sununu, Speaker of the House Tom Foley, House Majority Leader Richard Gephardt, and Senate Majority Leader George Mitchell. The only two Republican congressional representatives attending were House Minority Leader Michel and Senate Minority Leader Dole. According to their staff recollections, their involvement in the meeting was minimal. No one from the White House legislative affairs staff found out about the meeting and the agreement from lawmakers on Capitol Hill until later that morning as word began to leak out.

Building Trust

The president and his staff must work to build trust with legislators. Because of factors like political and institutional rivalries, trust between the branches may not be the natural state of affairs. Building effective relations with Congress means constantly assuring lawmakers that one will do what one says one will do. A promise to provide a legislator with a letter of support must be followed up. A promise for a presidential phone call must be delivered on.

Having the ability to "make things happen" is part of the building of trust from the standpoint of the White House staff. A White House staff that does not have the ability or stature to deliver on promises or commitments made will never glean the type of respect and trust from lawmakers to effectively lead or influence Congress.

Strategic Coordination

Coordinating with other executive branch agencies and building coalitions with outside groups are other keys to lobbying success. Both represent powerful tools that, if used in the right way, can strengthen a president's legislative muscle on Capitol Hill. How and when the White House chooses to coordinate with executive agencies is a key consideration. While the president and his staff want to utilize the agency resources at certain times and make sure that the executive branch departments do not get "off message," the White House also must guard against every agency initiative becoming a presidential priority.

During the first two years of the Clinton administration, Cabinet officials and agency heads often wanted to make their agency priorities the same as the president's, hoping to give themselves more leverage on Capitol Hill. White House staff studiously guarded the list of presidential priorities, pushing large pieces of the administration's agenda back to the agencies for implementation. After losing control of the Congress in 1994, the senior staff of the president reversed course with their agency counterparts and brought virtually the entire agenda of the administration inside the West Wing so that they could manage its execution on a daily basis. Coordinating the substance, message, and execution became a very nuanced and complex process in the highly charged political atmosphere of the Republican takeover. The White House wanted maximum control in all phases of its application under these conditions, whereas it allowed and even encouraged a liberal decentralization approach when operating under unified party control of the Congress and executive branch in the prior two years.

Communications and Message Coordination

How an issue or policy is talked about is almost as important as what it actually is. The president has an enormous advantage in being able to frame an issue. His "bully pulpit" often gives him the first and last word on a matter, particularly if it is contentious. He can use the bully pulpit to frame a new initiative, for example, the need for normalizing trade relations with China or condemning congressional tardiness in completing business. His voice maximizes when it is coordinated with his political allies on Capitol Hill or sympathetic spokespeople around the country. Presidential communications in all these forms are formidable tools, particularly when used as part of a comprehensive strategy to advance or thwart an issue. However, this is not foolproof, as we saw in the repeated attempts by the Clinton administration to frame the problems and solutions implied in their proposal to solve the health care crisis in 1994.

PRECEDING OUTCOMES II: A COLLECTION OF CONTEXTS

Although building successful congressional relations depends on weaving a tapestry of activities like those outlined above, success also varies based on institutional and policy contexts. Below we consider how managing relations with Congress varies based on differing contexts such as mixed versus unified party government, interacting with the House versus the Senate, and the type of public policy Congress is considering.

Mixed versus Unified Party Governments

First, consider mixed versus unified party government. The Clinton administration had the unique opportunity to serve its first two years with its own party as the majority. But the balance of President Clinton's term was spent working with a Republican majority in Congress.

In some respects, the president's political prowess in the legislative arena during periods of unified party government may be overrated. It is true that President Clinton and the Congress were able to enact a number of important pieces of legislation into law during 1993–94, including Motor Voter, Family Medical Leave, and a deficit-reduction budgetary measure. However, there were also glaring examples of failure by unified government, most notably in the form of President Clinton's health care reform package, which languished in a Democrat-controlled Congress and ultimately became fodder for a successful Republican campaign to take over Congress in the 1994 elections.

As Mayhew and others have pointed out,[12] unified control is not a sufficient criterion to predict significant differences in legislative accomplishment. Entire chapters or books could be written about different strategies to deal with unified party government. In the short space remaining, we make two points based on our experiences and those of others who have worked in the White House. First, we agree with Mayhew and others, such as Binder,[13] that there are structural components to gridlock that make it difficult to enact major legislative accomplishments even under conditions of unified party government. Given factors such as intrachamber member and committee rivalries, interchamber competition between the House and the Senate, Rule XXII in the Senate that requires sixty votes to break a filibuster, and the two-thirds majority required in both chambers to pass a bill over the president's objections, enacting any piece of legislation is difficult.[14]

Second, given all the problems moving an agenda through Congress with the president's party in control, too little time is spent cultivating relationships and reaching out to members of the opposition party. Building strong relationships with the opposite party is one of the most challenging aspects of leadership in the legislative arena. From majority leaders in the Senate, to speakers of the House, to presidents of the United States, finding a successful formula for working with the other party without alienating allies in one's own party eludes most modern-day political leaders in Washington. Yet presidents who can do it usually reap large benefits. If there is one common thread of underachievement running through all modern presidents, it is that the challenges of working with the opposition seem to have gotten the better of most of them.

Bicameral Effects

Differences between the House and the Senate are another important variable in managing relations with Congress. Differing majority rules represent the most glaring difference from the president's standpoint in managing relations with Congress. In the Senate, some argue that the majority is not really "a majority" without sixty votes. So much of Senate floor activity is dependent on unanimous consent or achieving a three-fifths supermajority. The minority often blocks majority initiatives without sixty votes in the Senate. This is not the case in the House. Even a slim majority, such as the House in the 106th Congress, can process legislation efficiently and effectively using its Rules Committee as long as it can keep its members unified.

Two implications for managing relations with Congress follow from this observation. First, the White House must incorporate this reality into its lobbying strategy, recognizing that each individual senator could potentially sabotage portions of the president's program. The White House should make personnel decisions and develop strategies based on this reality. The president's team should spend a good portion of its time working aggressively to develop relationships and gather input from a wide array of senators. Second, given the size of the House and its majority rules, working with the leadership in the House is relatively more important compared with working with leaders in the Senate. Although no White House should ignore rank-and-file House members, compared with those in the Senate, House rules allow the White House team to focus relatively more attention on the leadership.

Policy Contexts

The president's attempts to lead and manage relations with Congress also depend on the type of policy under consideration. For example, President Bush approached Congress a certain way in January 1991 when he attempted to secure congressional authorization for the use of force in the Persian Gulf War. Alternatively, President Clinton used a different set of tactics in 1993 when he successfully passed his economic-stimulus/deficit-reduction strategy. Finally, both presidents used yet another set of strategies when responding to more specific and particular requests from individual members, trying to secure administration positions on narrower policy questions.

Some issues, by their very nature in the current political environment, are highly partisan. In today's landscape, issues like health care, taxes, and education are difficult policies to reach bipartisan consensus on. This suggests a more partisan approach to managing these issues. Other policy areas like certain distributive policies, such as transportation funding, military spending, or foreign policy issues, are decidedly more bipartisan. In these areas, the president will find reaching bipartisan consensus and gaining support from across the aisle much easier tasks.

PRECEDING OUTCOMES III: STRATEGIC GOALS

Other precursors to outcomes are the strategic goals and actions of the participants in the dance. Too often in the analysis of U.S. politics, Congress and the president are simply viewed as the targets of outside societal influences. Outside forces, not the president's or congressional purposive goals, almost exclusively shape their actions, according to this view. This view is at odds with our experiences and observations in the real world. Individuals, their relationships, and their goals make a difference.

David Mayhew, in his book *America's Congress*, recognizes this shortcoming in contemporary U.S. political analysis when he says,

> Public affairs [his word for significant public actions by individuals and legislators that come to be remembered], moreover, is a highly important realm in that much of what virtually anybody by any standard would consider to be politically important originates, is substantially caused, and happens within it—that is endogenous to it. This may be a commonsense view, but it is not all that common within the boundaries of modern social science, where politics tends to be seen as driven or determined by exogenous forces such as classes, interest groups, interests, or otherwise pre-politically caused preferences.[15]

We agree with Mayhew and believe that recognizing the unique role that individuals and their strategic goals play helps illuminate many aspects of presidential–congressional relations. Evaluating these goals and how they change over time provides useful insights into the level of success or influence that presidents achieve in legislative outcomes. These strategic goals form part of the context, including the process and institutional variables outlined above, and help us better understand and interpret the meaning of outcome measures. Analyzing how the Clinton administration and congressional strategic goals interacted is a useful case study. Let us begin in 1993 during a period when Democrats controlled the House, the Senate, and the White House.

As is often the case in unified government, the Democrats worked to ensure that their proposals could pass without Republican support. As noted above, the cornerstone of the early agenda was a $500 billion tax increase and spending cut package to reduce deficit. This measure was passed by one vote, and no Republicans supported it. While many Democrats wore this victory as a badge of honor, the Republicans gradually but successfully worked to characterize the Democrats' frenetic legislative agenda as extreme, excessive, and out of touch with most Americans. They successfully drove home this point in the health care reform debate. The administration and the Democratic congressional leadership's decision not to move their complex and controversial proposal until they were assured that it could pass without the support of Republicans, particularly in the House, was a strategic disaster. The Republicans capitalized on the Democrats' decision and crystallized this strategic message: Stop the Democrats by putting the Republicans in control of Congress. The Republicans successfully used this message to change the entire political context of the new presidency. They convinced the American public that the Democrats should lose their jobs, not because they had failed to do what they said but precisely because they were doing what they had promised.

In January 1995, the new Republican majority in the Congress took the lead, attempting to shape the political and legislative agenda of the new Congress. The cornerstone of their strategy was the "Contract with America," which included popular initiatives such as litigation reform, tax cuts, and canceling many traditional Democrat-sponsored programs. Democrats at both ends of Pennsylvania Avenue were unsure initially how to respond. Congressional Democrats, particularly in the House, were not needed to pass any of these new proposals, leaving them in the comfortable position of being against everything. Because the House was going to take the lead legislative charge, the Senate Democrats were in a "wait and see" posture. The administration, desperately wanting to remain relevant, was anxious to see if there were policy issues on which staff could work together with the Republicans, knowing that there would be plenty of areas in which they could draw the bright lines of battle.

The House acted quickly and aggressively to implement its agenda. Like the Democrats in the previous Congress, Republicans relied on their own party to pass their proposals. Appearing to take a play out of the failed Democrat playbook, the House GOP advanced a partisan set of bills.

Soon the president and congressional Democrats realized that their best strategic position in response to these legislative proposals was to claim, as the GOP did in the previous Congress, that the Republican proposals were extreme, insensitive, and out of touch with the American people. Democrats pledged to do everything they could to prevent these draconian measures from becoming law. No legislation was passed into law that entire year except for a continuing resolution that was finally adopted in January 1996.

Victory in this case was not measured by traditional outcome measures. Instead, winning was defined by whose message was more believable to the American public. By most accounts the administration and congressional Democrats "won" for stopping the Republicans from going to far with their proposals. The boldness of the new Republican agenda fell on deaf ears. The Republicans now had ten months before the next election to decide whether to make a "half-time" correction in their strategy or stay the course.

It became apparent, especially after the departure of Majority Leader Dole, that the new GOP leadership team, Lott and Gingrich, wanted to play an entirely new card and, by doing so, set in place the third strategic dynamic between President Clinton and the Congress in three short years. The theme of this strategy was "cooperation." How and on what issues could the Republican majority work with a Democratic president? How could they quickly show they were not "extreme" and "insensitive" and were ready to do the people's business? The new majority in Congress and the new president both thought this was the ticket to their respective reelections in 1996. This was not a popular view among congressional Democrats, who felt that demonstrating that the Republicans could not handle governing the majority would surely be their ticket to regaining power. Congressional Democrats felt it would be far more preferable for the president not to cooperate with the Republican majority, showing the American people that the GOP could not govern.

Far Right Republicans held the same position, though for different reasons. They believed that compromise was tantamount to capitulation and that working together with the Clinton administration would dilute the Republican cause and only help the president get reelected. Nevertheless, the Republican leaders and the president forged a course of cooperation that resulted in small business tax cuts, minimum wage increases, welfare reform, and a framework for a bipartisan balanced budget package. The 1996 election returned President Clinton and the House and Senate Republican majorities.

Despite the success of this strategy produced in the 1996 election, there was serious dissatisfaction among the Republican rank and file. After working with the president to enact a balanced budget and pass welfare reform, Republicans were not sure about the next act of this political play. Many had no desire to continue to work with the president after he won the 1996 election and in the wake of revelations about campaign financing irregularities and the continuation of the Whitewater investigation. The Republican leadership decided to disengage from a cooperative posture on policy and develop an aggressive strategy to use its oversight and subpoena authority to pursue the new campaign and personal financial investigations.

In addition to pursuing the truth, these investigations served at least two other strategic purposes for Republicans. They continued to fill the negative atmosphere surrounding the Clinton administration, with the GOP hoping to undo the administration's credibility in the eyes of the public and media. They also served to keep the administration at arm's-length in the legislative arena.

"Scandal as diversion," as some would call it, appeared as a strategic approach through the hearing on Whitewater, through inquiry into the campaign financing of the 1996 election, and ultimately through the impeachment proceedings regarding the Lewinsky matter. It produced very little authorizing legislation of note, except by accident, and an appropriations process that generally served to the disadvantage of the Republicans and to the benefit of the president and Democrats. The 1998 elections were held in the height of this strategy, and the Republican majority in the Senate held its own while the GOP House majority lost a handful of seats, putting an already slim majority in serious jeopardy for 2000.

While the strategy of "scandal as diversion" was on the wane, the congressional leaders and the president contemplated an appropriate framework for the last dance of a lame duck president. The nature of the final strategic relationship is still unclear. There is no doubt, however, that clarifying the strategic goals pursued by the actors in the legislative and executive branches is a critical precursor to understanding the legislative outcomes (or lack thereof) produced by the Clinton White House and the Republican Congress.

CONCLUSION

Currently, most pundits', scholars', and reporters' views of presidential–congressional relations are too limited. Understanding the dance between presidents and lawmakers requires a broader perspective. Presidents do not sink or swim, succeed or fail, have influence or not, based solely on outcome-based measures like roll-call votes or sustaining vetoes. A broader perspective on presidential–congressional relations also requires the understanding that Congress tries to influence and lead the president as much as the president tries to lead Congress. Not only is too much of the research in this area "presidency centered," but there is also not enough emphasis on how Congress and the president try to influence each other through a dynamic process of give and take.

This chapter also highlights some of the secrets of success in managing presidential–congressional relations given these changing and differing contexts. Viewing presidential–congressional relations in this broader context sets the stage for a better and more realistic understanding of how these institutions can and should interact, including their potential and their limits.

Achieving success and influence with Congress as an American president is not easy. In fact, based on the variables discussed in this chapter one might conclude that most presidents are destined to fail. Quadrennial discussions about "mandates" or what can be done in the "first 100 days" simply do not fit reality when it comes to presidential agendas with Congress.

We are not ready to throw in the towel and concede that all future presidents will underachieve. But we do think that someone needs to burst (or at least deflate) the public's overblown expectations about presidential influence in the legislative arena. If a president hopes to produce prodigious legislative accomplishments, many political and institutional stars will have to align. He will have to be blessed with large legislative majorities in both chambers of Congress, an activist agenda with wide public support, and a great deal of bargaining skill to overcome a host of potential institutionally based pitfalls in Congress that could thwart pieces on his agenda. Appreciating that these political and institutional stars rarely align will help lower public expectations for future presidents.

And even when they do "align," recent experiences suggest that unified party control does not always result in the expected outcome. As several scholars have noted recently, the theory of "responsible party government," whereby one party controls both the legislative and the executive branches and enacts an agenda, may be a sound normative theory.[16] As a descriptive device, however, it is somewhat lacking.[17]

We should also modify our criteria for success to include implementation of the process variables outlined in this chapter. Presidents play a major role in setting the "tone" of relations between the branches. Focusing on using many of the process suggestions outlined above will set a positive and civil tone, maximizing the possibility of successful influence.

Successful influence also varies across time. The dynamic nature of the relationship between the president and Congress deserves more attention. Presidents may find success at different periods of their administrations only to lose it during other periods. Understanding how and why presidential–congressional relations change over time may yield important clues about the keys to success.

Finally, we need to remember that successful influence may be dependent on contexts. Success in the Senate does not guarantee success in the House. Winning on foreign policy does not translate into success in the domestic arena.

After reading this chapter one might conclude that we have raised more questions than we answered about the nature of White House–congressional relations. In some respects, that was our goal. The relationship between the branches is complex, dynamic, and fraught with misunderstanding. Yet, at another level, we hope that by outlining some of these complexities and raising these questions, we have fostered a deeper and more critical understanding of the relationship that helps scholars, students, and pundits appreciate the possibilities and limitations of the president's relationship with Congress.

At this writing, the administration of George W. Bush is less than one year old, and it is too early to tell how pundits and scholars will judge his relations with Congress. What is clear, however, is that many of the variables we suggest in this chapter that form the "tapestry of success" are extremely relevant and deserve full attention in evaluating the "influence" of President Bush and the Congress.

Here are some initial thoughts about how our framework might apply to the current president. First, the bicameral effects influencing the Bush presidency are striking. Initially, the Republicans controlled the Senate by the narrowest of majorities, but they lost control in June 2001 when Senator Jeffords (Vt.) became an independent. Even before the Jeffords switch occurred, a clear pattern emerged: Bush looked strong in the House and much weaker in the Senate. And while it appears that Bush had more "influence" in the House, the differences were largely caused by differences in institutional rules and procedures as opposed to anything done by the president or the White House staff.

Second, the White House demonstrated real skill on the education issue by engaging in what we call "active consultation" and "engaging the leadership." Bush created a bipartisan climate that allowed his education bill to sail through both the House and the Senate with large margins. Conversely, he approached the tax bill with a more partisan strategy and was less "successful" in building a broader consensus in the Congress for tax relief. In many ways Bush treated the tax bill just as Clinton approached Congress in the first year—building majorities almost only with support of his own party.

Third, Bush is facing many of the challenges of "strategic coordination" with the agencies that we discuss in this chapter. Most of the short-term problems this White House confronted in its first year—leaks from agencies, lack of information flow on announcements from executive departments to the Hill, Cabinet secretaries saying things that appear inconsistent with

White House policy, and so on—are happening with a regularity faced by previous administrations. But because these occurrences are expected in any White House, the key to successful influence is managing them.

Finally, the issue of how to work with the opposition bedevils Bush, like most other modern presidents. Bush's situation is even more complex because his party controls the House but not the Senate. In the end, this is an issue in which "success" and "influence" are almost impossible to evaluate. Successes or failures are perhaps best judged by how the president manages trade-offs. Winning support of the opposition often carries a heavy cost with members of the president's party—as Bush learned by the opposition he faced from some conservatives of his own party in the House on the education bill.

In the end, as we have argued in this chapter, winning or losing, success and influence are best evaluated by using a broad tapestry of criteria, across time and in separate policy contexts. So far this approach appears fair and accurate in evaluating the new president.

NOTES

1. Gary Andres, Patrick Griffin, and James Thurber, "The Contemporary Presidency. Managing White House–Congressional Relations: Observations from Inside the Process," *Presidential Studies Quarterly* 30, no. 3 (2000): 553–63; Kenneth E. Collier, *Between the Branches: The White House Office of Legislative Affairs* (Pittsburgh: University of Pittsburgh Press, 1997); Charles O. Jones, *The Presidency in a Separated System* (Washington, D.C.: Brookings Institution Press, 1994); Mark A. Peterson, *Legislating Together* (Cambridge, Mass.: Harvard University Press, 1990).
2. Quoted in Collier, *Between the Branches*, 10.
3. Richard E. Neustadt, *Presidential Power: The Politics of Leadership* (New York: Wiley, 1960).
4. George C. Edwards and B. Dan Woods, "Who Influences Whom? The President and the Public Agenda," *American Political Science Review* 93 (June 1999): 327–44.
5. Andres, Griffin, and Thurber, "The Contemporary Presidency."
6. Peterson, *Legislating Together*.
7. Keith Krehbiel, *Pivotal Politics: A Theory of U.S. Lawmaking* (Chicago: University of Chicago Press, 1998).
8. David R. Mayhew, *America's Congress: Actions in the Public Sphere, James Madison through Newt Gingrich* (New Haven: Yale University Press, 2000).
9. Jones, *The Presidency in a Separated System*, 19, emphasis added.
10. Sarah Binder, "The Dynamics of Legislative Gridlock: 1947–1996," *American Political Science Review* 93 (September 1999): 519–33.
11. Quoted in Collier, *Between the Branches*, 2.
12. See David R. Mayhew, *Divided We Govern: Party Control, Lawmaking and Investigations, 1946–1990* (New Haven: Yale University Press, 1991).

13. Binder, "The Dynamics of Legislative Gridlock."

14. Binder, "The Dynamics of Legislative Gridlock"; Keith Krehbiel, "Paradoxes of Parties in Congress," *Legislative Studies Quarterly* 24 (February 1999): 31–64.

15. Mayhew, *America's Congress*, 6.

16. See, for example, American Political Science Association, *Toward a More Responsible Two-Party System* (Washington, D.C.: American Political Science Association, 1950).

17. Jones, *The Presidency in a Separated System*; Krehbiel, "Paradoxes of Parties in Congress"; Mayhew, *Divided We Govern*.

8

Herding Cats: Presidential Coalition Building in the Senate

C. Lawrence Evans and Walter J. Oleszek

Leading the Senate is notoriously difficult—difficult for Senate party leaders, for the White House, for anyone. The dominant ethos of the contemporary Senate, after all, is individualism, rather than followership, and building coalitions in the chamber has been likened to "pushing a wet noodle" or "herding cats." In one floor debate, a frustrated Byron Dorgan (D-N.D.) asked Republican Leader Trent Lott (R-Miss.) if he had seen a recent television commercial "where the cowboys are trying to herd the cats." An equally frustrated Lott quipped that he often felt like "one of the cowboys trying to keep the cats [in line]; they won't herd up though."[1]

Briefly consider the institutional context of Senate leadership. Relative to representatives in the House, individual senators represent larger constituencies and thus confront more diverse interests and pressures. As a result, senators are not inclined to defer to centralized party leaders at either end of Pennsylvania Avenue.[2] Senators are "the ultimate insiders" and are major public figures in their own right.[3] They are capable of drawing substantial media attention. Members of the Senate have large staffs and thus, compared with House members, are less reliant on party leaders or the administration for information.[4] Most important, the filibuster enables individual lawmakers to bring the Senate legislative process to a halt unless sixty votes can be garnered for cloture.[5]

The task of presidential coalition building in the chamber was especially daunting during the 106th Congress (1999–2000). As has often been the case in recent years, different parties controlled the legislative and executive branches, exacerbating conflict between the White House and Capitol Hill. The 106th Congress also was shaped by the 2000 congressional and presidential campaigns, which provided incentives for the two political parties to utilize the legislative agenda to formulate and publicize partisan messages. Party leaders, so the argument went, were more interested in position taking than in legislative accomplishment. Moreover, the 106th Senate opened with the impeachment trial of President Bill Clinton. Although the two-thirds supermajority necessary for removal was not achieved, a majority of the chamber (and almost all of the Republicans) voted in favor of removal at some point in the process. Democratic members of the Senate believed that the president owed his survival in office to their support. Some Senate watchers predicted that Democrats would primarily look to Thomas Daschle (S.D.), minority leader at the time, for leadership on legislative matters.

Still, in this chapter we demonstrate that the White House was selectively but integrally involved in the Senate legislative process throughout the 106th Congress. This involvement took the form of regular communications and negotiations between administration and congressional officials, the articulation and publicizing of a national Democratic Party message, and the strategic use of vetoes and veto threats, among other tactics. The nature of Clinton's relations with the Republican-controlled Senate is instructive. In the 107th Congress, GOP President George W. Bush also confronts a sharply divided Congress, with the Senate under Democratic control following the June 2001 defection of James Jeffords (Vt.) from the Republican Party to independent status. Moreover, Bush did not win a plurality of the popular vote in November 2000, and his electoral college victory derived in part from a controversial Supreme Court decision. And during the 107th Congress, the GOP majority in the House remains razor thin, complicating the coalition building process in both chambers. As a result, President Clinton's interactions with the Senate during the 106th Congress can shed valuable light on the likely contours of interbranch relations in the 107th Congress and beyond.

MECHANISMS FOR COORDINATION

U.S. national government is a system of separate institutions sharing and competing for power, and the Constitution has been usefully described as an "invitation to struggle" between the Congress and the president for the privilege of directing national policy. But even during periods of intense party polarization and divided government, the interactions that occur between the branches include a complex combination of conflict and cooperation.

The existing scholarly literature delineates many of the tools that presidents use to build coalitions in the Senate. The White House can target distributive policy benefits to the constituencies of pivotal lawmakers. The commander in chief is also the fund-raiser in chief and can raise large sums of campaign money for individual House members and senators (albeit, of the president's party). The president also can use the bully pulpit to influence public opinion and thus change the incentives that legislators face on difficult roll-call votes.[6] The White House has access to the considerable informational resources of the executive branch, which can translate into influence on Capitol Hill. The president can activate outside interests to help push administration initiatives through the legislative labyrinth. In brief, the president has a wide arsenal of different strategic tools that he can deploy artfully for different kinds of legislation.

Over time, the executive and legislative branches have developed a number of fairly institutionalized mechanisms to facilitate communication, coordination, and coalition building across the branches, especially within the party of the incumbent president. Certain of these mechanisms, however, have been underemphasized by scholars and pundits alike. In this section, we single out three of them: the relatively formalized meetings that regularly occur between administration and congressional personnel, the party message agendas, and written Statements of Administration Policy (SAPs). These mechanisms are central to relations between the president and the Senate in contemporary U.S. politics.

Direct Communication

First, we should not discount the sheer quantity of personal communications that take place on a regular basis between the White House and congressional leaders.[7] These communications occur over the telephone, via e-mail and letters, and through formal meetings, and they are a predictable and regular feature of interbranch relations. Of course, much of the personal communication that occurs between White House and congressional officials is ad hoc. In 2000, for example, President Clinton telephoned a number of Democratic senators and asked for their support in extending permanent normal trade relations to China. In fall 1999, Clinton conducted a dinner meeting at the White House with key Senate leaders concerning chamber ratification of the comprehensive nuclear test ban treaty. Particularly as major legislation moves to the conference committee stage, congressional leaders and administration officials often discuss the possible parameters of a compromise. In late October 2000, Senate Appropriations Chairman Ted Stevens (R-Ala.) presented Jack Lew, the director of the Office of Management and Budget (OMB), with a "global solution" with respect to spending and policy differences on three appropriations bills. "The bottom line is three signable bills," said Senator Stevens.[8] Despite the proffered global solution, negotiations on these matters dragged on until a final budgetary agreement was achieved in December 2000.

Along with such ad hoc interactions, there are a number of relatively institutionalized meetings that occur regularly and include top officials from the executive and legislative branches. For the purposes of illustration, table 8.1 summarizes the most significant meeting forums used during the 106th Congress that included White House and Senate officials. Not surprisingly, given Democratic control of the executive branch and GOP control of Congress, most of these meetings were attended solely by Democrats.

The bipartisan congressional leadership did meet periodically with the president in the Cabinet room, and these sessions were heavily publicized in the media. But the size and partisan composition of the meetings usually turned them into forums for position taking, and they seldom were productive in terms of real progress on legislation. Instead, they were dominated by speeches by the key participants and usually ended with press conferences in which party leaders engaged in "happy talk" or publicly attacked the opposing party. On 12 September 2000, for instance, President Clinton invited the bipartisan House and Senate leadership to the White House to discuss how to conclude the legislative business of the 106th Congress. GOP leaders urged that 90 percent of the projected 2001 budget surplus be used for debt reduction. This idea was labeled a "gimmick" by White House officials and Democratic congressional leaders, who demanded action on their own legislative priorities—raising the minimum wage, a prescription drug benefit for Medicare recipients, and so on.[9]

Along with the bipartisan leadership events, a number of "Democrats only" meetings occurred during the 106th Congress that facilitated cooperation between congressional Democrats and the Clinton White House. For example, House and Senate Democratic leaders met with the president and top White House aides (usually in the Oval Office or the residence) three or four times per year. The occurrence of these sessions also was publicized by the media, but because of the sessions' more private nature and the absence of Republicans, they tended to be more frank and productive. Throughout the 106th Congress, Senate Democratic leaders and staff regularly spoke or met with White House officials, including the president. Most often, such interactions (often occurring on a daily basis) were between the director of legislative liaison for the White House and Democratic leadership staff. White House Chief of Staff John Podesta also telephoned or visited directly with Minority Leader Daschle when major legislation was on the floor.

Table 8.1 Institutionalized Forums for Interaction among Administration and Senate Officials, 106th Congress

Type of Meeting	*Description*
Bipartisan Leadership	Meetings occurred once or twice per year in the Cabinet room and included House and Senate leaders from both parties, White House officials, and the president. It was mostly a forum for partisan position taking.
Joint Democratic Leadership	Meetings occurred perhaps three times per year and included House and Senate Democratic leaders, White House officials, and the president. It promoted a more productive exchange because of the partisan composition.
Senate Democratic Leadership	Meetings occurred regularly on an "as needed" basis via telephone and in person. Such exchanges typically were between White House legislative liaison and staff to Daschle.
Democratic Caucus	Full Democratic Caucus meetings occurred over lunch every Tuesday when the Senate was in session. Administrative officials often made presentations. Only a few leadership staff and no reporters were permitted to attend.
Democratic Policy Committee	Members of the Senate Democratic Policy Committee held weekly meetings, with a primary emphasis on policy and legislation. Administration officials occasionally attended.
Committee Leaders	Meetings usually occurred biweekly on Wednesdays over lunch. Included were the Democratic leadership and Democratic leaders on Senate committees (ranking minority members in the 106th Congress). No staff were allowed except the director of White House legislative liaison.
Bicameral Leadership Staff	Meetings occurred every Friday that the Congress was in session at 10:00 a.m. Included were top staff to House and Senate Democratic leaders, with representation from top White House staff.

Source: Staff interviews conducted by the authors.

In addition, the weekly meetings of the Senate Democratic Caucus (on Tuesdays over lunch) provided members with a useful forum for deliberation on legislation and communications strategy. Executive branch officials regularly attended these sessions, which were closed to the media, as well as all staff except top leadership aides. As Senate action on the 2001 budget resolution and reconciliation measures approached, OMB Director Jack Lew, among other administration officials, made presentations at the Tuesday caucus meetings. The regular meetings of the Senate Democratic Policy Committee also featured participation and input from executive branch personnel with responsibilities that were relevant to the upcoming legislative agenda.

Biweekly meetings also occurred (usually on Wednesdays, in Daschle's office) between the committee ranking minority members and Senate Democratic leaders. During the 106th Congress, the director of legislative liaison for the White House regularly attended these sessions to learn about the political climate within the Democratic Caucus and to provide input from the administration.[10] Other top administration officials also sat in, depending on the issue and their expertise (e.g., the national security adviser might attend when foreign policy matters were discussed). Finally, the top aides to House and Senate Democratic leaders met every Friday at 10:00 a.m. (usually in the conference room of House Democratic Leader Richard Gephardt [Mo.]) to discuss the legislative agenda for the upcoming week. Top White House staff members always were in attendance.

Fundamental to these various meetings was two-way communication and bargaining. Administration officials conveyed executive viewpoints, and lawmakers informed White House officials about their perspectives on legislative issues as well as general political conditions in the Senate. Regularly, the White House and Senate Democrats went back and forth at these meetings offering initiatives and reacting to what others were proposing. For example, Senate Democrats might ask the president or top White House aides: "Is the president going to veto the bill?" White House officials might respond: "Will you sustain the veto?" A senior Senate Democratic aide has highlighted an important component of the two-way relationship: "There's always been an understanding that [Democratic leader] Daschle's role is to maximize the administration's leverage in negotiations [with Senate Democrats and Republicans]. In exchange, the priorities so many Democrats have get a fair hearing at the White House."[11]

How common or routinized were meetings, telephone conversations, letters, and e-mail messages among administration officials and Senate Republican leaders and staff during this period? According to Republican leadership aides, such interactions were less extensive and far more ad hoc than the consultation that occurred among fellow Democrats. Majority Leader Lott noted that he had "no relations" with White House Chief of Staff Podesta, whom he described as "a shrill partisan."[12] Executive branch personnel occasionally participated in the weekly meetings of the Senate Republican Conference, also conducted on Tuesdays over lunch. In 1999, for instance, Defense Secretary William Cohen and General Henry Shelton, the chairman of the Joint Chiefs of Staff, spoke to a Republican Conference meeting about U.S. involvement in Kosovo. Staff-level consultation on legislative matters also was sporadic. Instead, the personal interactions that did occur between the Clinton administration and the Senate Republican leadership typically took place when legislation was in conference or as part of formal bargaining to stave off a threatened veto during initial Senate consideration. Interestingly, Senate Republican staff have remarked that White House aides seemed to have more productive working relationships with certain House Republican leadership staff, especially the top aide to House Speaker Dennis Hastert (R-Ill.).

Message Agendas

The burgeoning importance of party message agendas and "message politics" enhances the ability of the president to build coalitions among his fellow partisans in Congress—while significantly complicating efforts at negotiation and compromise across the partisan aisle.[13] The national political parties develop organized messages, which include the issues, themes, and policy symbols that elite political actors believe will generate a positive response among voters toward their party and excite the support of their core activists. Message politics, in turn, refers to the interrelated set of campaign, communications, and legislative tactics that legislators and the White House use to advance their respective party messages.

For example, to put political heat on congressional Republicans during the 2000 budget endgame, the White House developed a presidential "message of the day" on issues such as raising the minimum wage or providing a prescription drug benefit to senior citizens. With the November 2000 elections as the backdrop, "there are a number of items that we've put front and center that have been making Republicans very uncomfortable," remarked a senior Clinton adviser.[14] About two weeks earlier, it is worth noting, House and Senate Republicans established a joint communications team. "House and Senate communicators, starting this week, are meeting every day to coordinate message," said a GOP leadership aide: "We will do so through Election Day."[15] From party leadership involvement during the committee process to the use of filibuster and cloture, much of the contemporary legislative process is shaped by the relevance of an issue to the message agendas of the two parties.[16]

Since at least the early 1990s, congressional Republicans and Democrats have developed extensive communications operations aimed at articulating and publicizing their party message agendas. During the 106th Congress, for instance, the House GOP message operation was spearheaded by Representative J. C. Watts (Okla.), chair of the Republican Conference. Working closely with Majority Leader Lott and Majority Whip Don Nickles (Okla.), Senator Craig Thomas (Wyo.) took the lead on the party message for Senate Republicans. The message activities of House and Senate Democrats, in part because of their minority status, seemed more organized and extensive than was the case with the majority party. Representative Rosa DeLauro (Conn.) supervised message activities for House Democrats, while Senator Richard Durbin (Ill.) fulfilled that role for Democrats in the Senate.

The message agendas help focus the attention of legislators on a subset of issue areas and proposals that differ (substantially but not entirely) by party. What were the party messages during the 106th Congress? The Republican agenda featured tax reduction, education reform, defense readiness, and juvenile justice reform. The Democratic message featured education policy, and it also emphasized issues such as gun control, the minimum wage, and campaign finance reform. The central component of the Democratic message agenda was opposition to Republican proposals for large, across-the-board tax reductions. And a central aspect of the GOP message agenda was the development of policy options on issues "owned" by Democrats that resonated with the public, such as education, prescription drugs for the elderly, and the like. In short, if Clinton "borrowed" popular GOP themes during his presidency—balanced budgets, welfare reform, and "the era of big government is over"—congressional Republicans also attempted to coopt Democratic issues and transform them into their own proposals.

It should be emphasized that decisions about message do not originate solely from the partisan meeting rooms of Capitol Hill. The two national party organizations contribute to message formulation by conducting extensive polling and focus groups. The congressional parties lack the resources necessary to engage in such activities on a regular basis. The interest groups associated with the Republican or Democratic Parties also participate in message formulation. The National Rifle Association (NRA), for instance, regularly gauges public opinion on gun issues and shares the results, along with suggestions for framing and marketing pro-gun positions, with the national Republican Party. Advocacy groups such as the NRA also run independent advertising campaigns, which serve to reinforce the communications activities of the two major parties.

Most important for our purposes, the president is the most visible political actor in U.S. national politics and thus plays a critical role in developing the message for the president's party in Congress. The White House has vast resources for developing policy proposals and publicizing them to the American people. Modern presidents regularly conduct polls and focus groups, and the White House staff now includes an elaborate communications operation. As the leader of his party, the president is a natural focal point for media and press attention. In short, the bully pulpit is a valuable tool for framing issues for the electorate and for coordinating legislative and communications priorities across the executive branch and with the president's party in Congress.

As mentioned, the centerpiece of the congressional Democratic message during the 106th Congress was the argument that the federal budget surplus should not be used to finance large tax cuts but instead should be devoted to paying down the debt and promoting the long-term solvency of Medicare and Social Security. This argument that huge tax cuts would undermine Social Security and Medicare was first articulated in Clinton's 1998 State of the Union message ("save Social Security first"), and polls and focus groups revealed that the message was popular with voters. Quickly, Republicans one-upped the president and promised to lock up all the revenues flowing into Social Security. The GOP embraced this idea as a way to ward off Democratic charges that Republicans wanted to raid Social Security to pass tax cuts for the wealthy. In effect, each party checkmated the other during the 106th Congress. "We said 'save the surplus to stop tax cuts,' " stated a senior Senate Democratic staff aide: "They used it to stop spending programs. So it came out a draw."[17]

In summer 1999, Clinton released a highly publicized plan to extend prescription drug benefits to Medicare recipients. Congressional Democrats quickly adopted the issue as a core component of their message. The Democratic message also featured calls for a patients' Bill of Rights, to provide further protections to customers of health maintenance organizations (HMOs). The HMO proposal derived from the work of a Clinton administration task force. Republicans devised their own alternatives to these health proposals, which emphasized the private sector more than the government as the avenue for accomplishing their preferences.

Prior to the beginning of a new Congress, executive branch officials and congressional leaders from the president's party meet to discuss communications and message. This consultation continues throughout the political year and usually steps up as an election approaches. Much of the coordination that occurs on legislative and communications priorities is informal. After all, the same issues tend to surface year after year, and leaders on both ends of Pennsylvania Avenue consider the same public opinion data. However, the two branches do confront different electoral constituencies, which can complicate efforts to coordinate message and strategy.

Based on our conversations with current and former White House and congressional leadership staff, it appears that, during the 106th Congress, House Democrats, Senate Democrats, and the White House had divergent viewpoints on the value of compromise with congressional Republicans. House Democrats, under the leadership of Minority Leader Gephardt, were focused almost exclusively on securing majority status in November 2000 and tended to be the least inclined to make legislative concessions to the opposition. They instead sought to reinforce the differences between the two parties on message issues, maintain a distinctive name brand for the party among voters, and campaign against a "do-nothing" Republican Congress. In contrast, a legacy-minded Clinton administration usually was the most willing of the three institutional actors to compromise with Republicans. Senate Democrats, under the leadership of Thomas Daschle, typically fell in the middle range regarding the benefits of compromise.

Even with these institutional disagreements about strategy, however, national Democrats were remarkably unified about legislative priorities and party message during the 106th Congress. They recognized the electoral advantages inherent in promoting a coherent favorable party name brand, which in turn aided the president in building coalitions within his congressional party. The flip side, though, is that message politics tends to divide the parties and thus complicates efforts by an administration to build legislative coalitions across party lines. In 1999–2000, the importance of message politics helped Clinton assemble Democratic Party coalitions large enough to block conservative GOP initiatives in the Senate. Only forty-one votes were necessary to filibuster such initiatives, and Senate leaders and the administration were almost always able to hold that many Democratic members in line. On vetoes, too, Democrats backed the president. Of the thirty-seven vetoes by Clinton during his two terms, Congress attempted to override thirteen, but only two of these attempts were successful. The zero-sum conflict that existed between the parties on message issues generally impeded bipartisan compromise and the passage of legislation. Particularly as an election nears, message politics can promote position taking and gridlock.

Presidential Signaling: Statements of Administration Policy

In important research, Charles Cameron emphasizes the importance of the veto and what he labels "veto bargaining" for understanding relations between the executive branch and Congress.[18] Cameron correctly observes that presidential–congressional interactions are best conceptualized as a game of strategy between purposive actors with divergent goals, especially during periods of divided government or when partisan majorities within Congress are razor thin. The key formal prerogative of the president is the ability to veto legislation passed by Congress and to have that veto sustained if either chamber cannot muster the two-thirds supermajority necessary to override it. Uncertainty usually exists, however, about the goals and preferences of key political actors in the interbranch bargaining game. Within such an environment, the strategic use of veto threats by the president can be consequential for the contents of legislative outcomes, even when no veto actually occurs. Under the right conditions, legislators will respond to a threatened veto by making the legislative adjustments that they believe are necessary to secure the president's signature. Thus, threatened vetoes can serve as a consequential signal of the president's policy preferences and strategic intentions.

In his book, Cameron makes imaginative use of media accounts and the *Public Papers of the Presidents* to gather data about the incidence and impact of veto threats. For a random sample of 443 bills passed by both chambers between 1945 and 1972, he found evidence of veto threats on 106 of the items. For the more significant measures in his sample, fully one-third evoked a veto threat at some point in the legislative process. What were the consequences of these threats? If the Congress capitulated to the president's policy demands, the president invariably signed the measure. On the other hand, if Congress failed to make any significant concessions in the president's direction, the measure was almost always vetoed. Finally, if Congress did not totally capitulate but did make some significant concessions, the president still signed the measure about 80 percent of the time. As a result, Cameron argues, veto threats are a common and potentially important component of the legislative process.

Scholars need to build on Cameron's work.[19] Since the 1970s, for instance, the two branches have developed highly institutionalized and nuanced mechanisms for the White House to send signals about its policy preferences on pending legislation and to issue carefully calibrated veto threats. Before major bills are considered on the House or Senate floors, the White House typically sends a written Statement of Administration Policy (SAP) to the relevant chamber.[20]

The legislative unit within the OMB prepares (under the direction of the White House and others) and transmits SAPs to the House and the Senate just prior to floor action on legislation. SAPs formally express the administration's position on the bill or specific provisions therein. They also are often sent to the House Rules Committee just before the panel devises a rule for floor consideration on a measure. In the 106th Congress, the administration sent 369 SAPs to Congress. Sixty-two were sent to the Rules Committee, 236 were sent to the House (just before floor action on the relevant bill), and seventy-one were sent to the Senate (also prior to floor action).

Based on a careful review of the SAPs, as well as interviews with current and former White House and congressional leadership staff, it appears that, by design, standard language tends to surface repeatedly in these policy messages. Knowledgeable staff routinely refer to such phrasings as "code words," "signals," and "messages." They comment that participants in the process fully recognize the intended meaning of these statements, especially as they relate to appropriations bills.

For example, on 6 October 2000 the administration sent an SAP to the Senate with respect to the commerce, justice, and state appropriations bill (H.R. 4690). The SAP discusses the administration's concerns with the Senate Appropriations Committee's spending recommendations and employs such subtleties of phraseology as the following: "The Committee has not adequately addressed . . ."; "The Committee bill provides only . . ."; "The Administration is disappointed . . ."; "The Administration takes strong exception to . . ."; or "The Administration appreciates the Senate's bill funding for. . . . However, we urge the Senate to including full funding for. . . ." Appropriations Committee members and staff aides understand how obligatory these various comments are intended to be. Generally, party and committee leaders are most conversant with the nuances of SAPs.

SAPs range in length from a few paragraphs to ten or more pages of detailed comments about the contents of a measure. Almost always, they begin with a short paragraph summarizing the administration's overall position on the legislation. This overall position tends to be phrased in one of the following six ways, which reflect different directions and intensities of administration preference, ranging from strong opposition to strong support. The administration

1. strongly opposes the measure.
2. opposes the measure.
3. does not take a position on passage.
4. does not object to passage.
5. supports passage of the measure.
6. strongly supports passage of the measure.

Level 3 (no position) can be phrased in many different ways, such as "The Administration has concerns with [the bill, and if it is] passed by the House, the Administration will work with the Senate to amend [the House-passed measure]"; or "The Administration has concerns with [the bill] and wants to work with Congress to address them." On occasion, the administration's overall position is not addressed at all.

For the other five levels, however, standard phrasings surface repeatedly across different SAPs, and participants in the process have commented that the language provides a fairly calibrated signal of the intensity of the president's viewpoint. For the 369 SAPs issued by the Clinton administration during the 106th Congress, table 8.2 summarizes the frequency of the different levels of presidential opposition and support. Over 80 percent of the SAPs include a bottom-line position for the White House, and for these items, the relative levels of opposition and support are distributed fairly broadly.

The SAPs that denote presidential opposition to a measure usually include an explicit veto threat of some form. On 30 September 1999, for instance, the White House sent an SAP to the House regarding H.R. 2436, entitled the "Unborn Victims of Violence Act of 1999." The SAP begins: "The Administration strongly opposes enactment of H.R. 2436, which would make it a separate Federal offense to cause 'death or bodily injury' to a 'child in utero' in the course of committing certain specified Federal crimes. If H.R. 2436 were presented to the President, his senior advisers would recommend that he veto the bill." On S. 1692, the "Partial-Birth Abortion Ban Act of 1999," a 23 October 1999 SAP states: "The President will veto S. 1692 for the reasons he expressed in his veto message of April 10, 1996, which is attached."

In SAP after SAP, the veto threat tends to come in one of the following forms, in roughly ascending order of intensity:

1. No veto threat language is included.
2. If certain specified provisions are added to the bill or dropped from the

Table 8.2 President's Overall Position in Statements of Administration Policy, 106th Congress

Position	Number of Statements of Administration Policy
Strong Opposition	82 (22.2%)
Opposition	90 (24.4%)
No Position	64 (17.3%)
Do Not Object	23 (5.2%)
Support	77 (20.9%)
Strong Support	33 (8.9%)

Source: Website of the U.S. Office of Management and Budget, http://www.whitehouse.gov/OMB/legislative/sap.

bill, then the president's senior advisers would recommend that he veto the bill.

3. If the measure is presented to the president, then the secretary would recommend that he veto the bill.
4. If the measure is presented to the president, then the president's senior advisers would recommend that he veto the bill.
5. If the measure is presented to the president, then he would veto the bill.

Table 8.3 provides summary data about the frequency of each level of threatened veto for the SAPs from the 106th Congress. Notice that veto recommendations from the president's senior advisers are treated as (somewhat) more consequential than similar threats from the secretary of the relevant executive branch department. The staff we spoke with commented that "senior advisers" are viewed as more proximate to the president and thus provide the White House with less wiggle room for scaling back its objections or backing down. (They also indicated that Cabinet secretaries sometimes make statements more for their political benefit than for that of the White House.) Again, although there is some variance in the language, the same phrases tend to surface repeatedly across different SAPs (and the bills they address) with the relative frequency denoted in table 8.3.

Of course, there are instances when the president will sign legislation into law despite the objections raised in the SAP. On the agricultural appropriations bill (H.R. 4461) for 2001, the SAP outlines a number of specific problems the administration had with the measure, such as the provision designed to increase trade with Cuba, and Clinton even hinted that he might veto the measure. In the end, he agreed to sign the bill "because of

Table 8.3 Types of Veto Threats, 106th Congress

Form of Veto Threat	*Intensity Level*	*Number of Statements of Administration Policy*
No explicit veto language is included	1	254 (68.8%)
If certain provisions are added to bill or dropped from bill, then veto	2	11 (3.0%)
Secretary would recommend veto	3	12 (3.3%)
Senior advisers would recommend veto	4	65 (17.5%)
President would veto	5	27 (7.3%)

Source: Website of the U.S. Office of Management and Budget, http://www.whitehouse.gov/OMB/legislative/sap.

the substantial amount of aid it would deliver to rural America."[21] According to our discussions with key White House and congressional staff, agriculture is an area in which lawmakers always lobby the administration for more money for farmers. And with the two Senate leaders (Lott and Daschle) representing agricultural states, as well as the political imperative of helping farmers, the administration usually was put in the position of trying to constrain additional spending for farm programs.

For some reason, SAPs have not yet received sustained analysis by congressional and presidential scholars. But these documents clearly provide a nuanced mechanism for the White House to communicate its positions on pending legislation to the House and the Senate, as well as a potentially valuable source of data for scholars. The systematic and calibrated nature of the veto threats indicates the strategic nature of these presidential signals and the importance of the veto in the legislative process.

LEVELS OF PRESIDENTIAL INVOLVEMENT

The modes and level of administration involvement in the Senate legislative process vary substantially from issue to issue. To tentatively gauge this variance for the 106th Congress, we spoke with the Democratic leadership aide who had primary responsibility for working with White House officials on legislative matters. For a sample of twenty-three issues considered by the full Senate during this period, we asked the staffer to rate the level of administration involvement during initial Senate consideration on a scale of one (low involvement) to five (high involvement). The sample of issues includes most of the hot-button items on the Senate agenda in 1999–2000.[22] The ratings clearly are rough, but they do provide a useful framework for exploring the coalition-building role played by the president on specific bills and issues. (For purposes of comparison, we also asked a top aide to the Senate Republican leadership to rate the involvement of GOP leaders during chamber consideration of these same items.) Summary data about White House involvement on the measures are provided in table 8.4.

According to the ratings, only one of the issues was characterized by very low administration involvement—an effort in summer 2000 by Senator John McCain (R-Ariz.) to roll back the federal subsidy for sugar production (considered during Senate action on the agricultural appropriations bill). The sugar issue is a perennial one on Capitol Hill; the positions of the White House and most Senators are long-standing and well known; and the matter is unrelated to either party's message agenda. Thus, the White House and Republican leaders both chose not to engage in coalition-building activities

Table 8.4 Intensity of Administration Involvement in Selected Senate Floor Issues, 106th Congress

Involvement Level		*Senate Floor Issues*
High	5	• Africa Trade/Caribbean Basin Initiative • Bankruptcy Reform • Permanent Normal Trade Relations with China • FY2001 Labor/HHS Appropriations • Hate Crimes • Nuclear Test Ban Treaty • Steel Imports • Y2K Liability
	4	• Estate Tax Repeal • FY2000 Labor/HHS Appropriations • Juvenile Justice/Guns • Managed Care Reform • Marriage Penalty Repeal • Prescription Drug Imports
Medium	3	• Dairy Compact • Farm Assistance • FY2001 Budget Resolution • FY2000 Reconciliation Bill
	2	• Campaign Finance Reform (1999) • Elementary and Secondary Education Act • Minimum Wage Hike • Partial-Birth Abortions
Low	1	• Sugar Subsidy Repeal

Source: Leadership staff interview conducted by the authors.

on the issue. For the other twenty-two items in the sample, however, the administration was actively involved to some extent. For example, consider the aborted attempt to reauthorize the Elementary and Secondary Education Act, which received the relatively low rating of two for administration involvement. Education issues were prominent in the messages of both parties, and much of the education debate concerned a Clinton proposal to fund the hiring of 100,000 new teachers. Although Edward Kennedy (D-Mass.), ranking member of the relevant committee, took the lead for Senate Democrats, administration officials were actively engaged on the issue. Indeed, White House officials tacitly encouraged moderate Democrats, led by Joseph Lieberman (Conn.), to develop a centrist alternative to the Kennedy package.

What factors help explain the considerable variance that is apparent in table 8.4? One might expect that presidential involvement would be highest on message issues because the incentives and need for intraparty cohesion are greatest on these items. As mentioned, the White House plays a key role in formulating and publicizing the message for the president's party. But in table 8.4, it is apparent that no strong relationship exists (on these items anyway) between a proposal's message status and the intensity of coalition-building efforts by the president. Major message items (for example, the comprehensive nuclear test ban treaty, managed care reform, campaign finance reform, and the minimum wage) are distributed across all of the rating levels. The high partisan stakes associated with message issues may indeed boost presidential involvement. However, the underlying propensity for party cohesion on these items, along with the likely activism of Senate leaders from the president's party, may also serve to reduce the *need* for extensive White House lobbying. When we consider the whipping efforts of Senate Republican leaders, for instance, they do tend to be most extensive on GOP message priorities such as tax reduction.

Notice, however, that four of the eight items that received the highest rating in table 8.4 concern international trade or foreign policy. The executive branch has special prerogatives and responsibilities in these areas, and members of both political parties expect administration input and involvement. In addition, the three trade issues (Africa trade/Caribbean Basin Initiative, permanent normal trade relations with China, and the steel imports initiative) each divided the Senate Democratic Caucus to some extent. And on each item, Republicans disproportionately supported the position embraced by the president. These measures provided opportunities for consequential White House lobbying and coalition building across the partisan aisle.

Interestingly, Senate consideration of the comprehensive nuclear test ban treaty was characterized by a fundamentally different political dynamic. Clinton administration officials had negotiated the terms of the treaty as delivered to the Senate, and, as a result, the White House structured the policy agenda on the issue. Senate Republicans, however, had primary control over the decision-making agenda, and the treaty languished for many months in the Foreign Relations Committee. In fall 1999, a number of Democratic senators, led by Byron Dorgan and Joseph Biden (Del.), made floor speeches urging the majority leader to schedule the test ban treaty for chamber action. Democratic members viewed the treaty, which was opposed by many prominent Republicans, as potential message fodder. "The Democrats' strategy," writes a knowledgeable congressional journalist, "has been based on the prognosis that they have constructed a 'win–win' equation: Either the Senate ratifies the treaty, or they will be able to blame the GOP for its defeat."[23] Lott, however, sensed that the Democrats lacked the votes to win on the floor. He called their bluff and scheduled the treaty for floor consideration. At this point, the White House stepped in and waged an intense lobbying effort aimed at postponing the vote. The president personally spoke with scores of senators from both parties about the matter. In the end, the White House was unsuccessful, the vote occurred, and the treaty went down to defeat.

Based on the data in table 8.4, another factor behind intensive White House involvement appears to be the personal policy interests and goals of the president. For instance, Clinton made the hate crimes initiative a personal priority in summer 2000. The White House conducted a major media event with the parents of Mathew Shepherd, the young gay man killed in Wyoming, as well as the two Laramie police detectives who had investigated the brutal murder. Daschle was so moved by the White House event that he asked Shepherd's parents and the two officers to speak at a Tuesday meeting of the Democratic Caucus. Clinton also worked with Senator Kennedy to publicize the issue and secure floor action on the proposal.

According to knowledgeable staff, the bankruptcy reform measure also became a personal priority of the Clinton White House. First Lady (and now Senator) Hillary Clinton was particularly opposed to the version initially embraced by Senate Republicans. During Senate consideration, a controversial amendment offered by Charles Schumer (D-N.Y.) (aimed at preventing people from declaring bankruptcy to avoid the financial penalties arising from convictions for blocking access to abortion clinics) was added to the bill on the floor. Vice President Al Gore even rushed back from the campaign trail to preside over the Senate in case his tie-breaking vote was needed to pass Schumer's amendment. Republicans decided to deny Gore his chance to cast the decisive vote (as he had done in May 1999 on a gun control amendment sponsored by Senator Frank Lautenberg [D-N.J.]). They voted for Schumer's amendment, which was adopted by an eighty to seventeen vote. Judiciary Chairman Orrin Hatch (R-Utah) said that he urged his party colleagues to support the abortion-related amendment so "nobody will be able to politically demagogue this issue."[24]

Prior to floor action, Schumer had successfully lobbied White House officials to state that the president would veto the measure if it did not include the abortion clinic amendment. Typically, veto threats are issued at the initiative of the administration. But sometimes such threats are a product of shared consultation between the White House and members of the president's party in Congress. One Senate leadership aide described this process as "litigating the threat language," and it nicely captures the strategic character of interbranch relations in contemporary U.S. politics.

The Clinton administration's reliance on veto threats to shape the bankruptcy reform bill was apparent at all stages of the legislative process—at various points, the White House issued two SAPs and at least four distinct veto threats. For instance, when Senate Democrats, led by Edward Kennedy (Mass.), attempted to use bankruptcy reform as a vehicle for passing a minimum wage increase, GOP members defeated the Kennedy initiative and instead added a GOP version of the minimum wage hike and small business tax breaks to the bankruptcy measure. Clinton's staff responded with another threat of veto if the final package included the Republican add-ons.

As is often the case, the administration's role became more pronounced as the item moved from committee, to the floor, to the conference committee stage. Clinton aide John Podesta wrote letters to congressional leaders saying, for instance, that "we are gravely concerned" about many of the GOP provisions.[25] Gene Sperling, Clinton's national economic adviser, brought language to Capitol Hill on the abortion clinic and other provisions as each side made offers and counteroffers.

According to Majority Leader Lott, the Republicans attempted to take into account President Clinton's objections on the measure. "We're taking out some of the language that they had concerns with [including the minimum wage increase and small business tax breaks] and we hope it will be acceptable," he said.[26] In fall 2000, as the bargaining endgame continued, Lott tried to "sweeten" the bankruptcy measure by adding language reauthorizing the "Violence against Women Act," which President Clinton strongly supported. "It is safe to assume that if Republicans try to sweeten the flawed bankruptcy bill with something more acceptable or desirable, it will still draw a veto," said a top White House aide.[27] Senator Daschle kept the pressure on Republicans by stating that the president might veto the bill if it kept heading in the wrong direction. In the end, congressional Republicans and the Clinton administration were unable to achieve a final agreement on the contents of the bankruptcy reform measure, and on 19 December, the president announced that he would pocket veto the bill. Judiciary Chairman Orrin Hatch (R-Utah) pledged that "one of the first things" he would do in the 107th Congress was seek passage of bankruptcy reform.[28]

CONCLUSION

The practical exigencies of legislating in the contemporary Senate—especially the filibuster, member individualism, divided government, and the narrow partisan majorities of recent years—significantly complicate efforts by the president to move his policy agenda through the chamber. Still, presidents have important prerogatives and resources that can be used to mobilize lawmakers, especially among a president's fellow partisans.

In this chapter, we have emphasized three, relatively unexplored, mechanisms that contemporary presidents use to facilitate communication, policy coordination, and coalition building across the branches. First, over time a number of important and routinized meetings have developed for the transmission of information between the White House and congressional leaders, primarily within the president's own party. Second, both national political parties now develop organized message agendas, which feature policy proposals and symbols that party leaders and activists believe will resonate for their party among voters. These message agendas help foster party unity within Congress and facilitate presidential coalition building—but again, primarily within a president's own party. The structure of conflict between the congressional parties on message issues tends to be zero-sum. While the linkage of the legislative agenda to campaign goals may help presidents marshal legislative support among their fellow partisans, efforts to forge policy alliances across the aisle are substantially complicated.

Third, the most significant formal prerogative that presidents use to influence the Senate (and the House) is the veto. Within the interbranch bargaining game, threatened vetoes probably are more important than actual vetoes. As we have seen, presidents use formal Statements of Administration Policy to send carefully calibrated messages to the Senate and the House (immediately prior to floor action) about their legislative preferences and the likelihood of a veto. These policy messages have become an important and institutionalized aspect of legislating in Congress, and they serve to enhance the role of the veto and the president in the interbranch bargaining process.

The modes and extent of presidential coalition building within the Senate are conditional and vary substantially from issue to issue. Based on our analysis of twenty-three major proposals considered by the full Senate during the 106th Congress, the level of direct presidential involvement in the Senate legislative process (e.g., persuading members, whipping) was not closely tied to the message status of an item. Party unity tends to be high on message issues, and Senator Daschle and other prominent Democrats within the chamber mostly provided the necessary coalition leadership on these measures. The Clinton administration did play an important role on message issues—but mostly during the processes of *message formulation and articulation*. Many of the central items in the congressional Democratic message originated in the executive branch, and President Clinton took the lead in publicizing them among party activists and the general public.

For our sample of major measures from the 106th Congress, the degree of presidential participation and lobbying during the Senate legislative process was particularly marked on foreign policy and trade initiatives—issue areas in which the executive branch has special prerogatives and responsibilities. The personal priorities and policy interests of the president also shaped the extent of administration activism. The bankruptcy reform bill, for instance, touched on important policy priorities of the president and first lady. Through a succession of SAPs, veto threats, legislative offers and counteroffers, and other persuasive efforts, the White House was integrally involved during initial Senate consideration and during the conference committee stage.

What is the bottom line? For the foreseeable future—no matter which party controls the White House and with or without divided government—interactions between the president and the Senate probably will remain highly strategic, fundamentally partisan, and increasingly inseparable from the broader campaign and electoral environments. Most likely, we will hear future congressional leaders and executive branch officials compare the task of Senate coalition building with "herding cats."

NOTES

1. *Congressional Record*, 22 September 2000: S9030.

2. Richard F. Fenno Jr., *The United States Senate: A Bicameral Perspective* (Washington, D.C.: American Enterprise Institute, 1982); Steven S. Smith, "Forces of Change in Senate Party Leadership and Organization," in *Congress Reconsidered*, 5th edition, ed. Lawrence C. Dodd and Bruce I. Oppenheimer (Washington, D.C.: CQ Press, 1993).

3. Stephen Hess, *The Ultimate Insiders* (Washington, D.C.: Brookings Institution Press, 1986).

4. C. Lawrence Evans, "How Senators Decide: An Exploration," paper presented at the Norman Thomas Conference on Senate Exceptionalism, Vanderbilt University, Nashville, 21–23 October 1999.

5. Sarah Binder and Steven Smith, *Politics or Principle? Filibustering in the United States Senate* (Washington, D.C.: Brookings Institution Press, 1997); Barbara Sinclair, "The '60-Vote Senate': Strategies, Process and Outcomes," paper presented at the Norman Thomas Conference on Senate Exceptionalism, Vanderbilt University, Nashville, 21–23 October 1999.

6. Samuel Kernell, *Going Public: New Strategies for Presidential Leadership*, 2d edition (Washington, D.C.: CQ Press, 1997).

7. We also need to consider the long-standing professional ties that exist between White House officials and the congressional leadership. During the Clinton administration, for instance, a number of top White House aides—including John Hilley, Larry

Stein, and Chuck Brain, all of whom served as director of legislative liaison for Clinton—were former aides to Senate Democratic leaders George Mitchell and Thomas Daschle. Their prior experience, contacts, and Hill loyalties helped promote effective channels of communication between Senate Democrats and the White House.

8. *National Journal's Congress Daily/AM*, 24 October 2000: 1.

9. Andrew Taylor and Karen Foerstel, "GOP's Hope for Graceful Exit Rides on Debt Reduction Plan," *Congressional Quarterly Weekly Report*, 16 September 2000: 2116.

10. The staff directors to the ranking minority members also met, but these sessions were less regular, and executive branch officials seldom attended.

11. Andrew Taylor, "A Different Sense of Urgency," *National Journal*, 30 September 2000: 2256.

12. Eric Pianin and Helen Dewar, "GOP Leaders on Hill Find Unity Elusive," *The Washington Post*, 30 September 2000: A10.

13. C. Lawrence Evans, "Committees, Leaders, and Message Politics," in *Congress Reconsidered*, 7th edition, ed. Lawrence C. Dodd and Bruce I. Oppenheimer (Washington, D.C.: CQ Press, 2001), 217–43; C. Lawrence Evans and Walter J. Oleszek, "Message Politics and Senate Procedure," in *The Contentious Senate*, ed. Colton C. Campbell and Nicol C. Rae (Lanham, Md.: Rowman and Littlefield, 2001), 107–27; Patrick Sellers, "Winning Media Coverage in the U.S. Congress," paper presented at the Norman Thomas Conference on Senate Exceptionalism, Vanderbilt University, Nashville, 21–23 October 1999.

14. *National Journal's Congress Daily/AM*, 27 September 2000: 1.

15. *National Journal's Congress Daily/AM*, 15 September 2000: 3.

16. Evans, "Committees, Leaders, and Message Politics."

17. Alison Mitchell, "On Budget, Everything in Moderation," *New York Times*, 19 November 1999: A29.

18. Charles Cameron, *Veto Bargaining* (New York: Cambridge University Press, 2000).

19. See Barbara Sinclair, "Hostile Partners: The President, Congress, and Lawmaking in the Partisan 1990s," in *Polarized Politics: Congress and the President in a Partisan Era*, ed. Jon R. Bond and Richard Fleisher (Washington, D.C.: CQ Press, 2000), 134–53.

20. The Statements of Administration Policy for the 105th, 106th, and 107th Congresses can be accessed via the website of the U.S. Office of Management and Budget, which administers the SAP process. The URL is http://www.whitehouse.gov/OMB/legislative/sap.

21. Adrieal Bettleheim, "Agriculture Spending Measure Heads for Senate Floor as Clinton Indicates Support," *Congressional Quarterly Weekly Report*, 14 October 2000: 2415.

22. More concretely, the sample derives from a broader study of Senate decision making during the 106th Congress that C. Lawrence Evans is conducting.

23. Richard Cohen, "The Senate Goes Ballistic," *National Journal*, 9 October 1999: 2890.

24. Robert Rosenblatt and Janet Hook, "Minimum Wage Hike Approved as Part of Bankruptcy Measure," *Los Angeles Times*, 3 February 2000: A6.

25. *CQ Daily Monitor*, 28 June 2000: 11.

26. *CQ Daily Monitor*, 21 September 2000: 7.

27. *National Journal's Congress Daily*, 25 September 2000: 3.

28. *National Journal's Congress Daily*, 6 October 2000: 5.

9

Politics of the Federal Budget Process

The Honorable Leon E. Panetta

"EVEN A GREAT BUDGET ISN'T WORTH A DAMN IF IT CAN'T PASS!"

As chairman of the House Budget Committee, I had the responsibility not only to develop the congressional budget but to sell it to the key House committee chairs and my colleagues. In 1992, when we presented the key elements of our proposed budget to a senior chairman, he looked at me, smiled, and said: "It's a great budget, Leon, but you know, even a great budget isn't worth a damn if it can't pass!"

The point was clear—budgets are not just about numbers and priorities, they are about politics. The real test of an executive branch budget is whether a president can convince a majority of the American people that his priorities are right for them and the nation. The real test of a legislative budget is whether the leadership can convince a majority of the members of the House and Senate that the budget is in the best interests of them and their constituents. Either way, success or failure is dependent on politics.

In putting together a federal budget, the process involves a careful analysis and balancing of policy, priorities, and politics. Obviously, it should begin with good policy. In the executive branch, the professional staff of the Office of Management and Budget (OMB) make their recommendations for increases or reductions in programs based on their expertise and experience with those areas of the budget. The departments and agencies can and often do challenge those recommendations based on substantive policy arguments. But inevitably in every policy debate, there comes a point at which the question is asked: What are the politics on this issue? Whether the answer to that question is accurate often determines the fate of a president's priorities.

As an example, during the development of President Clinton's first economic plan, it was determined on a policy basis that significant savings could be achieved by striking all funding for highway projects that were not authorized in the law. Under the normal legislative process, a particular highway has to be approved in a transportation authorization bill before it can be funded in a transportation appropriations bill. Powerful members, however, recognized that they could bypass that process by simply placing a favorite new highway project directly into the transportation appropriations bill. This was viewed by the administration's budget staff as both bad policy and bad budgeting. They, of course, were right—on the process. They turned out to be wrong on the politics.

It turned out the then chairman of the Senate Appropriations Committee, Senator Robert Byrd of West Virginia, had funded a number of projects in his home state that had been not been authorized. They were among those projects targeted for elimination. Of course, once that simple reality became clear, the conclusion followed that it would not be smart to antagonize the chair of the Senate Appropriations Committee if the president was interested in getting his other budget priorities funded. These well-intentioned savings never saw the light of day!

The congressional budget process involves the same political analysis because every member is a vote for or against the budget. In close votes, the budget can be held hostage by the demands of one member. Oftentimes, those demands may not even relate to national budget policy but, rather, to projects or funding issues within that member's district or state. The ability to balance the enactment of important budget policy with the political demands of individual members is the chemistry that defines victory or defeat. That is the nature of the budget process. It also happens to be the nature of our democratic process. To fully understand how process and politics work, it is essential to consider the following: the budget process itself, the history of politics and deficits, the present challenge of politics and the surplus, and the role of leadership in balancing the tension between good policy and good politics.

THE FEDERAL BUDGET PROCESS—"BUDGETS, LIKE SOUP, NEED ONE CHEF, NOT 535!"

The fundamental difference between the branches when it comes to the budget is simple—the executive branch is an intensive and predictable "top-to-bottom" process, whereas the legislative branch is a more freewheeling and unpredictable "bottom-to-top" process. As one frustrated OMB career official once remarked to me, "Budgets, like soup, need one chef, not 535!" That in a sentence summarizes how one president has the consummate power to determine what an administration's budget will look like, whereas 535 members of both the House and the Senate can have a multitude of conflicting views as to the numbers and priorities. The fundamental differences in each process explain the genius of our forefathers in establishing a system of checks and balances between the president and the Congress.

Executive Budget Process

The president throughout our early history was responsible for presenting to the nation a comprehensive and detailed budget. President Washington detailed his budget requests as part of his annual messages, as did many of his successors. In 1921, the Budget and Accounting Act specifically required presidents to submit budgets, stating priorities to Congress, no later than the first Monday in February. The Congress, on the other hand, only recently came to the task with the passage of the Budget and Impoundment Control Act of 1974.

OMB Spending Targets

In the administration, the process of preparing a budget begins with the OMB (see figure 9.1). With its professional staff, this executive branch office, once known as the Bureau of the Budget, issues a proposed general target for spending to each agency and department. That number is arrived at by an analysis of the next fiscal year's total budget and what is likely to be required for both discretionary and mandatory spending. It begins with economic projections on growth, inflation, unemployment, interest rates, and so on, which are translated into income and spending estimations. Because budgets are prepared with five- to ten-year projections in most areas, these past numbers are a good place to start the analysis to determine if they are still relevant to the current state of the economy.

In providing these targets to the various departments and agencies, the director of OMB will normally use the most conservative estimates of how much funding will be available. This forces the budget officers outside the White House to operate within tight constraints and allows OMB to make *future* adjustments if needed to protect the president's priorities and deal with *future* contingencies.

These targets are usually sent out in the late summer of the year before

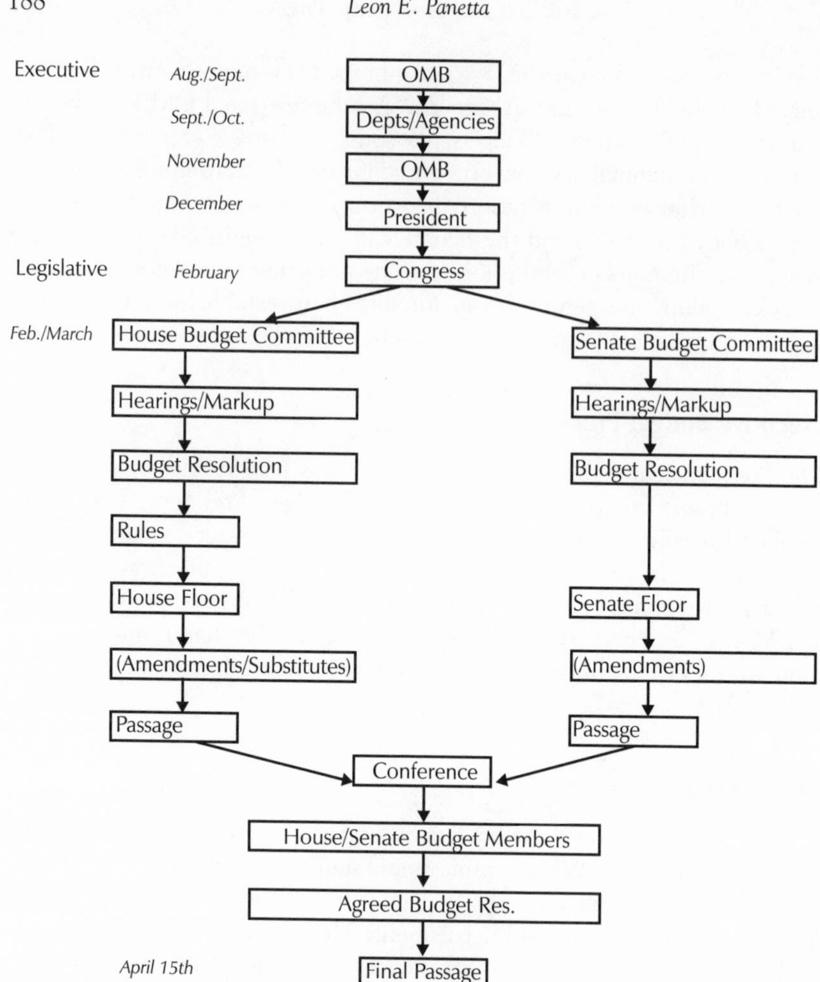

Figure 9.1 Phase One of the Budget Process: Development of Budget

the formal budget is presented to the nation in February. Often complicating this timetable is the fact that the prior fiscal year budget is being held up in the Congress. If few, if any, appropriations bills have been passed, then the administration is attempting to project future needs without really knowing what Congress will provide for current programs. Nevertheless, the process must go forward if budget deadlines are to be met.

As figure 9.1 indicates, responses to the OMB directive are returned in late September or early October. OMB then recommends a "pass back" number to the departments and agencies. That begins a negotiating process between the budget and policy staffs of the departments and agencies and OMB to resolve and clarify differences. The principle goal is to arrive at as much consensus as possible on the final recommendations to the president in order to limit the number of conflicts and appeals.

Appeals to the President

At this point, Cabinet secretaries and agency heads have to make a basic decision. Is it in their interests to accept the recommendations of the OMB director to gain support on future budget battles or to challenge the OMB position by going directly to the president and risking the possibility of both denial and future antagonism at the highest levels? Because of the obvious risks, the issues are generally resolved within most departments and agencies. However, whether the reason is based on legitimate policy differences as to what should be spent on certain programs or on political tactics that involve the departments, the president, or the press, there will always be a few who will want to appeal their positions. Their reasoning often reflects the delicate balancing of politics between the secretary and his or her department and the nature of their relationship with the president. It is the view of some that, win or lose, the good fight must be made and possibly, just possibly, a few more dollars will be provided. Others base the appeal on testing the depth of support they have with the president.

To deal with these appeals to the president and last-minute revisions, most OMB directors set aside a reserve amount for these kinds of contingencies. My approach as director was to set aside at the very beginning of the budget process a reserve fund that would be available to resolve all of the final issues. Additional funds could also be provided with an adjustment here or there to economic estimates. The president was aware of the reserve and was urged to listen to all of the appeals but not to specifically commit or agree to any increased funding. At the end of the appeals, as director, I would recommend to the president an approach to dividing up the reserve account among some of the priority programs advocated by the department and agency heads. The president often would make additional changes on the final formula but always within the bounds of the reserve. The consequence of this process served the interests of all those involved—the president gave the impression that he was willing to listen without giving away the store; the department and agency heads felt that while they did not receive all they were asking for, they had put up the good fight and had something to show for their efforts; and the OMB director had protected the core budget with the reserve fund, and the small increases that were provided did not encourage others to challenge the process in the future.

This decision-making process by the president usually concluded in late December. With President Clinton, it was usually Christmas Eve. The month of January is normally spent refining the numbers, preparing all of the appropriate tables, double-checking the line items in the budget, and preparing the text of the final budget document—a foot-high pile of four to five volumes along with a summary text.

Building Support for the Budget

January is also used for another purpose—to build political support for the budget. On a carefully targeted basis, selective leaks to the press are made on the president's priority programs and the funding levels contained in the budget. For example, if the president was doubling funds for the Headstart Program, that fact along with additional background would be provided to a national newspaper. Headlined stories in the *New York Times*, *Washington Post*, and *USA Today* would gradually make clear to the public and the Congress the parameters of the president's budget. At the same time, the agencies and departments, particularly the Defense Department, would often provide their own off-the-record details of the budget decisions, both those they supported and those they opposed. The purpose of all of this is to begin a drumbeat of interest in the final details of the budget.

The most significant policy decisions are protected for the president to reveal as part of his State of the Union Address. By the time the budget itself is formally unveiled in February, the nation has a pretty good sense of the priorities of the president and how they are addressed in the context of the final document. If done right, all of these strategies present a clear summary of the president's agenda to the nation.

The basic lesson of the entire executive branch budget process is that the president controls both the policy and the politics—from the first numbers provided by OMB to the departments and agencies, to the president's final decisions, to the State of the Union Address, to the presentation of the budget itself. In that sense, it is very much a "one chef" operation—a "top-to-bottom" process—with the power, focus, and final decisions reserved for the president of the United States.

Legislative Budget Process

In the Congress, however, it is a "multichef" process. The budget cannot be dictated by the speaker, the leadership, or a few key chairs. It has to be negotiated chair by chair, committee by committee, member by member, until a consensus is developed that commands a majority vote. It is the product of the democratic process, and as such, it is very much a "bottom-to-top" formula that can be every bit as chaotic as the executive branch process is efficient.

The president's budget, as outlined in figure 9.1, is referred to both the House and the Senate Budget Committees for their consideration. If Congress is controlled by the opposing party to the White House, the president's budget is often proclaimed by the congressional leadership as "dead on arrival." During the 1980s, when President Reagan presented his budget to the Congress, Democrats immediately would denounce it as "DOA." On the other hand, if the White House and Capitol Hill are controlled by the same party, the president's budget can become a foundation on which to build the congressional budget. In either scenario, it is a sure bet that the House and the Senate will want to have their impact on the final numbers and priorities.

In addition to the lack of a central authority controlling the process in Congress, the budgets themselves are very different between the executive and legislative branches. As mentioned before, the president's budget is very detailed and voluminous, with each department and agency budget carefully presented on a line-by-line basis. The congressional budget, on the other hand, is contained in a brief resolution that lists some twenty functional areas that set broad targets for spending in categories ranging from national defense, international affairs, general science, energy, space, and technology to natural resources and environment, agriculture, education, health, Medicare, and income security and others. For a complete list of these functional categories, see table 9.1.

Although specific program funding is discussed in each area by the Budget Committees in order to arrive at a final functional number, these decisions are not binding on the appropriations process. For example, the Budget Committee may believe that Title I funding in education should be at a certain level in order to arrive at an overall function 500 education number, but that recommendation is not binding on the Appropriations Committee. The congressional budget, therefore, is more of a guideline to areas of the budget than a specific line-by-line mandate.

Hearings and Negotiations

The legislative process itself begins with hearings in the Budget Committees. These hearings are held in each body to allow the White House and Cabinet secretaries the opportunity to defend the president's budget. They normally begin with the director of OMB and the secretary of the treasury rotating between the House and Senate Budget Committees the first two days. From there, the various Cabinet secretaries are scheduled for their testi-

Table 9.1 Functional Areas Contained in Congressional Budget Resolutions

50	National defense
150	International affairs
250	General science, space, and technology
270	Energy
300	Natural resources and environment
350	Agriculture
370	Commerce and housing credit
400	Transportation
450	Community and regional development
500	Education, training, employment, and social services
550	Health
570	Medicare
600	Income security
650	Social Security
700	Veterans benefits and services
750	Administration of justice
800	General government
900	Net interest
920	Allowances
950	Undistributed offsetting receipts

mony along with various public interest groups and congressional members who generally appear near the end of the hearing process. These hearings normally take place in the February–mid-March period of the congressional session.

During this period, the chairs of the Budget Committees and their respective leaderships are trying to determine a likely course of action. What are the changes or revisions that have to be implemented to the president's budget in order to gain the majority support of their parties? Although efforts have been made to develop bipartisan budgets, particularly in years when budget summits or negotiations took place between the White House and the Congress, the general pattern in recent years is that the minority deliberately stands back and forces the majority to pass the budget with its votes only. The first budget resolutions enjoyed bipartisan support because of the cooperation of such leaders as Democratic Senator Ed Muskie of Maine and Republican Senator Harry Belmon of Oklahoma. The 1990 Budget Agreement is another example of both parties and the White House working together for months to develop an agreed-on budget. But in most years, the budget resolution must be developed, passed, and implemented by a partisan majority.

That means that the chair of the Budget Committee has no alternative but to work within his or her party, negotiating with key chairs and members. As chairman of the House Budget Committee, I began with an analysis of the major areas of contention in any budget—defense, education, Social Security, Medicare, and taxes. Other areas—veterans, health, agriculture, transportation, housing, and space—were also important to certain constituencies within the House. If a chair can develop consensus on the big issues, the other issues would fall into place more easily. The key in the days of large deficits was to achieve a lower deficit figure than the president. The basic formula was (1) a lower deficit than the president, (2) higher education spending, (3) fewer Medicare and Medicaid cuts, (4) less defense spending, and (5) more fees and revenues. If one could balance all of these issues, the chances were that one could get a Democratic majority to support the budget resolution. For a Republican majority, particularly in a surplus budget, the basic formula is (1) higher tax cuts, (2) higher defense spending, (3) protect Social Security, (4) generous education spending, and (5) cut everything else if you can!

To arrive at party consensus, the process begins with the key chairs. To lose the chair of the Ways and Means Committee or the Appropriations Committee could spell doom for the budget resolution. For me, it meant taking time to sit down and meet with each and every chairperson and the staff of the committees to talk numbers and priorities. It resembles the executive process of discussions between the OMB director and the Cabinet secretaries, except that the chair of the Budget Committee has less leverage because all the other chairs and their committees represent valuable votes for or against the budget itself.

This process gives the Budget Committee chair a good idea of where the key problem areas are and what each chair will or will not tolerate. Following this probing period and the hearings, the chair then begins a negotiating process with the members of his or her party on the Budget Committee. I was fortunate enough as chairman to have a broad cross section of members represented on the committee—from Representatives Barney Frank of Massachusetts and Barbara Boxer of California on the Left to Charlie Stenholm and Marvin Leath of Texas on the Right. If I could get their concurrence on the budget, chances were pretty good that I could get broad support on the floor of the House.

Each of these members had a special issue of concern—from agriculture to AIDS research programs, from cancer studies to defense, from education to highways, from the FBI to legal aid, from foreign aid to elderly housing. Because the minority members will provide no help in passage of the budget, every vote on the majority side is crucial to success. A chair is left with little alternative but to provide as much as he or she can to meet the priorities of each key majority member.

The Chair's Mark

The end result of these negotiations and consultations is a chair's mark—a draft of a proposed budget resolution for the consideration of the full committee. The goal is to hold enough of the majority members to defeat any amendments and provide final passage to move the resolution to the floor of the House.

Because the minority knows it does not have the votes to defeat the resolution, members will offer amendments largely directed at embarrassing the majority. For example, if defense spending is less than that in the president's budget, the minority might offer an amendment to restore that funding, forcing the more defense-oriented members of the majority to go on public record for or against such an amendment. Some members have standard amendments that they offer because of their constituencies or ideologies—ranging from increased funds for Headstart or AIDS research to cuts in funds for rural legal assistance or a questionable weapons system. Assuming that the chair and the leadership have done their work, the majority can generally hold firm against these amendments on the argument that it is time to move the resolution to the floor for action.

The Floor

The challenge on the floor, of course, is how to hold that same majority together to adopt the resolution. In the House, the resolution must go to the Rules Committee to determine the type of rule that will control the debate on the floor. The first budget resolutions in the House during the mid- to late 1970s enjoyed totally "open rules," which permitted any member to offer any amendment. When resolutions were taking more than two legislative weeks to complete because of the large number of amendments, the leadership decided that a tighter rule was required that only permitted total budget substitutes to be offered.

These large substitutes in the past have been pretty predictable. First of all, few members have the individual or staff capability to put together entire budget resolutions on their own. Second, once those members and caucuses have developed a substantive budget, they tend to repeat their efforts from year to year. In general, substitutes could be expected from the liberal side—usually the Black Caucus—and the conservative side—usually from members who were experienced with budgets like John Rousellot of California in the

1970s or John Kasich of Ohio in the 1990s. The minority may or may not have a substitute, and usually the president's budget is offered, particularly if the party that does not control the White House thinks that the president will be embarrassed by receiving few votes. The goal of the majority is to allow members the opportunity to vote for a liberal, conservative, or other alternative depending on their district constituencies with the hope that those members will then vote for final passage of the budget resolution. The logic is simple: "I tried to get my kind of budget adopted, but it failed, so I voted for the committee resolution to meet our responsibilities under the Budget Act."

To accomplish this, the House rule permits votes on all of the alternative budgets first on the assumption that none of them will pass. The final vote comes on the committee resolution. On the Senate floor, which is not controlled by a Rules Committee as in the House, the debate is limited by the Budget Act, and that tends to reduce the number of amendments.

On both sides of the Hill, the ultimate driving force behind passage is the responsibility of the majority to run the business of the nation and the Congress, meet the Budget Act deadlines, and allow the appropriations process to move forward. Whether members agree or disagree with every element of the budget, the rationale of completing the budget process is the most compelling argument to getting it passed.

Although the budget resolution is not signed by the president, to be passed it does require a final conference report resolving the differences in the numbers between the House and Senate versions. Again, because this is usually the total responsibility of the majority party, the conference on budget resolution generally splits the difference between the two Houses. If the Senate number on defense is $280 billion and the House number is $274 billion, there is a very good chance that the final number will be $277 billion. The chairs of the House and Senate Budget Committees usually sit down with their respective staffs and decide unilaterally where the most logical consensus can be found. That consensus must be tested with key members to ensure a majority vote.

In the Senate, passage of a conference is viewed as more pro forma. In the House, recorded votes are almost always requested, forcing the majority to again make sure it has every vote needed for passage.

Reconciliation

Final passage of the budget resolution allows the Congress to begin the process of implementing the budget. Referring to figure 9.2, there are two principle tools of implementation. One is reconciliation, which requires the

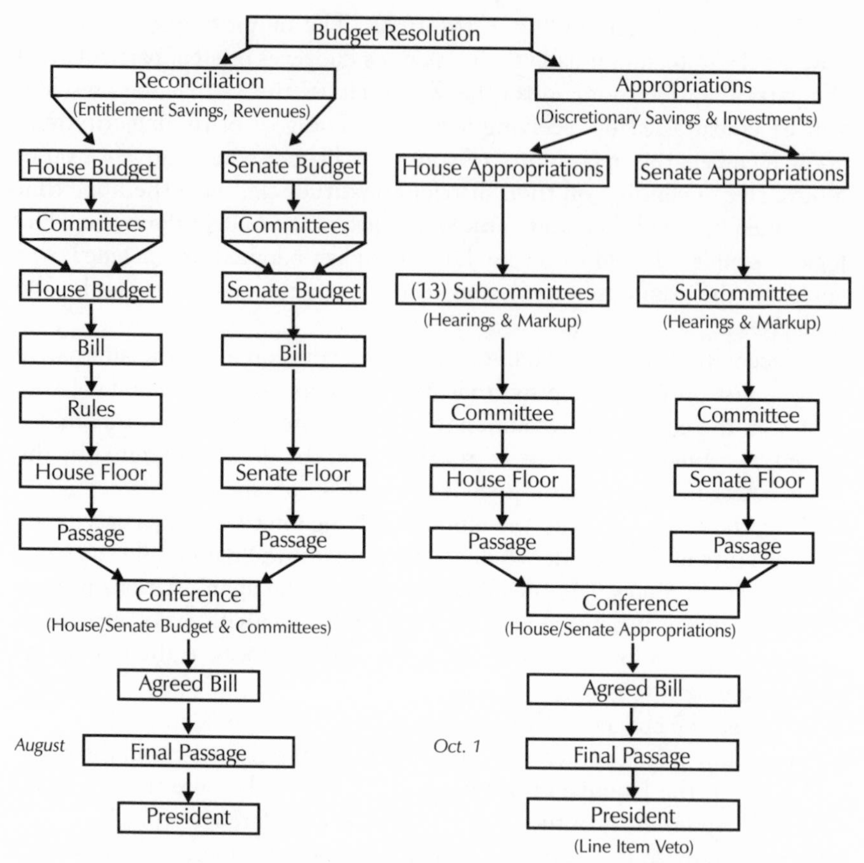

Figure 9.2 Phase Two of the Budget Process: Implementation of the Budget

Congress to achieve through changes in the law savings in entitlements or mandatory programs as well as additional taxes or fees. Directions are provided by the Budget Committees to each of the authorizing committees requiring them to come up with the savings or revenues mandated by the budget resolution. In this process, the individual chairs and committees have great discretion in deciding exactly how they will achieve the specific targets under the budget resolution.

In general, the Ways and Means Committee portion of reconciliation is the engine that drives reconciliation, for taxes and health care savings are both the most controversial and the most substantive parts of the package. When Dan Rostenkowski was chairman of the Ways and Means Committee,

I would wait until he had completed his portion of the reconciliation package before putting the other committee sections in place. Again, the politics of passing reconciliation may rest totally with the majority party, in which event the same process of negotiating with individual members will take place. One the Senate side, it should be noted, the principle procedural advantage of reconciliation is that the bill itself cannot be filibustered by the minority. This may be the single most important procedural tool available to the majority under the Budget Act. Instead of having to put together sixty votes to break a filibuster, it can pass a reconciliation bill with a simple majority.

In fighting deficits, reconciliation was a common implementation weapon because every budget resolution called for either spending savings or revenues and oftentimes both. In surplus years, it is not generally used except as a tool to pass controversial legislation that could otherwise be blocked by a filibuster. A legitimate argument can be made that it should only be used to achieve budget savings, but it remains a tempting legislative weapon for the majority party.

Appropriations

The second tool of implementation is the appropriations process. While the budget resolution sets an overall cap on discretionary spending, the House and Senate Appropriations Committees divide up that amount between their respective thirteen subcommittees. Each of the subcommittees reports out an appropriations bill, but the total of these bills cannot exceed the amount in the budget resolution, or a point of order can be made on the floor of the House or the Senate. Emergencies are not subject to these limitations, and, of course, the House and the Senate can waive the points of order subject to a majority vote. These appropriations bills, because they provide spending on a bipartisan basis, are often supported by both Republicans and Democrats. It is in these appropriations bills that the rubber meets the road in the legislative process because this is not just language—this is real money that counts when it comes to a member's home constituencies. Here, the principle force for agreement is within each appropriations subcommittee, in which the chair and the members ensure that they all get a fair share of the action. If done right, that process guarantees passage. The one barrier is if the president vetoes the bill because it does not sufficiently fund his priorities or contains provisions he opposes.

In the end, the differences in the budget process are defined by the powers outlined in the Constitution. The executive, as commander in chief, controls the development, policy, decisions, and implementation of the budget. The legislative body, by virtue of the "power of the purse," controls the actual spending, but because there are 535 members of Congress, the development, policy decisions, and implementation of any congressional budget are often chaotic and unpredictable. Final action is a roll of the dice that may often depend on politics, threats, crisis, and the need for a Congress to adjourn. Ultimately, although budgets are developed differently in both branches, their fate depends on whether the president and the Congress can work together to resolve their differences. The often reluctant cooperation of both branches is the engine that drives the budget process forward. And that only happens when both are convinced that the politics of resolving their budget differences is on their side.

THE BATTLE OVER DEFICITS—"IT HAS TAKEN US OVER TWENTY YEARS TO GET OUT OF THIS HOLE!"

Although it is clear that there are distinct differences between the executive and legislative branches as to the development of a budget, over the last twenty or more years of deficits, both have faced similar challenges in trying to discipline their spending. To designate federal dollars to certain federal programs is a power that both the president and the Congress thoroughly enjoy. Cutting spending, on the other hand, is a nasty and unrewarding responsibility that neither relishes. When you spend money, you make people happy. Happy people are more likely to vote for you. When you reduce or cut funding or raise taxes, you anger people, and angry people will most likely vote against you. All of this is basic politics, and that is why deficit reduction was never easily embraced.

When the Congressional Budget and Impoundment Control Act of 1974 was adopted, the goal was not so much to impose budget discipline but, rather, to limit President Nixon's ability to impound expenditures approved by a then Democratic Congress. The Congress reluctantly adopted a budget process because members understood that, politically, they could not limit the president's ability to impose spending restraint without appearing to adopt some restraint on their own.

Few, in fact, expected that the new process would work or change business as usual. The original drafters—members such as Representative Dick Bolling of Missouri, Senator Ed Muskie of Maine, and Representative John Rhodes of Arizona—believed that it was important for Congress to have its own budget in order to put the entire budget's legislative priorities into one context. But they also knew how difficult it would be to change the addiction to the historical open-ended appropriations process. Indeed, both the tenure and the membership of the new Budget Committees—particularly on the House side—were structured to limit their power. Members rotate off after three terms. The chair would have to leave as well when his or her term on the committee was up. The key committees, like Appropriations and Ways and Means, were given a set number of members on the Budget Committee. The early provision requiring two budget resolutions in each congressional session was designed to accommodate additional spending. In a word, the intent was to limit the power of the Budget Committee to interfere with business as usual in the Congress.

The Early Years

In the early years, the challenge of budget chairs was not so much to force action to control deficits but to cajole and accommodate other key chairs and the leadership to go along with the targets set by the budget resolution. An example of this is the reconciliation process. As discussed before, reconciliation is the one enforcement tool in the Budget Act with teeth. It controls and expedites the process of achieving savings and deficit reduction. But for over six years, it was a tool that was never used. As a new member of the House Budget Committee in the late 1970s, then Chairman Bob Giamo asked me to head up the Reconciliation Task Force. But my role was not to require but to encourage budget savings. These savings were defined in the budget resolution. I had the responsibility of going to such committee chairs as Jamie Whitten of Mississippi (Appropriations), Dan Rostenkowski of Illinois (Ways and Means), Bill Ford of Michigan (Post Office and Civil Service), and Carl Perkins of Kentucky (Education and Labor) to urge that they voluntarily achieve these savings. Needless to say, it was not very persuasive to simply encourage such savings because it was good policy for the nation. Most of these chairs had earned their reputations because of domestic programs they had established or funded, many of them named in their honor.

It was not until the first Reagan budget passed in the early 1980s and Democrats lost control of the legislative process that the full force of a mandatory reconciliation enforcement tool was realized. The then director of OMB, David Stockman, drafted the reconciliation bill off the floor of the House, and, with scribbles and notes in the margins, it was passed. The Republican Senate was able to clean up a great deal of the haphazard drafting that mistakenly eliminated some popular programs, but it was clear to all of the members that reconciliation was a powerful tool that could change the very structure of government itself. But the Reagan budget also called for large tax cuts and defense increases. As a result, instead of reducing the deficit, it exploded, and the national debt went from less than $1 trillion to close to $4 trillion.

Gramm-Rudman-Hollings

The growing deficit forced additional action by the president and the Congress. In 1985, the so-called Gramm-Rudman-Hollings Act was passed—the Balanced Budget and Emergency Deficit Control Act. The bill introduced the concept of the mandatory trigger to force savings in the absence of congressional leadership. It set mandatory deficit reduction targets that, if not met, required "sequestration" or cuts across the board that automatically met those targets. The problem was that despite the fact that certain sensitive programs like Social Security were spared some of the deep across-the-board cuts, Congress prevented Gramm-Rudman-Hollings from taking full effect because of the arbitrary damage that would be done to programs and constituencies. Although some form of "sequestration" has remained as part of the budget enforcement process, the reality is that it is much more limited than the large cuts first envisioned by Senators Gramm, Rudman, and Hollings. This experience confirms that any enforcement tool is only as good as the politics that support it. No trigger works unless there is a majority of votes willing to back it up in the Congress. Otherwise, it will disappear very quickly.

Budget Summits

Following the Gramm-Rudman-Hollings experience came a series of "Budget Summits" that provided a forum for both the president and the Congress to try and find consensus on deficit reduction. The challenge always came down to several key but difficult issues: Should additional revenues be raised, how much, and who should carry the burden of additional taxes? Should entitlements be reduced to achieve long-term savings—what would these reforms mean for programs like Medicare and Medicaid and farm programs? How much should be spent on defense? And what limits should be placed on domestic discretionary spending? The ability to balance these issues often determined whether or not an agreement could be achieved.

The most fundamental political change was that both the president and the Congress were willing to have a select group of negotiators determine broad policy for the nation. The president's agenda was placed in the hands of his secretary of the treasury, the director of OMB, and his chief of staff, and legislative decisions were no longer being made by chairs and committees but by the select members of the leadership and key chairs and members sitting at the negotiating table. While this process was effective at expediting agreements, it became more unpredictable when the legislation was brought to the floor. Most members did not feel that they were part of the process. At the same time, because a number of controversial issues were combined into one large omnibus bill, members also recognized that there was some political protection in voting for a large deficit-reduction package supported by the president even though they did not always agree with every element.

The 1990 Budget Summit was probably the most significant bipartisan effort made at achieving consensus, in terms of both the deficit reduction achieved and the length of the negotiations between the president and the Congress. Negotiations began in early June and continued throughout the summer, with final negotiations taking place at Andrews Air Force Base. Although differences were narrowed on a final package, it took a group of six—the key leadership of the House and Senate, the OMB director, and the secretary of the treasury—to make the final decisions. Even then, when the package was brought to the floor of the House, it was defeated because of opposition by some Republicans led by Newt Gingrich of Georgia. That required further negotiations to pick up the additional Democratic votes needed for passage. The final package included not only a budget resolution and reconciliation savings but all of the appropriations bills as well. It is by far the largest single piece of legislation to be enacted at one time. It took a wheelbarrow to bring it to the floor.

Within that package, however, were some very important budget enforcement tools that would have been politically impossible to implement outside of a large agreement. The most important tool was a so-called pay-go requirement that provided that no entitlement spending or tax cuts could be enacted unless they were fully paid for by either other spending reductions or revenue increases. The second tool was to place caps on discretionary spending that established fixed targets for reducing discretionary spending over a five-year period. A limited sequestration tool was added to ensure that those targets would be met. The passage of this agreement is perhaps the most significant bipartisan deficit-reduction package to be enacted by Congress.

Toward a Balanced Budget

In 1993, the Clinton economic plan providing for $500 billion in deficit reduction was passed by Democratic votes only. In the House, the plan passed by one vote—a vote that came by the intervention of then Speaker

Tom Foley of Washington at the last minute on the floor. In the Senate, the vice president cast the deciding vote.

The closeness of this vote combined with the loss of the Democratic Congress and the government shutdown in late 1995 increased the tensions between the two branches on budget issues. In the Congress, when Republicans attempted to advance the agenda contained in their "Contract with America," President Clinton vetoed these efforts. Although the parties did agree to the 1997 Balanced Budget Act, the tense relationship between the president and the Congress—exacerbated by the impeachment process—continued to force political confrontation on budget and appropriations issues. Both sides became increasingly dependent on crisis in order to resolve budget issues. The parties realized that little could be achieved absent the threat of government shutdown. The budget cycle became a predictable exercise in gridlock politics. Each party played to its individual constituencies during a good part of the legislative year, relying on the last-minute threat of chaos to provide the excuse needed to conclude final budget negotiations. The one good result of this gridlock was that the failure to agree on large budget spending or tax cut proposals often left more of the surplus available for debt reduction.

By the late 1980s and 1990s—some twenty years after the passage of the Budget Act—the hard-fought deficit battles were beginning to produce reduced deficits and eventually a balanced federal budget. As one veteran member of Congress admitted to me, "It has taken us over twenty years to get out of this hole!" And he was right!

The budget process as a result of bipartisan support between the president and the Congress developed some strong enforcement tools and discipline. Indeed, during the 1980s there was pressure to go even further with proposals to have a constitutional amendment to require a balanced budget and bills to give the president the additional power of a line-item veto to strike specific spending added by the Congress. This later proposal did pass the Congress in the 1990s only to be struck down by the Supreme Court as a violation of the separation of powers clause of the Constitution. Crucial to deficit reduction was the fact that political campaigns made deficit control a national political issue. Ross Perot's presidential candidacy made it the centerpiece of his campaign and forced both the Democrats and the Republicans to acknowledge that something had to be done about the growing national debt.

During these last twenty years, the budget process played an important role. While it was by no means perfect or immune from the pressures to spend more on priorities from defense to domestic needs, and while it failed to develop effective tools to control the mandatory side of the budget, it has been a powerful incentive for both the executive and the legislative branches to discipline spending and achieve a balanced federal budget. The real challenge now is to maintain that discipline in dealing with surpluses.

THE BATTLE OVER SURPLUSES—"THE POLITICS OF SURPLUSES ARE WORSE THAN THE POLITICS OF DEFICITS!"

It was generally assumed that once the nation achieved a balanced budget and surpluses that the politics of the budget process would become less contentious as both sides found additional resources to spend. Not so. A presidential aide admitted to me in the middle of some recent budget negotiations, "The politics of surpluses are worse than the politics of deficits!" Why is this happening?

The heart of the budget process was developed in the battle of dealing with increasing deficits. The principle goal of budget discipline was to reduce spending and achieve savings. How do we take these very effective tools to implement budget discipline and apply them to surpluses?

"Pay-Go"

For example, the "pay-go" discipline is designed to prevent Congress from adding to the deficit with spending initiatives or tax cuts. But with a large projected surplus, the requirement to set aside an amount to pay for initiatives and tax cuts begins to lose its effectiveness. The tool has to be refashioned to accommodate the changing priorities of the time, or else the process will break down or be ignored. One recommendation would be to require that a set amount of the surplus be set aside to offset entitlement increases and tax cuts. This number would be made part of the budget resolution and would prevent the surplus from being raided for excessive spending or revenue reductions. Right now, "pay-go" as a discipline is being virtually ignored.

Caps on Discretionary Spending

Adding further frustration to the budget process is the fact that the tools used to help produce surpluses in the future, like discretionary cap savings, are driving that part of the budget down to 30 percent of total federal spending. That means that funding the mandatory side of the budget is approaching 70 percent—with 54 percent going to such entitlements as Social Security, Medicare, and Medicaid, and 15 percent going to interest on the debt. Thus, while current politics made it difficult, if not impossible, to constrain mandatory programs, key priority areas—defense, education, environment, research and development, science, housing, transportation—are confined to a smaller and smaller part of the budget.

The consequence is that when the irresistible force of the growth of discretionary expenditures needs meets the immovable object of caps on spending, the Congress inevitably turns to gimmicks and smoke and mirrors to hide the additional spending. As an example, large chunks of defense spending are now added as "emergencies" to avoid discretionary caps along with aid to agriculture and even funding for the census. All of this undermines the trust and credibility of the budget process. But as the history of the Budget Act makes clear, process alone, without politics, will not work.

Mandatory Spending

Throughout the budget process there has been a constant tension between savings in discretionary spending and savings in mandatory spending. Although overall caps were applied to all discretionary programs, controls on mandatory programs were more haphazard. Significant savings have been achieved over the years in entitlement spending on Medicare and Medicaid, agriculture price support programs, veteran and civil service programs, and the postal service. But the reality is that no overall discipline has been successfully applied to entitlements, largely because these are sensitive political constituencies and also it simply is not easy to design an effective compliance approach.

Today, the politics of controlling entitlement spending are even worse. Neither the president nor the Congress has been willing to confront the threat on retirement programs represented by the baby boom generation when they retire. The surplus provides a convenient way to avoid tough choices. And yet, unless the president and Congress are prepared to consider long-term reforms in Social Security, Medicare, and other entitlements, the surplus alone will not be enough to meet future requirements, more spending will go on automatic pilot, there will be less oversight, and the result will be to squeeze discretionary priorities.

Partisanship

Of greater concern is the fact that the politics of the budget have become more partisan, confrontational, and divisive. As discussed before, crisis is the primary driving force to resolve disputes. Nothing better illustrates that fact than the reality that we currently have a budget in balance; anticipated surpluses of over $5 trillion; and the greatest opportunity for Democrats, Republicans, the president, and the Congress to work together and agree on long-term priorities, from reforming Social Security and Medicare to tax cut policy and education and health care funding. And yet there continues to be partisan conflict and disagreement. While there is at least consensus that the Social Security surplus should go to Social Security, everything else is in dispute between the two parties. In many ways, the same issues that divided the parties in the past continue to haunt the present—should the nation provide for tax cuts and increased defense spending or increased funds for education, health care, and other domestic needs plus debt reduction?

The reality is that budgets are not just about numbers and line items; they are about setting national priorities. To that extent, they are also political documents that tell us where the president stands, where the Congress stands, and where each of the political parties stands. But the most effective budgets are not only those that set out a clear set of priorities but those that are credible, realistic, and ultimately enforceable.

In a closely divided government, *enforceable* means there must be consensus and compromise or else there will be crisis. Right now, it is the threat of failure that drives the process. Presidents' budgets rarely are acceptable to Congress. Congressional budgets rarely are acceptable to the president. Rather than resolve those differences, the budget process is driven to the edge of a cliff late in the congressional session. There is the threat of a potential shutdown, and that ultimately forces a final deal. The only hope for change is if the public provides one of the parties with an overwhelming majority or if both parties decide that it is in their interests to govern rather than to fight.

THE ROLE OF LEADERSHIP—"THINGS ARE DONE THROUGH EITHER LEADERSHIP OR CRISIS."

In the end, the key to the budget process is not procedural or resorting to legislative mandates of one kind or another. One cannot resolve conflicting priorities and the budget process without those who are willing to exercise leadership and take risks. I have often said that "in a democracy, things are done through either leadership or crisis." It was the tough leadership of presidents, members, and others that produced a strong economy:

- the tough leadership of business CEOs who had to decide on downsizing and implementing productivity through technology;

- the tough leadership of the Federal Reserve in fighting inflation and implementing interest rate hikes when necessary;
- the tough leadership of presidents and Congress on trade issues to expand a global market; and
- the tough leadership of presidents and Congress in reducing the deficit and in taking the risks necessary to achieve these goals.

In 1990, President Bush agreed to the budget compromise, and it achieved the most significant debt reduction to date and established caps on spending and pay-go disciplines. It took political courage, and Bush paid a price in political support in the 1992 election, but he did the right thing.

In 1993, President Clinton pushed through his economic plan, and it passed by a single vote. The president pushed it hard, members voted for it, and many paid a price in the 1994 election, losing their seats and control of the Congress. But they did the right thing.

Today, there is a real danger that the nation's budget—because of the size of the tax cut passed by the Congress and the weak performance of the economy—may again go back to the slippery slope that brought us deficit spending and quadrupled our national debt. The present administration and the Congress are virtually ignoring all of the lessons and sacrifices of the past.

In the end, the budget process—presidential and congressional—is only effective if there are those willing to take risks necessary to make it work. Clearly, the Constitution provides a legal framework within which both the president and the Congress can exercise their defined powers. And throughout the history of the budget, both the president and the Congress have sought agreements and procedural tools to strengthen their abilities to discipline spending and establish priorities. All of this has been fashioned and beaten into shape in the hot cauldron of politics. But history has also shown us that politics alone cannot work unless leaders are willing to lead. That is the essence of the budget process. It is the essence of our democracy.

10

The Making of U.S. Foreign Policy: The Roles of the President and Congress over Four Decades

The Honorable Lee H. Hamilton

The relationship between Congress and the president in foreign policy has evolved over the past four decades in response to changes in the world and in U.S. society and politics. Prior to 1965, when I entered the Congress, the president's authority in foreign policy was rarely challenged by a largely deferential legislature. Harry Truman's claim that the president alone made foreign policy still had substantial merit. Since then, Vietnam, Watergate, the end of the Cold War, the proliferation of special interest groups, the intensification of the political environment, and the explosion of twenty-four-hour news and information have led Congress, for various reasons, to assert its power in foreign policy more often and in new and complex ways. Congress now regularly challenges the president's proposals in every area of foreign policy and speaks out frequently in a cacophony of conflicting voices.

Despite these changes, the fundamentals of the foreign policy roles of the president and Congress remain essentially the same. The president is still the chief foreign policy maker. Most major initiatives in foreign policy originate with him. Congress continues to be both a critic and a partner of the president. It possesses many of the same strengths and weaknesses that it had in the 1960s. As has been the case since the beginning of the republic, our foreign policy works best when the president and Congress speak with one voice. Sustained consultation between the president and Congress remains the most important mechanism for fostering an effective foreign policy with broad support at home and respect and punch overseas.

HISTORICAL TRENDS

The relative influence of the president and Congress over foreign policy has fluctuated throughout U.S. history. During the nineteenth century, as the United States was consumed with domestic developments and expansion westward, Congress sometimes exerted greater power than the president. Teddy Roosevelt and Woodrow Wilson asserted greater presidential authority in the early twentieth century as they expanded the U.S. role in the world and brought America into World War I. Congress then regained influence following its rejection of U.S. entrance into the League of Nations, which began a twenty-year period of scaled-back U.S. involvement in international affairs. The U.S. entry into World War II fostered a renewed presidential dominance of foreign policy, which lasted until the domestic upheaval and eventual congressional outcry caused by the Vietnam War. Since Vietnam, presidents have generally maintained great authority in foreign affairs, but they have been challenged on many fronts by a newly assertive Congress.

The ebbs and flows in the relative influence of Congress and the president have been linked to broader changes in the world environment and U.S. domestic politics. The president has tended to have the greatest power in foreign policy during times of national crisis, war, or heightened public interest in foreign affairs. The twentieth-century presidents who have enjoyed the greatest control over foreign policy—Woodrow Wilson until 1918, Franklin Roosevelt after 1941, Harry Truman, Dwight Eisenhower, John Kennedy, Lyndon Johnson—governed during major wars or at the height of the Cold War. Congress has tended to assert more authority when the United States has been at peace and the American people have been disengaged from world events, such as in the aftermath of World War I and following the end of the Cold War.

Domestic politics have also had a major impact on the relative power of the president and Congress. This has been illustrated vividly over the past four decades. The national trauma over Vietnam, and a growing perception of abuses by the so-called imperial presidency, prodded Congress to assert greater influence over foreign affairs. This trend of congressional activism has continued—although inconsistently—in the years since Vietnam because of a variety of changes in U.S. society and politics.

This historical fluctuation in the relationship between Congress and the president stems from the division of foreign policy powers stipulated by the Constitution. Because the Constitution assigns some of these powers to the president and others to Congress, it invites them to struggle, as the great constitutional scholar Edwin Corwin has noted, for the privilege of directing U.S. foreign policy. The president is the commander in chief and head of the executive branch. Congress has the power to declare war and the power of the purse. The president can negotiate treaties, but the Senate must ratify them. This shared responsibility leaves the door open to both branches to assert their authority. Historical circumstances and the will and capability of each branch, then, determine their relative influence.

The ideal established by the Founders is neither for one branch to dominate the other nor for there to be an identity of views between them. Rather, the Founders wisely sought to encourage a creative tension between the president and Congress that would produce policies that best advance U.S. national interests and reflect the views of the American people.

CHANGES SINCE THE 1960s

The changes in the influence of Congress and the president since the 1960s are striking and complex. Congress challenges the president's authority far more often today but does not exercise consistent power because its foreign policy capacity is more diffuse and its stances are often incoherent. The president still generally possesses more foreign policy power than Congress but frequently struggles to command the nation's attention and win Congress's support.

The changes of recent decades began with the Vietnam War. Most members of Congress, and much of the American people, became concerned during the war that the United States had moved too far and too fast in concentrating war-making and other powers in the hands of the president. Believing that such a concentration of power was neither necessary, nor desirable, nor tolerable in a democratic society, these members gradually sought to restrict presidential power and enhance the foreign policy influence of Congress.

Congress was slow to take dramatic action on Vietnam—in part because many members who had reservations about the war did not want to use the blunt tool of rejecting appropriations for defense—but by 1973 Congress passed legislation that helped to end the war and established a new framework for executive and legislative war-making authority. The War Powers Act of that year, passed over President Nixon's veto, imposed groundbreaking procedural restraints on the capacity of the president to unilaterally commit U.S. armed forces abroad. The act stipulates that the president must consult with Congress before introducing U.S. forces into hostilities or imminent hostilities, must report to Congress when such forces are introduced, and must terminate the use of forces within sixty to ninety days unless Congress authorizes their use or extends this time period. The act's guiding principle is that a democracy should go to war only with the consent of the people, as expressed by their elected representatives. Although the act has often been ignored in the decades since by both the president and Congress, its advocates at the time argued that it would provide Congress with the means to fulfill the war-making responsibility assigned to the legislature by the Constitution.

Congress continued to flex its foreign policy muscle in subsequent years. The Watergate scandal of 1973–74 weakened the personal position of President Nixon and the institutional power of the presidency, while revelations of secret CIA operations abroad, particularly in Chile, further emboldened Congress to take the offensive in ways it would not have considered a decade before. In 1974, Congress challenged administration policy in southeastern Europe by prohibiting military aid to Turkey and stymied commercial agreements that President Nixon had reached with the Soviet Union by enacting the Jackson–Vanik amendment, which tied increased trade with the Soviet Union to its freedom of emigration. A year later, Congress enacted an amendment to the Arms Export Control Act that required any U.S. sale of military equipment worth more than $7 million to be submitted to Congress for approval. This new congressional assertiveness did not mean that Congress had gained the upper hand in foreign policy, but it did indicate that Congress was playing an increasingly important role. President Carter recognized Congress's growing independence when he devoted substantial time and energy to winning congressional approval of the Panama Canal Treaty and arms sales to Saudi Arabia. He realized that Congress could no longer be expected to rubber-stamp the president's policies.

President Reagan regained some of the president's authority because he was viewed by the American people as a strong leader with a clear vision of the world. But he faced serious congressional challenges as well, particularly on U.S. policy toward Central America. Congress refused on multiple occasions to support his requests for funding of the Contras in Nicaragua—resistance that led his administration to subvert the law in order to provide the aid anyway.

Since the end of the Cold War, foreign policy relations between Congress and the president have frequently been rocky. President Bush managed to win congressional support for the Gulf War after an intensive lobbying campaign on Capitol Hill, but President Clinton struggled mightily to gain congressional approval for a full panoply of foreign policy initiatives, from the Comprehensive Test Ban Treaty and fast-track authority for trade agreements to funding for the United Nations, the International Monetary Fund, international peacekeeping, and foreign aid. Executive–legislative relations reached a new low point with President Clinton's impeachment, which exacerbated the mutual mistrust between Congress and the president and made foreign policy cooperation between the branches increasingly rare during Clinton's second term.

The growing independence and influence of Congress have been reflected in the increased attention paid to Congress by foreign leaders and domestic foreign policy lobbyists. These representatives now go directly to Congress to advocate a position or urge Congress to modify or overturn administration policy. Recent U.S. presidents have employed a variation of this tactic as well—enlisting foreign leaders to lobby Congress on behalf of their proposals. For instance, Israeli Prime Ministers Rabin and Peres helped convince members to support aid to the Palestinians following the Oslo peace accords.

CHANGED INTERNATIONAL ENVIRONMENT

A major reason for the greater activism of Congress over the past decade is the changed international environment. During the Cold War, particularly until Vietnam but again to a lesser degree during the Reagan years, the president commanded great authority in large part because Americans felt a strong collective threat to their national security. Members of Congress who challenged the president could be charged with lacking patriotism and subverting the national interest. That political environment encouraged members to fall in line behind the president, except during periods of presidential weakness, such as the 1970s, or when public opposition to the president's policies was especially strong.

Today the United States faces a much more complicated set of international challenges. The world is being transformed by revolutions in finance, trade, and communications, while new security threats proliferate and issues like human rights, the environment, and drug trafficking increasingly take center stage. The Cold War doctrine of containment was easy to articulate and understand, but what overarching framework can describe a U.S. foreign policy that suits today's world? Without a single, strong rationale for foreign policy, Congress and the president get involved in a variety of issues in a more haphazard and uncoordinated way. Their focus is on China and Russia one day, the Balkans and Columbia the next. Economic issues have greater prominence, while security threats are more diffuse. Instead of facing one superpower with thousands of nuclear weapons, we confront the threats of terrorism; proliferating nuclear, chemical, and biological weapons; information warfare; and international drug trade and organized crime.

The U.S. national interest in a particular country or issue is now harder to define. Advancing democracy and the rule of law, developing free markets, promoting human rights, preventing genocide—these issues that have gained a new prominence are all important, but they are rarely directly related to vital national interests. In some nations, we have so many national interests that some of our interests can appear to conflict with others. For instance, in congressional debates on trade with China during the 1990s, some members argued that our national interest in economic growth and peace in Asia meant that we should work to increase trade with China. Other members argued that our national interest in advancing democracy and human rights required that we condition trade with China on Chinese progress in those areas. In such cases in which the U.S. national interest is unclear or extremely complex, there is often a lack of consensus on what policy should be. This lack of consensus makes it harder for the president to rally congressional support and encourages members of Congress to advocate various proposals of their own.

MORE ACTORS

Another major change of recent years has been the dramatic increase in the number of actors influencing U.S. foreign policy. During the 1960s, foreign policy was largely the domain of a small group of people—the president, the secretaries of state and defense, the national security adviser, the chairs of the House and Senate Foreign Relations Committees, and other members of the elite foreign policy establishment. To consult with Congress, the president and his advisers simply needed to call up the key congressional leaders. Today, power in Congress is more diffuse, and consultation means talking with as many members as possible. Every member takes interest in foreign policy at one time or another, and every member wants to be heard.

There are also many more groups outside of government seeking to influence foreign policy today: the business community, labor unions, ethnic constituencies, nonprofit organizations, foreign countries, former officials, international organizations, universities—and the list goes on. All of these groups and individuals seek to advance their views on Capitol Hill and in the White House.

The influence of these various actors has been boosted by the end of the Cold War. The relatively benign international environment and the focus of most Americans on domestic concerns have produced a political vacuum that can frequently be filled by special interests. The absence of a single, coherent foreign policy doctrine, such as containment, leaves greater room for interest groups to argue that their positions are in the U.S. national interest, as they define it.

The end of the Cold War has therefore allowed issues that were not given great attention previously to come to the fore. For instance, it has only been in recent years that U.S. foreign policy makers have focused heavily on the issue of religious freedom overseas. Without the need to make all features of U.S. foreign policy fit the framework of containment, members of Congress and U.S. officials are more able to bring issues that were once peripheral to foreign policy to center stage.

There are also more actors today because more Americans are affected by international affairs. For instance, the U.S. economy is increasingly dependent on international trade. That means that businesses—including small companies and even small farmers—have a greater stake in foreign policy. The overall influence of the business community increased during the 1990s as U.S. involvement in the world economy grew. Business lobbyists played a major role in building congressional support for the North American Free Trade Agreement and trade with China and in influencing President Clinton to ease sanctions against countries such as Iran, Libya, and Sudan.

The flip side of this powerful support for free trade by business is the frequent opposition to trade agreements voiced by labor and environmental groups, which tend to believe that trade agreements will export jobs out of the United States and create downward pressure on environmental standards overseas. Many congressional Democrats share the views of these groups and are therefore reluctant to approve many trade deals. The result is that U.S. trade policy is sometimes determined not by an objective consideration of the national interest but by the relative influence of various special interests, particularly business and labor.

Ethnic groups are another set of powerful actors in U.S. foreign policy. Their influence is certainly not new; it dates back to the earliest days of the republic. But the number of politically active ethnic groups has grown tremendously, and their lobbying techniques have become much more sophisticated. The ethnic groups with the most influence are those that are well funded and have large numbers nationally, heavy concentrations in particular areas of the country, or positions of power in society. Ethnic groups have an especially large influence on Congress because members with large concentrations of particular ethnic groups in their districts have great incentives to promote the foreign policies advocated by those constituencies.

Ethnic congressional caucuses now abound. In the House there is an Indian Caucus, an Armenian Caucus, an Albanian Caucus, and many more. These caucuses often act as fund-raising mechanisms for members who support their objectives. Some members have close personal ties not just to other nations but to particular political parties in other countries.

Many ethnic groups that had little influence a few decades ago now have substantial impact. Consider the rising power of Armenian Americans. Ten years ago, Armenia was of little concern to most members of Congress, but today the Armenian American lobby is a powerful advocate. Armenia is now one of the largest recipients of U.S. foreign aid because of the lobby's enhanced political influence. Its power stems from the heavy concentration of Armenian Americans in four major states—California, Massachusetts, New Jersey, and New York. Cuban Americans, of course, have long had a great impact on U.S. policy toward Cuba because of their concentration in southern Florida and in a few other areas.

Perhaps no set of actors has seen its influence grow as rapidly in recent years as the wide range of people representing nongovernmental organizations (NGOs), including think tanks, public interest groups, and private voluntary associations. These groups—ranging from the Christian Coalition to Human Rights Watch—advocate positions, and exert power, on every imaginable issue in international affairs. U.S. funding for the United Nations, for instance, was tied down for several years by a peripheral anti-abortion provision that was pushed by right-to-life activists and opposed by family-planning groups. The more powerful NGOs sometimes draft legislation themselves that members subsequently introduce in Congress. They also help shape the public debate through grassroots activities and op-ed writing nationwide.

International organizations have greater influence as well. Thirty years ago, few members of Congress could even name the top officials of major international institutions. Today, the leadership of the United Nations, the International Monetary Fund, the World Bank, and the World Trade Organization is in constant contact with U.S. officials and members of Congress. U.S. foreign policy is often designed in tandem with the policies of these institutions.

Universities play a growing role, too. Schools of international affairs do not just educate the next generation of foreign policy makers; they participate in the policy-making process themselves by holding conferences on major international issues. Many university professors serve as helpful resources and consultants to policy makers.

Foreign countries themselves are more active in the U.S. foreign policy process. Foreign heads of state and foreign ministers regularly come to Washington to ask for American help or lobby for particular policies. Scarcely a day goes by now without members of Congress meeting with top foreign officials.

And then there is the media—one of the most powerful foreign policy actors today. Television in particular has the ability to set our foreign policy agenda through the impact of its images. In 1992, television images of starving children in Somalia provoked American outrage and led former President Bush to send U.S. troops to Somalia to help combat its famine. Yet, some months later, television images of dead American soldiers being dragged through the streets of Mogadishu led President Clinton to withdraw our soldiers just as quickly.

INFORMATION REVOLUTION

The making of foreign policy has also been changed dramatically by the Information Revolution, which has exponentially increased the amount of information available to ordinary Americans and policy makers every day. Policy makers now receive far more information about the world than they can possibly use. Some of it is official intelligence, which is more scientific, detailed, and precise than ever before. But much of it comes from specialized publications, cable outlets, and the Internet. The fax machine, satellites, and the Web have made the world a much smaller place and have made Americans and their representatives more acutely aware of events in the farthest corners of the world.

This proliferation of information has advantages and disadvantages. On the positive side, it makes it harder to keep secrets—and therefore harder to keep people oppressed and in the dark. That is good news for human freedom, and we should welcome it. But the changes also make the process of making foreign policy more disorderly and unpredictable, and they tend to hamstring careful deliberation by placing a high premium on quick reactions. Policy makers are not always able to sift through all of the information carefully to weed out the important and accurate from the inconsequential or misleading. The proliferation of information also complicates the president's job because he must compete with so many other voices and outlets for the nation's attention.

CHANGES IN CONGRESS

Changes in the institution and practices of Congress have also altered the influence of each branch in foreign affairs. Since 1965, the foreign policy capacity of Congress has grown both more expert and more diffuse. This has led Congress to challenge the president more often but frequently in a haphazard and dysfunctional way. Congress has become more representative of widely varying American viewpoints, but it has also become more chaotic and divided.

Congressional activity in foreign policy has been transformed by the growing individualism and diversity of members. After Pearl Harbor, a whole generation of members tended to defer to the president and congressional leadership on foreign affairs. After Vietnam, many new members felt that they could formulate foreign policy just as well themselves. Members began to accumulate larger and highly professional staffs—both in their own offices and in committees. The staff of the House International Relations Committee, for instance, tripled between 1971 and 1978. Congress also gained access to more executive branch documents and sources and made greater use of its own independent research bodies, such as the Congressional Research Service, the General Accounting Office, and the Congressional Budget Office. This increased expertise has enabled Congress to get involved in far more aspects of foreign policy than ever before.

The greater ethnic diversity of Congress has added to its independence and wide-ranging interests in foreign policy. Congress now includes far more women, African Americans, Latinos, and members of other ethnic groups than it did just a few decades ago. These members have brought new concerns to the foreign policy debate. The sanctions placed by Congress on South Africa in the 1980s and the increased national focus on women's rights overseas have reflected the growing power of black and female members.

Many members today have weaker personal ties to their parties and to the institution of Congress. This makes them more willing to speak out and advance policies on issues of particular concern to them or their constituents. In 2000, for example, an individual senator used his power as chairman of a Senate appropriations subcommittee to block hundreds of millions of dollars that had been approved by Congress for U.N. peacekeeping missions because he opposed the administration's policy on Sierra Leone.

The policy-making process is further complicated because the parties themselves are internally split on many issues of foreign policy. On trade policy, for instance, pro-trade Republicans and Democrats have often been allied against members of both parties who want the United States to take stronger stances on labor standards, human rights, religious freedom, national security, or the environment. Developing a unified position on a foreign policy issue in Congress has become extremely difficult, and on a controversial issue, it can be virtually impossible.

This fragmentation of the Congress is heightened by the more frequent turnover of members today. Turnover brings many fresh voices into the Congress, but it also reduces the number of members with historical memory, experience in international issues, and a longer term perspective on foreign policy matters. Many new members are confronted with foreign policy issues for the first time in their lives when they enter Congress. They react to them in all kinds of different ways.

These changes in Congress have fueled a large-scale diffusion of power. Foreign policy influence is now spread in a confusing manner among dozens of congressional committees, from Agriculture to Government Affairs, rather than being concentrated in the main foreign policy–authorizing committees, which have the greatest foreign policy expertise. This diffusion of power has made it all the more difficult for Congress to develop a coherent foreign policy approach.

In fact, the greatest concentration of foreign policy power is now in the appropriations committees, in which foreign policy concerns are usually secondary to domestic political and fiscal concerns. Congress continually cut international affairs funding from the amount requested by the president during the Clinton years, preferring to devote money to tax cuts or popular domestic programs.

Congressional responsibility in foreign policy has been further weakened by the growing influence of domestic political concerns on the foreign policy process. Many members of Congress view foreign policy as nothing more than an extension of U.S. politics. They use foreign policy to curry favor with supporters or constituents or to score political points by attacking the president. Some Republicans in Congress did this during the 1990s, for instance, by frequently calling President Clinton's policies toward China, Iraq, and North Korea appeasement without offering any constructive alternatives.

The rise of the perpetual political campaign has rendered the congressional foreign policy capacity even thinner because members now spend so much time campaigning and fund-raising that less time is left for careful policy deliberation. Even when members are focused on policy, international affairs are usually at the bottom of the list of concerns because time spent on it yields little domestic advantage, in attracting either campaign funds or constituent votes. Most members seek to join committees, such as Banking and Commerce, that are more lucrative—financially and politically—than the foreign affairs committees.

CHANGES IN THE EXECUTIVE BRANCH

Some of these changes in the way Congress approaches and handles foreign policy have been mirrored in the executive branch. Foreign policy authority in the executive has also become more diffuse, as the number of federal agencies involved in foreign policy has proliferated. The State Department,

Defense Department, and CIA remain the central bodies for much of U.S. foreign policy, but they are no longer the exclusive authorities. The Treasury Department, for instance, now handles most international economic issues. The Justice Department manages immigration policy and the war on drugs. The Departments of Energy, Commerce, and Agriculture, as well as the U.S. Trade Representative, play important foreign policy roles as well.

This diffusion of authority is fueled by the changing, and increasingly complex, agenda of foreign policy. The Departments of State and Defense are best suited to manage diplomatic and security issues, but today's agenda is full of technical and scientific problems—ranging from international finance, to AIDS, to the global environment—that require other kinds of expertise. The Gore–Chernomyrdin Commission, which was established during the Clinton presidency to help manage U.S.–Russian relations, reflected this need for specialized knowledge and input. It matched up U.S. and Russian experts from outside of the traditional foreign policy apparatus to discuss issues such as health, energy, and the environment.

Along with the diffusion of foreign policy authority has come a greater concentration of power in the National Security Council (NSC). The NSC now acts as the primary manager and coordinator of the various foreign policy activities being conducted by the different departments of government. With more actors involved in executive branch policy making, it can be difficult for an administration to speak with one voice. It is the job of the national security adviser to ensure that it does.

The policy-making process has also become more politicized in the executive branch. Every issue—from trade to energy policy—is now subject to intense scrutiny based on political, and sometimes partisan, concerns. President Clinton, for instance, emphasized foreign policy issues such as NATO expansion, sanctions on Cuba, and the pursuit of peace in Northern Ireland in part because they would help him earn votes from major ethnic groups. Domestic politics have certainly always played a role in U.S. foreign policy, but the end of the Cold War has boosted their influence in the executive as in the Congress.

Another change is in the role of U.S. embassies. A primary function of our overseas posts used to be the collection and reporting of information on overseas trends and events. This function is less important today because much more news and information is available to policy makers through other outlets. Embassies have therefore shifted their focus from collecting information to analyzing it.

The result of all of these changes in the international environment, in American society, in U.S. domestic politics, and in Congress and the presidency is that the foreign policy process is more contentious and erratic. This makes the task of achieving consensus around the formulation and conduct of U.S. foreign policy, for both the president and the Congress, all the more difficult.

WHAT HAS NOT CHANGED

There has also been much that has remained the same in U.S. foreign policy since the mid-1960s. The essential ingredients for a successful foreign policy—presidential leadership, congressional partnership and responsibility, and sustained consultation between the branches—are unchanged.

Role of the President

The president is still, by far, the most important foreign policy maker. He must lead in order for the United States to advance its interests and values around the world. Only the president is accountable to, and speaks for, all Americans, and only he can rally public support to a foreign policy cause. The American people still generally support the president on major foreign policy issues. When he vigorously takes his case to Congress and the American people, he usually wins their support.

U.S. presidents have played the central role in nearly every major foreign policy achievement of the past thirty years. Nixon overcame years of distrust to renew U.S. relations with China; Carter negotiated the Panama Canal Treaties and the Camp David accords establishing peace between Israel and Egypt; Reagan intensified the U.S. challenge to the Soviet Union and began deep cuts in nuclear weapons; Bush skillfully managed the end of the Cold War and built the coalition that forced Iraq out of Kuwait; and Clinton led U.S. efforts to strengthen and expand NATO, protect peace in the Balkans, and advance international trade. Congress often provided needed support and helpful refinements of these policies, but their achievement would have been impossible without presidential leadership.

What must the president do to be an effective leader in foreign policy? Most importantly, he must make foreign policy a priority. Any president faces immense pressures to focus on the domestic agenda, but success in foreign policy demands substantial time and energy.

The president must sustain his focus on critical foreign policy issues. Too frequently—although often for compelling reasons given the many demands of the job—the president's attention (as well as the attention of the American people) moves away from a foreign policy problem once the guns go silent but before a full solution has been achieved. Because of the constant press of many world crises demanding American leadership, sustaining U.S. policy over time can be extremely difficult. Only the president can do it.

The president must also decide which foreign policy issues to focus on. Faced with a long list of international challenges, he must determine which are the critical issues that deserve his attention and leadership. He must know where he wants to go and how he intends to get there. The president must explain what his goals are, articulate his policy proposals clearly, and specify what kinds of resources he is prepared to expend.

One of the greatest challenges for the president is explaining the international environment and U.S. national interests to members of Congress and the American people. Public and congressional support for the president's initiatives will come only if Americans understand the fundamentals of the challenges we confront and are committed to meeting them. This task of educating the American people about foreign policy is especially difficult for a president today because of all of the other voices competing for the public's attention. To be heard above the clamor, the president must begin the education process at the outset of his term and keep at it until his final day in office.

Finally, the president must work in partnership with Congress and with friendly leaders around the world. U.S. foreign policy is far more effective when it has strong bipartisan support in the Congress and support from other nations. Good personal relations between the president and foreign heads of state help build international backing for U.S. policy. These relationships are especially important today because most of the challenges for U.S. foreign policy require international cooperation and support. Similarly, good relations between the president and members of Congress are essential to build support for the president's policies at home. Members of Congress will tend to back the president more strongly if they are involved in the policy process from the beginning, rather than simply informed of decisions after the fact.

Role of the Congress

Congress, too, has important foreign policy responsibilities. A strong foreign policy requires that Congress live up to its constitutional mandate to be the president's partner in the development of policy. Congress should be an independent critic of the president, but that criticism should always be in the context of improving and strengthening U.S. policy.

Congress brings many strengths to the foreign policy process. It best represents the diverse views of the American people, is far more accessible than the president, contains a wide range of opinion and knowledge, and possesses a strong streak of independence that often makes for vigorous and healthy debate. Congress often helps to refine and improve the foreign policy proposals of the president.

To its credit, Congress has a better record on foreign policy than many of its critics maintain. It has generally supported the major themes of U.S. foreign policy over the past several decades: containment of the Soviet Union; close relations with key allies in Europe, Asia, and elsewhere; a strong defense; free international trade; and the promotion of democracy and human rights abroad. Congress has supplied the necessary funding for aid to Israel and other Middle East peace partners, endorsed the enlargement of NATO, and supported debt relief for the world's poorest nations.

Yet there are serious flaws with the way Congress approaches foreign policy. Congress often does not take foreign policy seriously enough. It sometimes views foreign policy challenges from a narrow or limited perspective, rather than taking the time to understand the total national interest involved in an issue. For example, some members look at China only in terms of its human rights performance or its export of military technology—ignoring our other security, economic, political, and humanitarian interests in China.

Congress often shirks its responsibilities in foreign policy. For instance, it regularly fails to authorize the use of military force as it is mandated to by the War Powers Act. Only twice since 1973 has Congress authorized the deployment of U.S. forces—in 1983, when U.S. troops were sent to Lebanon, and in 1991, on the eve of the Gulf War. Many other military engagements, including Grenada, Panama, Somalia, Haiti, Bosnia, and Kosovo, have passed by without congressional authorization.

Congress has a very poor record of considering international treaties that have been signed by U.S. presidents and await Senate ratification. In some cases, when the Senate votes to reject a treaty, it is asserting its independent judgment, which is its proper constitutional role. But dozens of treaties signed by U.S. presidents and submitted to the Senate over the past fifty years have simply been collecting dust and have not even been taken up for debate—on issues ranging from human rights, to the environment, to maritime regulations.

Congress also neglects its foreign policy responsibilities by failing to spend enough time performing rigorous oversight of foreign policy. Congress must do more than write the laws; it must make sure that the administration is carrying them out the way Congress intended. In recent years, Congress has devoted little time to regular programmatic oversight, focusing instead on personal investigations often designed to discredit individual public officials.

On the other hand, Congress too often micromanages foreign policy. It sometimes fills bills with detailed performance and reporting requirements that can hamstring the president's flexibility in implementing policy. In Congress's defense, micromanagement often results from congressional frustration with a failure of the executive branch to consult with Congress and take its concerns into consideration.

The president's job is further complicated when Congress links unrelated issues together rather than considering them on their individual merits. During the 1990s, for instance, Congress linked U.N. funding to abortion and linked nonproliferation legislation on Russia and Iran to its ratification of the Chemical Weapons Convention. When Congress links tough foreign policy issues to other controversial measures, it makes it all the more difficult to move forward on them.

Congress sometimes acts too timidly in foreign policy by passing the buck. Take its approach to economic sanctions. It postures and attracts credit for acting tough by enacting sanctions legislation but places the entire burden of making the tough decision to impose sanctions on the president by leaving it to him to determine whether to apply or waive them in cases of violation of U.S. law. Congress thus punts the issue to the president and forces him to take the political heat that may follow his decision, rather than sharing the responsibility with him.

Finally, despite its increased activism in recent decades, Congress rarely leads and rarely educates the public about foreign policy. It is generally reactive rather than proactive—dealing with foreign policy issues only when forced to by the president or the media. Occasionally members give foreign policy speeches—some are very good—but they rarely feel any real burden to explain our foreign policy challenges to the American people. The members who do so are a distinct minority.

To play a more constructive role, Congress needs to rethink the way it approaches foreign policy. It should put aside efforts to score political points, step up to its constitutional obligations, and take a full share of responsibility for the formulation of U.S. foreign policy. Our foreign policy works best when the president and Congress work together on behalf of America's interests.

CONSULTATION

The best way to foster foreign policy cooperation between the president and Congress is through sustained consultation. Consultation is the process of policy discussion and mutual exchange between the president and Congress. It can take many forms, including executive branch testimony at congressional hearings, briefings by foreign policy officials, and informal conversations. More important than its form is the attitude of the parties involved. Consultation is most effective when each branch makes a sincere effort to involve the other branch in its decision-making processes.

Consultation fosters mutual trust between the president and Congress, and it encourages them to develop our foreign policy together. It does not—and should not—ensure agreement between the branches. But even on the toughest issues, it helps smooth some of the hard edges of disagreement, and it almost always refines and strengthens our policy.

Both the president and Congress often give short shrift to consultation. On the executive branch side, presidents tend to inform Congress of their decisions after the fact rather than consulting it during policy development. Presidents begin talking to Congress only when a congressional vote is upcoming, a media story is breaking, or a crisis is at hand. They tend to treat Congress as an obstacle to be overcome instead of as a partner in the policy-making process. And they often consult with only a limited number of members, excluding others who are heavily interested in particular foreign policy issues.

The most prominent examples of poor consultation in recent decades involve the Vietnam War and aid to the Contras in Nicaragua. The failure of Presidents Johnson, Nixon, and Reagan to consult Congress sufficiently over those issues led to major political controversies and serious congressional backlashes. These examples stand out because consultation was not simply poor; it was intentionally poor because the administrations wanted to conceal information from Congress and the public. Policy was controlled by a small group of high-level officials, and few others either inside or outside the administrations knew the full extent of our government's activities. Other examples of poor consultation abound. The Clinton administration, for instance, consulted poorly on our interventions in Somalia, Bosnia, and Kosovo and during its efforts to obtain funding for the United Nations and ratification of the Comprehensive Test Ban Treaty.

Congress, too, regularly displays several consultation shortcomings. Members often are simply not receptive to consultation. They are either uninterested in foreign policy or want only to be briefed by the president, the secretary of defense, or the secretary of state. After the 1994 so-called Agreed Framework with North Korea was negotiated, for instance, I organized two briefings for members on Capitol Hill with the administration official who negotiated the agreement. A total of one member showed up.

Consultation is made more difficult today because power in Congress is so diffuse and shifts with each issue. There is no single person—or group of people—whom an administration can consult with and conclude that it has gained congressional support. Partisanship in Congress can weaken consultation further. Congressional leaders have sometimes refused to be consulted by an administration while members of the other party were present. That kind of attitude makes it extremely difficult to develop a bipartisan foreign policy.

Despite these deficiencies, there have been a number of times in recent decades when consultation has worked well. The president can still usually gain congressional support for major foreign policy initiatives when he sets his mind to it. President Carter consulted very effectively to achieve congressional approval of the Panama Canal Treaty and of arms sales to Saudi Arabia. The Bush and Clinton administrations consulted well to gain congressional support for aid to former Soviet bloc countries after the fall of communism and for preserving normal trade relations with China. And every president of recent memory has consulted Congress regularly and effectively to maintain support for the Middle East peace process.

What, then, must the president and Congress do to overcome, or at least mitigate, the common deficiencies in the consultative process? First, each side must understand its proper role, powers, and limitations in foreign policy. The president must recognize that Congress plays an important role in policy formulation and refinement and can provide our foreign policy with stronger public support. Congress must recognize that its role is generally limited to helping to develop policy and must give the president some flexibility in its day-to-day implementation. Congress must strike a balance between responsible criticism, based on measured oversight of the executive branch, and responsible cooperation.

Second, the president and Congress must build a relationship based on mutual respect, trust, and partnership. Administration officials must take the perspectives of Congress seriously and respond to congressional concerns. Members of Congress must be sensitive to the complexity of foreign affairs and the difficulty of crafting and implementing policy. The branches must engage in a genuine dialogue on the problems that concern them most.

Third, consultation must take place, to the extent feasible, prior to decisions, not after they have already been made. The administration should inform Congress of the range of policy alternatives and seek Congress's advice. If the administration does intend simply to inform Congress of a decision, it should make this clear and not pretend to be seeking congressional input.

Fourth, support for consultation must come from our leadership. Consultation is most effective when the president himself is personally involved. For their part, leaders of Congress must set the example for other members by their constructive approach to the making of foreign policy. They can also help the administration understand the many perspectives of members.

Fifth, consultation must be bipartisan. Too often administration calls for bipartisanship are simply appeals for the opposing party in Congress to approve the administration's agenda. Real bipartisanship means engaging the other party in policy formulation. Congress must also strive for bipartisanship. It is most effective in advancing a foreign policy position when that position has strong support in both parties.

Sixth, the president must devote more resources to consultation—535 independent members of Congress cannot be reached by a handful of administration lobbyists. The administration should increase the number of people working to consult with Congress and assign high-quality people to that task. It should frequently send midlevel, as well as high-level, officials to Capitol Hill; keep closer track of the foreign policy views and concerns of every member; and hire more former members to work in the executive branch as a means of strengthening ties between the branches.

Seventh, the administration must have a sustained focus on consultation. It should not consult only during crises or when it needs immediate congressional support. On critical issues like China, Russia, the Middle East, and the international financial institutions, the administration should begin educating members as soon as they enter office. Congressional support will be more forthcoming in crisis situations if Congress is kept aware of issues before they explode.

Eighth, the administration must consult in many different ways and have a flexible approach. The kind of consultation required varies from issue to issue, from situation to situation, and from member to member. One-on-one discussions between officials and members can be especially effective. President Johnson was a master at these because he knew where each member was coming from and what was most important to him or her.

Ninth, Congress must make consultation a higher priority. Members should encourage consultation by attending briefings and displaying interest in foreign policy. Congress should be receptive to consultation from midlevel as well as high-level officials and should hire more former executive branch officials in order to improve its understanding of the workings and perspective of an administration.

Finally, Congress should create a permanent consultative group of congressional leaders. In 1993, I joined several other members of the House in introducing a bill to establish such a group made up of the congressional leadership and the chairs and ranking members of the main foreign policy committees. Other members with special interest or expertise could join the group's work on certain issues. The group would meet regularly—perhaps as often as once a month—with the top foreign policy officials in the administration, including the secretary of state, secretary of defense, and director of central intelligence. The agenda for these meetings would not be strictly limited, allowing members to raise issues of concern to them. The group would also meet on an emergency basis whenever the president was considering military action abroad.

Such a group would enable the administration to consult with a wide range of congressional leaders in a single setting, mitigating the difficulty of consulting with the many centers of congressional power. The group would encourage the congressional and administration leadership to work through important policy questions together and would provide a centralized forum for foreign policy discussion and for dissemination of appropriate information to other members.

Improved consultation will not end disagreement and conflict over foreign policy. On occasion, the president and Congress will differ no matter how much consultation takes place. But more often than not, good consultation will help an administration gain greater backing in Congress. It will almost always foster a stronger, more refined, and more unified U.S. foreign policy.

CONCLUSION

The changes in the foreign policy relationship between Congress and the president since 1965 have had both positive and negative consequences. The increased assertiveness of Congress has helped make foreign policy more representative of the diverse views of the American people, and the greater scrutiny placed on the president has helped prevent the president from amassing too much unchecked power. But the diffusion of foreign policy authority has made it easier for special interests and domestic politics to take priority over national interests, and it has made the task of achieving consensus around tough issues more difficult than ever before.

These changes underscore the continuing importance of the basic principles that have been the source of a strong foreign policy throughout U.S. history. In today's era of globalization, as in the early days of the republic, U.S. foreign policy works best when it is marked by strong presidential leadership, responsible congressional partnership and oversight, and sustained dialogue and consultation. These are the fundamental and timeless building blocks for an effective U.S. foreign policy.

Together, the president and Congress have achieved a lot in foreign policy over the past several decades. Despite frequent clashes, they have led us to victory in the Cold War and a position of unmatched international preeminence. To maintain that position and remain secure, prosperous, and free, the United States must continue to lead. That leadership requires a committed president and a responsible Congress working together to advance a foreign policy that reflects the views of the American people and serves our national interests in a time of extraordinary global change and many new international challenges.

11

Clinton's Military Actions: No Rivals in Sight

Louis Fisher

In the area of the war power, Congress over the past half century has been in a constitutional free fall. In Korea in 1950 and in Southeast Asia in the 1960s, Congress sat largely on the sidelines. The Tonkin Gulf Resolution of 1964 irresponsibly shifted war powers to President Lyndon Johnson. By passing the War Powers Resolution of 1973, Congress supposedly reasserted its constitutional role. In fact, the resolution marked a further surrender of legislative power to the president.[1]

The Cold War with the Soviet Union ended in the final years of the Reagan administration. With world tensions relaxed, at least at the superpower level, Congress had an opportunity to recapture its constitutional prerogatives over the war power. But throughout the Bush and Clinton administrations, Congress was more supine than ever. President Bush invaded Panama without coming to Congress for authority. He claimed that he could go to war against Iraq without legislative approval, prompting Congress at the last minute to pass authorizing legislation. As part of a limited and humanitarian mission, Bush sent troops to Somalia in the waning months of his administration.

Unilateral presidential wars became even more pronounced during the Clinton years. The commitment to Somalia turned to nation building and bloody confrontations, provoking Congress to cut off funds. Over the next eight years Clinton used military force against Iraq, Haiti, Bosnia, Yugoslavia, Afghanistan, and Sudan. Congress debated a number of restrictive legislative provisions yet never followed through. Resort to the courts has been ineffective. Presidents may thus unleash military force against other nations with few legislative and no judicial checks. In this fundamental area of the war power, the presidency has moved toward what the Framers feared and expressly rejected: monarchy—not monarchy in the sense of a life term but monarchy in the sense of concentrating the war power in the hands of a single person.

Bush's action against Saddam Hussein had edged close to this monarchical model. Although Congress managed to authorize offensive operations against Iraq, Bush was ready to act with or without Congress. As he later noted: "Even had Congress not passed the resolutions I would have acted and ordered our troops into combat. I know it would have caused an outcry, but it was the right thing to do. I was comfortable in my own mind that I had the constitutional authority. It had to be done."[2] Here Bush promotes an autocratic or monarchical model. What mattered to him was not the Constitution or legal constraints but simply doing the "right thing." Clinton would use the same phrase in justifying military force against Haiti and Bosnia.

Bush decided to seek a U.N. Security Council resolution to support military action in Iraq, much as President Truman secured a Security Council resolution for taking military action in Korea. Clinton followed those precedents by obtaining Security Council resolutions for Haiti and Bosnia. In addition, he relied on decisions by the North Atlantic Council (of NATO) to conduct air strikes in Bosnia and to make war against Serbia. Both Bush and Clinton used U.N. and NATO "authority" to circumvent the constitutional authority of Congress to initiate military action against other nations.[3] Through these presidential actions, the constitutional power to sanction military force is transferred, in effect, from Congress to international and regional organizations.

CLINTON GEARS UP

During the 1992 presidential campaign, Clinton promoted an activist, interventionist policy for world affairs, indicating a willingness to use U.S. military troops abroad. His credibility as a commander in chief had been undercut by stories about his draft record during the Vietnam War. Various accounts surfaced on his efforts to avoid military service. Yet, in an interview in June 1992, he insisted that he could be trusted to be commander in chief and criticized Bush for failing to use military force to bring humanitarian aid to the citizens of Bosnia and Herzegovina.[4]

Clinton's capacity to serve credibly as commander in chief was quickly challenged when he proposed that gays be allowed to serve in the military. Objections from the Joint Chiefs of Staff that they had not been properly consulted implied a rebellion within the military ranks against Clinton. The Senate then threatened to write the existing administration ban into law. At a news conference on 23 March 1993, a reporter described an incident in which it appeared that the sailors of the USS *Theodore Roosevelt* had been mocking the president before his arrival. The reporter asked pointedly: "Do you have a problem, perhaps because of your lack of military service or perhaps because of issues such as gays in the military, in being effective in your role as Commander in Chief . . . ?"[5] Clinton denied that he had a problem being commander in chief. Within a few months, he would have what White House officials saw as an opportunity to demonstrate his military "toughness."

THE ATTACK ON BAGHDAD

On 26 June 1993, Clinton ordered cruise missiles into Iraq in response to a car-bombing plot to assassinate former President Bush during a visit to Kuwait. Sixteen suspects, including two Iraqi nationals, had been arrested. Although the trial of those suspects was still under way in Kuwait, the CIA concluded that there was "compelling evidence" that a plot to assassinate Bush had been directed and pursued by the Iraqi intelligence service. Calling the plot "an attack against our country and against all Americans," Clinton reported to Congress that he had ordered the launching of twenty-three Tomahawk cruise missiles as an exercise "of our inherent right of self-defense as recognized in Article 51 of the United Nations Charter and pursuant to my constitutional authority with respect to the conduct of foreign relations and as Commander in Chief."[6]

The cruise missiles badly damaged the Iraqi intelligence service's principal command and control facility in Baghdad. In addition, three of the missiles destroyed homes in the surrounding neighborhood, killed eight people, and wounded at least twelve others. News analyses suggest that the White House appreciated that this use of military force could promote Clinton's image as a strong and decisive leader. The attack, said a White House aide, would "serve notice to one and all that Americans are prepared first of all to exercise leadership and to remain engaged and to act with military forces as appropriate." A senior administration official noted: "We were showing that Bill Clinton can take the challenge." Aides disclosed to the press that Clinton, shortly after making an address from the Oval Office on the bombing, returned to the White House residence to watch a movie with his wife and slept "a solid eight hours."[7] The word was out: Clinton could make tough military calls and not look back.

Clinton described the attack on Baghdad as "essential to protect our sovereignty, to send a message to those who engage in state-sponsored terrorism, to deter further violence against our people, and to affirm the expectation of civilized behavior among nations." The attack, he claimed, sent the following message to Iraq and other nations: "We will combat terrorism. We will deter aggression. We will protect our people."[8] However, that argument is not credible. As two attorneys of constitutional law have pointed out, "Calling the U.S. bombing of Iraq an act of self-defense for an assassination plot that had been averted two months previously is quite a stretch."[9] Moreover, what Clinton did to Iraq he would not have done to other countries suspected of terrorist activity. For example, in response to evidence that Syria was behind a terrorist action, he would not have launched cruise missiles at intelligence facilities in Damascus. Other responses, less confrontational, would have been used.

NATION BUILDING IN SOMALIA

Shortly before leaving office, President Bush dispatched U.S. troops to Somalia as part of a multinational relief effort, explaining that there were no plans "to dictate political outcomes" and no intent to become "involved in hostilities."[10] Yet, in President Clinton's first year, the humanitarian venture turned bloody and shifted focus to hunting down and arresting a Somali political figure, Mohamed Farah Aideed. In response to the killing of twenty-three Pakistani peacekeepers in June 1993, Clinton ordered U.S. airplanes to launch a retaliatory attack. Two months later, four U.S. soldiers were killed when a land mine blasted apart their Humvee vehicle in Mogadishu. Aideed was again blamed for the deaths. Earlier conflicts had killed four other American soldiers. Officials in the Clinton administration began to talk of "nation building": rebuilding political structures in Somalia to form a stable order.

Congressman Lee Hamilton, chairman of the House Foreign Affairs Committee, objected to this new mission: "I do not believe that the United States should be engaged in nation building in Somalia. That is the task of the United Nations."[11] Congressman Ron Dellums (D-Calif.) asked: "Who gave us the right—as peacekeepers—to determine which political figure or faction deserves to emerge victorious in Somalia?"[12] On 3 October, about a week after this debate, eighteen Army soldiers were killed. Aideed's forces captured an American pilot and displayed him, battered and dazed, to TV cameras. The body of a dead U.S. soldier was dragged through the streets of Mogadishu by an angry mob.

Congress began to draft legislation to require Clinton to remove the troops from Somalia by a certain date unless he obtained statutory authority. Under this pressure, Clinton announced on 7 October that all U.S. troops would be out of Somalia no later than 31 March 1994, except for a few hundred support personnel in noncombatant roles.[13] A week later he stated that the U.S. mission "is not now nor was it ever one of 'nation building.' "[14] Congress used its power of the purse to bring the military operation to a halt. Legislation prohibited the use of any funds after 31 March 1994 for the operations of U.S. armed forces in Somalia unless the president requested an extension and received authority from Congress. The legislation permitted the use of funds after the cutoff date to protect U.S. diplomatic facilities and American citizens.[15]

THE THREAT TO INVADE HAITI

Jean-Bertrand Aristide, the first democratically elected president of Haiti, was forced out of office by the military regime on 30 September 1991. During the 1992 election, Clinton criticized the Bush administration for "turning its back" on refugees fleeing Haiti.[16] Once in office, Clinton was able to secure an agreement from Lt. Gen. Raoul Cedras, who promised Aristide's return by 30 October. In October, Clinton sent about 600 U.S. military construction troops to Haiti to prepare the way for Aristide. The troops were largely military engineers sent to work on roads, bridges, and water supplies. When the ships arrived, a group of armed civilians prevented the troops from landing.

On 15 October, Clinton implied that he might have to use military force against Haiti, in part because 1,000 U.S. citizens lived in Haiti or worked there. An amendment in the Senate, to require prior congressional authority to send U.S. forces to Haiti except to protect and evacuate U.S. citizens, was rejected decisively, eighty-one to nineteen.[17] On 21 October, the Senate adopted (ninety-eight to two) nonbinding language that expressed the sense of Congress that Congress should authorize U.S. military operations in Haiti unless U.S. citizens were in imminent need of protection and evacuation or the president determined that deployment was vital to national security interests.[18] The basic effect was to transfer the war power to Clinton.

The enacted bill, relying on nonbinding statutory language, expressed the "sense of Congress" that funds in the defense appropriations bill should not be obligated or expended for U.S. military operations in Haiti unless (1) authorized in advance by the Congress, (2) it was necessary to protect or evacuate U.S. citizens, or (3) the president determined that the deployment was "vital" to U.S. national security interests and there was insufficient time to seek and obtain congressional authorization. Even those elastic guidelines could be set aside if the president reported in advance that the deployment was justified by U.S. national security interests.

In May 1994, the House debated several amendments to limit Clinton's use of military force in Haiti. The amendment that passed, 223 to 201, was another nonbinding measure, declaring it to be the sense of Congress that the United States should not take military action against Haiti "unless the President first certifies to Congress that clear and present danger to citizens of the United States or United States interests requires such action."[19] An alternative amendment, offered by Congressmen Dellums and Hamilton, was rejected, but it too opposed military action unless Clinton justified it.

The amendment that passed in May, anemic as it was, did not last for long. Two weeks later the House rejected it on a separate vote.[20] Why this flip-flop? The Republican vote on the two amendments stayed fairly constant: 169 to 3 on the first amendment and 171 to 3 on the second. The amendment failed the second time because of shifts among the Democrats: fifty-four Democrats supported the first amendment, and only twenty-four supported the second. This shift of thirty votes changed the results from 223 to 201 in favor to 226 to 195 opposed.[21]

On 29 June, the Senate debated nonbinding language to oppose military operations in Haiti unless certain conditions were met. The author of this amendment, Judd Gregg (R-N.H.), used the power of the purse to restrict the president and yet accepted the president as the prime mover in military operations. His amendment stated that no funds should be obligated or expended for any U.S. military operation in Haiti unless such operations were authorized in advance by Congress. Yet Gregg added a number of conditions. Troops could be deployed to Haiti to protect or evacuate U.S. citizens and whenever it was "vital to the national security interests of the United States." The person to make the latter determination was the president.[22]

Even though Gregg discussed his amendment in terms of the Constitution, he did not really believe that Congress should have to authorize military actions in advance. Rather, Clinton should simply explain to Congress what he had decided: "So this sense of the Senate makes it clear that we as a body expect the President . . . to come to us in advance and explain whether or not and why that is the decision he wishes to pursue military operations in Haiti."[23] If the administration felt "they must use a military response in order to put Mr. Aristide back in power, then that is the right of the President of the United States to make that decision."[24]

Gregg later converted his sense-of-Congress language into legally binding language. Still, the effect of the amendment remained the same. No funds could be used to deploy U.S. forces to Haiti unless (1) such operations were authorized in advance by the Congress, (2) force was necessary to protect U.S. citizens, or (3) the president decided that force was necessary to protect vital national security interests. To avoid the funding restriction, Gregg explained that Clinton needed only to "first contact and advise us in advance before he uses military force in an invasion of Haiti."[25]

Both supporters and opponents of the Gregg amendment read the president's war powers expansively. Senator Jesse Helms (R-N.C.), a supporter, stated: "The President, of course, has constitutional authority to order such an invasion. Nobody questions that."[26] Senator John McCain (R-Ariz.), an opponent, said that "for us to prospectively tell the President of the United States that he cannot enter into military action anyplace in the world, in my view is a clear violation of his powers as Commander in Chief under the Constitution of the United States."[27]

Several senators cited precedents to justify unilateral presidential action. McCain discussed actions taken by President Jefferson against the Barbary pirates: "That was done without a declaration of war. That set a precedent for operations like Grenada, Panama, et cetera." Christopher Dodd, a Democrat from Connecticut, agreed that the reference to the Barbary pirates "is a good historical example."[28] However, Jefferson took only *defensive* actions against the Barbary pirates while Congress was adjourned. When Congress returned, he sought authority for *offensive* actions. Congress passed at least ten statutes authorizing Presidents Jefferson and Madison to take military action against the Barbary pirates.[29] There was no declaration of war against the Barbary pirates, but military operations were expressly authorized by statute. Jefferson never argued for the scope of war power that the Clinton administration and its supporters claimed.

Gregg's amendment lost, thirty-four to sixty-five. At that point the Senate voted ninety-three to four in favor of another sense-of-Congress amendment, this one identical to language adopted by the Senate on 21 October 1993 (when it was accepted ninety-eight to two). The basic thrust was to lodge war power with the president: Congress should authorize military actions in Haiti unless U.S. citizens were in danger or the president decided that force was vital to U.S. interests.[30]

On 31 July 1994, the Security Council adopted a resolution "inviting" all states—particularly those in the region of Haiti—to use "all necessary means" to remove the military leadership on that island. Using nonbinding language, the Senate voted 100 to 0 that the Security Council resolution "does not constitute authorization for the deployment of United States Armed Forces in Haiti under the Constitution of the United States or pursuant to the War Powers Resolution (Public Law 93-148)."[31] A number of lawmakers were offended by the concept of an administration seeking "authority" from the Security Council but not from Congress. Senator Helms remarked: "For the past 3 weeks, the President's advisers have been running around the United Nations in New York City lobbying the Russians and lobbying the French for permission to invade Haiti, but the permission of Congress, which is required by the United States Constitution, has not been sought."[32]

In a nationwide televised address on 15 September, Clinton told the American public that he was prepared to use military force to invade Haiti. Referring to the U.N. resolution of 31 July, he declared his willingness to lead a multinational force "to carry out the will of the United Nations."[33] He made no such pledge to carry out the will of Congress or the American public. In fact, he seemed to glory in the idea of acting against public opinion: "But regardless [of this opposition], this is what I believe is the right thing to do. I realize it is unpopular. I know it is unpopular. I know the timing is unpopular. I know the whole thing is unpopular. But I believe it is the right thing."[34] Like Bush, he seemed to have little interest in doing the legal thing, the authorized thing, the constitutional thing.

Clinton spoke of the need to keep commitments: "I'd like to mention just one other thing that is equally important, and that is the reliability of the United States and the United Nations once we say we're going to do something."[35] Who constituted this "we"? It did not include Congress or the American public. The commitment was made unilaterally by the president acting in concert with a U.N. Security Council resolution that he helped pass.

Invasion became unnecessary because negotiations by former President Jimmy Carter (with Senator Sam Nunn and Colin Powell) convinced the military leaders to step down and permit Aristide's return. Nevertheless, nearly 20,000 U.S. troops were sent to Haiti to provide stability. House and Senate debates were strongly critical of Clinton's insistence that he could act militarily against Haiti without legislative authority. A resolution, introduced to provide retroactive authorization for the use of U.S. armed forces in Haiti, was rejected in favor of substitute language stating that "the President should have sought and welcomed Congressional approval before deploying United States Forces to Haiti."[36] A remark by Senator Max Baucus (D-Mont.) captured the feeling among many legislators: "The President did not seek my approval for occupying Haiti. And he will not get my approval now."[37] While the legislative response was generally critical of Clinton's actions, the president reinforced the precedent of acting under the "authority" of the United Nations rather than Congress. It was a precedent he would build on.

AIR STRIKES AND GROUND TROOPS IN BOSNIA

In his first year in office, Clinton indicated that he would need authorization from Congress before ordering air strikes in Bosnia. At a news conference on 7 May 1993, he stated: "If I decide to ask the American people and the United States Congress to support an approach that would include the use of air power, I would have a very specific, clearly defined strategy." At that same news conference, he switched from the word *support* to *authority*: "I assure you today that if I decide to ask for the authority to use air power from the Congress and from the American people. . . ."[38] On 8 September, he mixed the language of seeking legislative "support" with that of getting the "agreement" of Congress:

> Of course in the United States, as all of you know, anything we do has to have the support of the Congress. I would seek the support of the Congress to do that. . . . [I]f we can get the Congress to support it, then I think we should participate. . . . [Military action in Bosnia] has to be able to be enforced or, if you will, be guaranteed by a peacekeeping force from NATO, not the United Nations but NATO. And of course, for me to do it, the Congress would have to agree.[39]

He later wrote to the party leaders in the Senate—George Mitchell (D-Maine) and Bob Dole (R-Kans.)—encouraging them to vote "authorization of any military involvement in Bosnia."[40] However, other Clinton statements in 1993 seemed to degrade Congress to a mere consultative body. He told reporters on 27 September that "it is clear to everyone that the United States could not fulfill a peacekeeping role in Bosnia unless the Congress supported it. And I will be consulting with all the appropriate congressional leadership in both parties."[41]

In September 1993, Dole was prepared to require advance approval from Congress before Clinton could deploy any additional U.S. forces to Bosnia–Herzegovina. Exceptions allowed the conduct of humanitarian relief operations and the enforcement of the no-fly zone. However, Dole later limited the amendment to the deployment of ground forces. It said nothing about requiring congressional approval for air strikes.[42] Clinton opposed any legislative efforts to restrict his military options.[43] He did not think "we should have an amendment which would tie the President's hands and make us unable to fulfill our NATO commitments."[44] As with Haiti and the United Nations, "our" commitments would be decided solely by the president, not by Congress. Clinton said he opposed statutory language that "would make it unreasonably difficult for me or any President to operate militarily with other nations when it is in our interest to do so—and as we have done effectively for half a century through NATO."[45] Yet, over that entire half century,

NATO had never once used military force. On the basis of nonexistent precedents, Clinton wanted discretion to do what no president had ever done.

On 20 October, the Senate voted ninety-nine to one for the following nonbinding language: "It is the sense of Congress that none of the funds appropriated or otherwise made available by this Act should be available for the purposes of deploying United States Armed Forces to participate in the implementation of a peace settlement in Bosnia–Herzegovina, unless previously authorized by Congress."[46] Senator George Mitchell supported the provision "because it does not purport to impose prior restraints upon a President performing the duties assigned him under the Constitution." He did "not favor prior restraints. I believe they plainly violate the Constitution."[47] By opposing prior restraint, Mitchell left the decision of military force solely to the president, a position that contradicts what Mitchell called a central principle of the Constitution, which "intended to prevent the accumulation of power in any one branch of Government, in any institution, or individual."[48] The nonbinding Senate language became law.[49]

AIR STRIKES AGAINST THE SERBS

In 1994, Clinton threatened air strikes against Serbian militias in Bosnia, looking for authority not from Congress but from U.N. Security Council resolutions and decisions by NATO. As he put it: "The authority under which air strikes can proceed, NATO acting out of area pursuant to U.N. authority, requires the common agreement of our NATO allies."[50] In other words, Clinton needed approval from the United Kingdom, France, Italy, and other NATO allies but not from Congress.

Air strikes began in February 1994 when U.S. jets shot down four Serbian bombers over Bosnia, marking the first time in history that NATO forces had been engaged in combat. Clinton reported to Congress that the actions were "conducted under the authority of U.N. Security Council resolutions and in full compliance with NATO procedures."[51] For Clinton, compliance with the Constitution did not carry the same priority or urgency. He saw no need to obtain authority from Congress. Authority from international and regional institutions would do just as well, if not better.[52] Air strikes continued in April, August, and November. Congress did not challenge Clinton's authority to conduct air strikes in Bosnia.

NATO conducted limited air strikes during the first half of 1995. When Bosnian Serb forces overran the U.N.–designated "safe area" of Srebrenica, NATO carried out the war's biggest air raid at the end of August 1995.[53] On 1 September, Clinton explained to congressional leaders the procedures followed for ordering air strikes on Bosnia. The United Nations and NATO participated in the decision; Congress did not. The North Atlantic Council (NAC) "approved" a number of measures and "agreed" that any direct attacks against remaining safe areas would justify air operations as determined "by the common judgment of NATO and U.N. military commanders."[54] Clinton said he authorized the actions "in conjunction with our NATO allies to implement the relevant U.N. Security Council resolutions and NATO decisions."[55] He said nothing about acting in conjunction with Congress or statutory authority. On 12 September, he regarded the bombing attacks as "authorized by the United Nations."[56]

GROUND TROOPS TO BOSNIA

In 1995, Clinton decided to introduce about 25,000 ground forces into Bosnia. The Senate debated an amendment regarding troops to Bosnia but once again crafted legally nonbinding language. It would be the "sense of the Senate" that no funds should be used to deploy combat-equipped U.S. forces for any ground operations in Bosnia and Herzegovina unless "Congress approves in advance the deployment of such forces." Exceptions allowed the president to deploy U.S. ground forces if they were needed to evacuate U.S. peacekeeping forces from a "situation of imminent danger, to undertake emergency air rescue operations, or to provide for the airborne delivery of humanitarian supplies."[57]

Debate on this amendment illustrates how much legislators deferred to the president on the deployment of troops. The author of the amendment, Senator Gregg, felt "strongly that prior to the President taking this action, he should come to the Congress and ask for our approval." However, nothing in the amendment required congressional approval. Senator Sam Nunn (D-Ga.) supported the amendment only because it did not have the effect of law: "If it did tie the President's hands at this critical juncture while the peace negotiations are underway, I would oppose it and vote against it."[58] Senator John Kerry (D-Mass.) agreed that if the amendment's language was legally binding, many senators would oppose it.[59]

Senator Paul Simon (D-Ill.) announced that he would vote against the amendment, even though it was a "sense of the Senate," because foreign policy cannot be effective "if Congress micromanages it." Senator Bill Cohen (R-Maine) disputed that point, noting that Clinton was about to deploy 25,000 troops "to one of the most hostile regions in the world" and "without having any sort of defined plan presented to us."[60] The Gregg amendment passed the Senate, ninety-four to two.[61]

As Congress debated statutory language on sending troops to Bosnia, Secretary of State Warren Christopher warned that Clinton would not be "bound" by any congressional ban on funding. The administration said it was prepared to go ahead regardless of what Congress legislated.[62] At a news conference on 19 October, Clinton said that he hoped to get congressional "support" but implied that he would send the troops to Bosnia with or without legislative action.[63]

The House also debated presidential authority to commit ground troops to Bosnia. On 30 October, by a vote of 315 to 103, the House passed a nonbinding resolution that U.S. troops should not be deployed without congressional approval.[64] Ninety-three Democrats—nearly half of those in the House—joined 222 Republicans to support the resolution. Although House Minority Leader Dick Gephardt voted against the resolution, he said, "None of us wants to see American troops in Bosnia without the prior approval of this body."[65] He supported the second part of the resolution (requiring congressional authorization for the deployment) but not the first part (about peace negotiations in Bosnia). He thought the first part was too disruptive of ongoing negotiations. Other Democrats, such as Lee Hamilton and James Moran, voted against the resolution but agreed that Congress should have to approve the sending of U.S. ground troops to Bosnia.[66]

The House majority of 315 to 103 for a nonbinding resolution slipped a bit on 17 November, when the House voted on legislation that would have legal effect. This bill prohibited the use of funds to deploy U.S. ground troops in Bosnia unless Congress specifically provided funds for that purpose. The margin this time fell to 242 to 171.[67] Instead of the ninety-three Democrats supporting the measure on 30 October, only twenty-eight Democrats backed a legally binding requirement.

Hamilton's position expressed in the past—that the president needs prior authorization from Congress for military deployments—had changed. He opposed the bill because it "ties the hands of the President. It tells the commander in chief that he cannot deploy troops to Bosnia, period. When you are the commander in chief, you have the power to deploy troops. That is fundamental, and this bill takes away that power."[68] If the president, as commander in chief, has the fundamental power to deploy troops, why should there ever be prior authorization or any debate on legislative language? Also, the bill did not say that Clinton "cannot deploy troops to Bosnia, period." He could deploy them but only after Congress had appropriated funds specifically for that objective. As Benjamin Gilman, chairman of the House Committee on International Relations, later noted: "This resolution does not rule out the deployment of United States forces to Bosnia, but it does make certain that the President come to the Congress first."[69]

Twelve Republicans voted against the 17 November version. James B. Longley Jr., of Maine, said he was "not a supporter of putting American troops on the ground in Bosnia. I think it would be a terrible mistake." Nevertheless, he deferred to the president: "I have to respect the authority of the Commander in Chief to conduct foreign policy. . . . I think there is no greater threat to American lives than a Congress that attempts to micromanage foreign policy. I have told the President that I would respect his authority as Commander in Chief."[70] How is it "micromanagement" to debate sending ground troops to Bosnia? Why are American lives threatened when Congress opposes military intervention? Aren't American lives threatened when the president puts them in harm's way? And why wasn't Longley's respect for the president balanced by his respect for the Constitution?

The administration expressed interest in obtaining legislative support—but not legislative authority. In a letter to Senator Robert C. Byrd on 19 October, Clinton invites "an expression of support by Congress."[71] He told reporters on 31 October that if a peace agreement were reached, he would request "an expression of support" in Congress for committing U.S. troops to a NATO implementation force.[72] In a letter to Speaker Newt Gingrich on 13 November, Clinton continues to avoid any suggestion that he needed authorization from Congress before sending U.S. ground forces to Bosnia.[73]

In an address to the nation on 27 November, Clinton justified the deployment as a way of stopping "the killing of innocent civilians, especially children, and at the same time, to bring stability to Central Europe, a region of the world that is vital to our national interests. It is the right thing to do."[74] That language parallels his justification for invading Haiti: it was the right thing, even if not the legal thing. On 6 December, having approved the NATO operation plan for sending ground troops to Bosnia, he said he would be requesting "an expression of support from the Congress."[75] The support never came.

The response in Congress depended greatly on what Bob Dole, the Senate majority leader, would do. On 27 November, he made it clear that legislative prerogatives were subordinate to presidential interests. It was Dole's view that Clinton had "the authority and the power under the Constitution to do what he feels should be done regardless of what Congress does."[76] There would be no checks and balances system, no tussling for power. Once the president had announced his policy, legislators would dutifully fall in line. Congress, as an independent branch, did not exist. It was not remotely coequal.

Dole spoke as the Republican front-runner for president in 1996. Instead of demonstrating leadership and protecting institutional interests, he deferred to the president and the polls: "We need to find some way to be able to support the President and I think we need to wait and see what the American reaction is."[77] Other senators developed the idea that presidential commitments abroad, even if misguided, were sacrosanct. Slade Gorton (R-Wash.) believed that Clinton's commitment to Bosnia "was both unwise and improvident. Nonetheless, it was made by the President."[78] Several senators rejected that theory. Jon Kyl (R-Ariz.) insisted that Congress "has to make it clear to the President that he cannot simply go around making premature commitments without the advice and consent of the Congress."[79] Senator Byrd spoke out in defense of congressional war prerogatives, as did Senators Kay Bailey Hutchison (R-Tex.), Russ Feingold (D-Wis.), and James Inhofe (R-Okla.).[80]

On 13 and 14 December, the Senate considered several measures regarding U.S. troops to Bosnia. One approach was a nonbinding resolution with two parts: expressing congressional opposition to sending the troops while also "strongly" supporting the troops.[81] Senators tried to walk a fine line, not wanting their opposition to the deployment to be interpreted as a lack of support for U.S. soldiers. This resolution fell, forty-seven to fifty-two. The Senate also rejected a House bill prohibiting the use of defense funds for the deployment of ground troops to Bosnia unless the funds were specifically appropriated by law. That bill failed, twenty-two to seventy-seven.[82] The Senate then passed, sixty-nine to thirty, a multipart bill providing support for U.S. troops but expressing "reservations" about sending them to Bosnia.[83]

Senator Dole explained some of the purposes behind the bill that passed. One objective was to shift responsibility from Congress to the president. Dole said that Clinton "made this decision and he takes responsibility. It was his decision to send troops and his decision alone."[84] That is, if anything went wrong, it would be the fault of President Clinton, not Congress. Congress backed away from the merits of sending troops to Bosnia. Dole remarked: "This resolution does not endorse the President's decision. It does not endorse the agreement reached in Dayton."[85] He explained his position: "We can posture and complain about the President's decision. I do not like it. He knows I do not like it. I told him I do not like it."[86] The bill was a way for senators to oppose Clinton's policy while praising the soldiers being sent to carry it out.

On the same day as these Senate votes, the House acted on a series of measures related to Bosnia. By a vote of 210 to 218, the House failed to pass a bill prohibiting funds from being used to deploy troops to Bosnia. It next voted 287 to 141 to pass a nonbinding House resolution regarding enforcement of the peace agreement. The resolution expressed "serious concerns and opposition to the president's policy" but declared that the House was confident that U.S. troops "will perform their responsibilities with professional excellence, dedicated patriotism, and exemplary courage." Like the Senate, the House was intent on having it both ways. Another House resolution, also "unequivocally" supporting U.S. troops but omitting direct criticism of the president's policy, lost 190 to 237.[87] The net result was that President Clinton was able to deploy 20,000 ground troops to Bosnia without first seeking or obtaining authority from Congress.

On 21 December, Clinton said that he expected that the military mission to Bosnia "can be accomplished in about a year."[88] A year later he extended the troop deployment for another "18 months,"[89] but the eighteen-month extension came and went, with the Clinton administration no longer attempting to set an end point to the commitment in Bosnia. On 3 March 1998, President Clinton told Congress that he did not propose "a fixed end-date" for U.S. troops in Bosnia.[90] Efforts by Congress to force withdrawal of troops by a certain date or to require authorization for continued deployment came to naught.

The Clinton administration's initial cost estimate for the Bosnia intervention was $1 billion or more.[91] A month and a half later Clinton put the cost at $1.5 billion.[92] By 2000, the cost had climbed beyond $10 billion. The administration was able to fund the commitment initially without coming to Congress for an appropriation that specifically designated funds for Bosnia. Instead, Clinton was able to reprogram funds from other programs to the Bosnia commitment. To shift those funds, he needed the approval only of certain congressional committees, not from Congress as a whole.[93]

THE WAR AGAINST YUGOSLAVIA

In October 1998, Clinton was once again threatening air strikes against the Serbs, this time to protect the ethnic Albanian majority in Kosovo. At a news conference on 8 October, Clinton stated: "Yesterday I decided that the United States would vote to give NATO the authority to carry out military strikes against Serbia if President Milosevic continues to defy the international community."[94] It is an interesting phrase: "*I* decided that the United States. . . ." Whatever Clinton decided would be America's policy. The decision to go to war against another country was in the hands of one person, exactly what the Framers thought they had avoided.

Clinton's chief foreign policy advisers went to Capitol Hill to consult with legislators but not to obtain their approval.[95] Although Congress was to be given no formal role in the use of force against the Serbs, legislatures in other NATO countries had to authorize military action in Kosovo. The Italian Parliament had to vote approval for the NATO strikes.[96] The German Supreme

Court ruled that the Bundestag, which had been dissolved with the election that ousted Chancellor Kohl, would have to be recalled to approve deployment of German aircraft and troops to Kosovo.[97] Congress was content to watch from the backseat.

On 11 March 1999, with Clinton close to unleashing air strikes against Serbia, the House voted on a resolution to support U.S. armed forces as part of a NATO peacekeeping operation. The resolution—purporting to "authorize" Clinton to deploy U.S. forces to implement a peace agreement—passed 219 to 191.[98] However, legislators were voting on a *concurrent resolution* (H. Con. Res. 42), and Congress cannot authorize anything in a concurrent resolution. It is not legally binding because it is not presented to the president for his signature or veto. What lawmakers voted on was something that started out as a joint resolution but changed at some point to a concurrent resolution, with no one alert enough or willing enough to change the word *authorize* to something more appropriate, like *support*.

Furthermore, members of the House clearly anticipated a peace agreement between Serbs and Kosovars. The Kosovars eventually accepted the plan, but the Serbs did not. Therefore, the House vote cannot be taken as support for a bombing operation that would begin within two weeks.

By the time the Senate voted on 23 March, negotiations had collapsed, and air strikes were imminent. The Senate voted fifty-eight to forty-one to support military air operations and missile strikes against the Federal Republic of Yugoslavia (Serbia and Montenegro).[99] Like the House, the Senate mistakenly used the word *authorize* in a concurrent resolution (S. Con. Res. 21). The war against Serbia began on 24 March.

On 28 April, the House took a series of votes on the war in Serbia. It voted 249 to 180 to prohibit the use of appropriated funds for the deployment of U.S. ground forces unless first authorized by Congress. A motion to direct the removal of U.S. armed forces from Yugoslavia failed, 139 to 290. A resolution to declare a state of war between the United States and Yugoslavia was rejected, 2 to 427. A fourth vote, to authorize the air operations and missile strikes, failed on a tie vote, 213 to 213.

Newspaper editorials and commentators derided the House for these multiple and supposedly conflicting votes, but the House at least articulated some basic values. It insisted that Congress authorize the introduction of ground troops, and it refused to grant authority for the air strikes. Lawmakers pointed to the irony of President Clinton seeking the approval of eighteen NATO nations but not the approval of Congress. Congressman Ernest Istook (R-Okla.) remarked: "President Clinton asked many nations to agree to attack Yugoslavia, but he failed to get permission from one crucial country, America."[100]

In contrast to the House, the Senate decided to duck the issue by tabling a series of proposals. Senator John McCain offered a joint resolution to authorize President Clinton to use "all necessary force and other means, in concert with United States allies, to accomplish United States and North Atlantic Treaty Organization objectives in the Federal Republic of Yugoslavia (Serbia and Montenegro)." The clear intent was to give congressional support to continued air strikes as well as anything else the president decided was appropriate, including the introduction of ground troops. Supporters of the resolution claimed that it offered Congress an opportunity to take responsibility, but Senator Kay Bailey Hutchison (R-Tex.) argued convincingly that the resolution was an exercise of legislative abdication.[101]

Rather than consider the resolution on its merits, with possible amendments, the Senate tabled it, seventy-eight to twenty-two.[102] Had the resolution passed, the legal purpose was unclear. Senator McCain at times described his amendment as unnecessary because the president already had, he said, sufficient authority under the Constitution to do whatever he liked militarily: "The Presidency already has its authority. . . . If the Senate does nothing, . . . the President has the power to commit all armies to the conflict in Yugoslavia tomorrow."[103] Then why enact the legislation? To push Clinton to do what he could do anyway? In that case, the McCain resolution would have operated more like a nonbinding, sense-of-Congress measure.

A few weeks later the Senate tabled another amendment, this one by Senator Specter, to direct the president to seek approval from Congress before introducing ground troops into Yugoslavia. Failure to obtain approval would deny the president funds to conduct the operation.[104] Specter said, "It is high time that Congress stood up on its hind legs and said we are not going to be involved in wars unless Congress authorizes them."[105] Later he argued: "We don't have the authority to delegate our constitutional authority."[106] His amendment was tabled, fifty-two to forty-eight. An amendment by Senator Bob Smith (R-N.H.), to prohibit funding for military operations in Yugoslavia unless Congress enacted specific authorization, was tabled seventy-seven to twenty-one.[107]

Through these successive tabling motions, the Senate might as well have considered one final motion: "Do we want to exercise our constitutional powers and participate in matters of war?" Tabled, sixty-three to thirty-seven.

During the bombing of Serbia and Kosovo, Congressman Tom Campbell (R-Calif.) went to court with twenty-five other House colleagues to seek a declaration that President Clinton had violated the Constitution and the War Powers Resolution by conducting the air offensive without congressional authorization. On 8 June 1999, a district judge held that Campbell did not have standing to raise his claims. Although each House had taken a number of votes, sometimes supporting Clinton and sometimes not, Congress had never as an entire institution ordered Clinton to cease military operations. In that sense, there was no "constitutional impasse" or "actual confrontation" for the court to resolve. Instead, the court was faced with a small group of lawmakers who objected to presidential conduct. As the court noted: "If Congress had directed the President to remove forces from their positions and he had refused to do so or if Congress had refused to appropriate or authorize the use of funds for the air strikes in Yugoslavia and the President had decided to spend that money (or money earmarked for other purposes) anyway, that likely would have constituted an actual confrontation sufficient to confer standing on legislative plaintiffs."[108]

The district court's decision was affirmed by the D.C. Circuit on 18 February 2000. Writing for the majority, Judge Laurence H. Silberman held that the members of Congress lacked standing to bring the suit. On that point he was joined by Judge A. Raymond Randolph, who nevertheless wrote a concurrence offering different views on the standing issue. Judge David S. Tatel wrote a dissenting opinion, agreeing with Silberman's analysis of the standing issue but disagreeing with Silberman's position that the case posed a nonjusticiable political question.[109] The appellate court's decision was taken to the Supreme Court, which, on 2 October 2000, denied certiorari.

AFGHANISTAN AND THE SUDAN

In August 1998, President Clinton ordered cruise missiles into Afghanistan to attack paramilitary camps and into Sudan to destroy a pharmaceutical factory. He justified this use of military force as retaliation for bombings earlier in the month against U.S. embassies in Nairobi and Dar es Salaam. The administration claimed that Osama bin Laden was behind the embassy attacks, that he used the training complex in Afghanistan, and that he was somehow related to the pharmaceutical plant.

Clinton explained that he selected the two targets because "of the imminent threat they presented to our national security."[110] It was never clear why the pharmaceutical factory in Sudan represented an "imminent threat." Although Clinton claimed that the plant was "involved in the production of materials for chemical weapons,"[111] questions were raised as to whether the plant was producing a precursor chemical for a nerve gas or an agricultural insecticide. The Pentagon later conceded that it was unaware that the plant produced a large share of the medicine used in the Sudan.[112] Despite a $30 billion budget for the intelligence agencies, the administration had no one to walk into the plant to see whether it actually produced pharmaceuticals.

In February 1999, the owner of the pharmaceutical plant filed a lawsuit in a U.S. court, insisting that the Clinton administration compensate him for the facility and release millions of dollars in assets frozen by U.S. officials on the ground that he was linked to bin Laden. In May, the administration released $24 million of his assets. A separate suit was filed seeking compensation, and legislation (H.R. 5290, H. Res. 593) was introduced for the same purpose. Two years after the attack on Sudan, there are still questions about whether the plant had any role in the manufacture of nerve gas or had any connection to the bombing of the U.S. embassies in Africa.

CONTINUED BOMBING OF IRAQ

Throughout his eight years in office, Clinton used military force against Iraq. After ordering cruise missiles into Baghdad in June 1993, in September 1996 he launched other missiles against Iraq in response to an attack by Iraqi forces against the Kurdish-controlled city of Irbil in northern Iraq. Cruise missiles also struck air defense capabilities in southern Iraq. Clinton explained that the missiles "sent the following message to Saddam Hussein: When you abuse your own people or threaten your neighbors, you must pay a price."[113]

There was no claim here of self-defense or the need to protect the lives of Americans. The rationale was different: Whenever foreign leaders abuse their people and threaten their neighbors, a U.S. president can take military action to punish them. With that standard, how many nations could a president attack? It is quite a long list. Start with Russia and China and then turn to smaller but still substantial countries in Asia, Africa, and other continents. Clinton's argument here is even less credible than his rationale for the 1993 cruise missile attack against Baghdad.

Toward the end of January 1998, Clinton threatened once again to bomb Iraq, this time because Saddam Hussein had refused to give U.N. inspectors full access to examine Iraqi sites for possible nuclear, chemical, and biological programs. The bombing was postponed when U.N. Secretary General Kofi Annan visited Baghdad in February and negotiated a settlement with Iraq. The Clinton administration accepted the settlement, with reservations, but made clear that military force remained an option if Iraq failed to comply with the new agreement.

Congressional leaders had drafted a resolution (S. Con. Res. 71) that condemned Iraq and urged Clinton to take "all necessary and appropriate actions to respond." The language had an eerie resemblance to that of the Tonkin Gulf Resolution of 1964, which authorized President Johnson to use all necessary force in Vietnam. Senator Max Cleland, a Democrat from Georgia, led a handful of Democrats in opposing the resolution. It was never adopted.[114]

The following argument is the closest anyone ever came to a legal justification for the bombing. When Congress passed the authorization bill in January 1991 empowering President Bush to take military action against Iraq, it somehow gave advance blessing to whatever the U.N. Security Council might do in the future in issuing resolutions on Iraq. On its face, such a claim—delegating war in perpetuity—would seem preposterous. Congress could no more surrender its prerogatives over foreign policy to an international body than it could its power of the purse.

Here are the specifics of the argument. On 14 January 1991, Congress enacted P.L. 102–1 to authorize U.S. armed force against Iraq. President Bush could use military force pursuant to U.N. Security Council Resolution 678 "in order to achieve implementation of Security Council Resolutions 660, 661, 662, 664, 665, 666, 667, 669, 670, 674, and 677."[115] This statute is usually interpreted as congressional authority to drive Iraq out of Kuwait, which was the purpose of Resolution 678, adopted on 29 November 1990. All the earlier resolutions, from 660 to 677, prepared the way for 678. Resolution 660, passed on 2 August 1990, condemned Iraq's invasion of Kuwait and demanded immediate withdrawal. Resolution 661 imposed economic sanctions. Resolutions 662 to 677 reinforced the earlier resolutions and added other restrictions.

Can one argue that Congress, on 14 January 1991, transferred its constitutional power to the Security Council? Here are the steps of that argument. Resolution 678 authorized member states to use all necessary means "to uphold and implement resolution 660 (1990) and all subsequent relevant resolutions and to restore international peace and security in the area."[116] Advocates of presidential power claim that the phrase "all subsequent relevant resolutions" includes whatever the Security Council promulgated after 14 January 1991.

The language of Resolution 678 is somewhat ambiguous. What does *subsequent* refer to? Any resolution issued after 678? Or any resolution issued after 660 but before 678? It could be read either way. The natural reading is the latter one because the objective was to oust Iraq from Kuwait. President Bush never had authority to send ground troops north to Baghdad. That would have exceeded his statutory authority and violated the understanding of other nations that were part of the multilateral alliance.

The most unnatural reading would be to conclude that Congress, in passing P.L. 102-1, had abdicated its constitutional powers to the Security Council and that henceforth the magnitude of the U.S. military commitment would be decided by U.N. resolutions, not congressional statutes. Under this far-fetched theory, whatever the Security Council decided would compel Congress to vote the necessary appropriations. Congressional debate on P.L. 102-1 provides zero support for that theory.

In December 1998, President Clinton ordered four days of bombing in Iraq. He justified the military action as an effort to attack Iraq's nuclear, chemical, and biological weapons programs and because Iraq had failed to cooperate completely with U.N. weapons inspectors.[117] He also explained that U.S. credibility would suffer if it did not carry through its earlier threat to use military action if Iraq interfered with U.N. inspectors: "If Saddam can cripple the weapons inspection system and get away with it, he would conclude that the international community, led by the United States, has simply lost its will. . . . If we turn our backs on his defiance, the credibility of U.S. power as a check against Saddam will be destroyed."[118] The Pentagon later disclosed that U.S. and British forces were "taking care to avoid hitting Iraqi factories suspected of producing chemical and biological weapons" for fear of unleashing plumes of poisons on civilians.[119]

In a letter to Congress, Clinton argues that the military operation in Iraq was "consistent with and has been taken in support of numerous U.N. Security Council resolutions, including Resolutions 678 and 687." In this same message, he claims that he acted under the authorization of P.L. 102-1, enacted in January 1991.[120] There is no legal basis for that argument. In the midst of the four-day bombing, the House passed a nonbinding resolution supporting the armed forces and reaffirming the policy of removing Saddam Hussein. Congressman David Skaggs, a Democrat from Colorado, faulted both Clinton and Congress for violating the war power provisions of the Constitution.[121]

As a result of the December bombing, there were now no U.N. inspectors to monitor chemical, biological, and nuclear capability in Iraq. Secretary of State Madeleine Albright and Secretary of Defense William S. Cohen warned that the United States and the United Kingdom would continue to act militarily against Iraq, with or without the approval of other allies or the U.N. Security Council.[122] The rationale of deriving legal support from U.N. Security Council resolutions had apparently been jettisoned. Over the following eight months, the United States and the United Kingdom conducted repeated air strikes against Iraq, firing more than 1,100 missiles against 359 targets—triple the number of targets attacked during the four-day operation in December 1998.[123]

Initiatives by President Bush expanded the scope of executive power, especially his claim that he could go to war against Iraq without seeking authority from Congress. Instead, he went to the U.N. Security Council and obtained a resolution giving a blessing for military action. He also put together an alliance of nations that supported the offense against Iraq. President Clinton built on those precedents, seeking resolutions from the Security Council for military actions against Haiti and Bosnia. In addition, he turned to NATO for "authority" for military operations against Yugoslavia. Thus, international and regional organizations have become instruments for circumventing the constitutional role of Congress. Legislators have yet to discover an effective way of protecting their institutional interests. Large majorities can coalesce around nonbinding resolutions, but as soon as the resolution changes to legally binding language, or as the deadline for action comes clearly into view, Congress backs off. By the election year 2000, there appeared to be no limit on what a president could do in committing the nation to war.

As a result, the power of the national government has been fundamentally transformed. The Framers thought that they had eliminated monarchical decisions to independently and unilaterally take the nation to war. That model of government is back. The Framers believed that a system of checks and balances would give each branch an interest and stake in protecting their institution and fighting off encroachments. That is not happening. Finally, the Constitution is no longer a reference point for deciding how we go to war. Instead, questions on the use of military force are now left to political power and public opinion.

NOTES

1. Louis Fisher and David Gray Adler, "The War Powers Resolution: Time to Say Goodbye," *Political Science Quarterly* 113, no. 1 (spring 1998): 1–20.
2. George Bush and Brent Scowcroft, *A World Transformed* (New York: Knopf, 1998), 446.
3. Louis Fisher, "Sidestepping Congress: Presidents Acting under the UN and NATO," *Case Western Reserve Law Review* 47, no. 4 (summer 1997): 1237–79.
4. Louis Fisher, "President Clinton as Commander in Chief," in *Rivals for Power*, ed. James A. Thurber (Washington, D.C.: Congressional Quarterly, 1996), 215.
5. Public Papers of the Presidents, 1993, I, 337.
6. Public Papers of the Presidents, 1993, I, 938, 940.
7. "Show of Strength Offers Benefits for Clinton," *Washington Post*, 28 June 1993: A1, A14.
8. Public Papers of the Presidents, 1993, I, 938–39.
9. Michael Ratner and Jules Lobel, "Bombing Baghdad: Illegal Reprisal or Self-Defense?" *Legal Times*, 5 July 1993: 24.
10. Public Papers of the Presidents, 1992, II, 2176, 2180.
11. 139 Cong. Rec. 22748 (1993).

12. 139 Cong. Rec. 22754 (1993).
13. Public Papers of the Presidents, 1993, II, 1705.
14. Public Papers of the Presidents, 1993, II, 1740.
15. 107 Stat. 1476, sec. 8151(b)(2)(B) (1993). For further details on military actions by Clinton, see Louis Fisher, *Congressional Abdication on War and Spending* (College Station: Texas A&M University Press, 2000), 80–114.
16. Bill Clinton and Al Gore, *Putting People First: How We Can All Change America* (New York: Times Books, 1992), 137–38.
17. 139 Cong. Rec. 25729 (1993).
18. 139 Cong. Rec. 25729 (1993).
19. 140 Cong. Rec. 11632–33 (1994).
20. 140 Cong. Rec. 12420–21 (1994).
21. *Congressional Quarterly Weekly Report*, 28 May 1994: 1420; *Congressional Quarterly Weekly Report*, 11 June 1994: 1560.
22. 140 Cong. Rec. 15016 (1994).
23. 140 Cong. Rec. 15016 (1994).
24. 140 Cong. Rec. 15018 (1994).
25. 140 Cong. Rec. 15019 (1994).
26. 140 Cong. Rec. 15023 (1994).
27. 140 Cong. Rec. 15031 (1994).
28. 140 Cong. Rec. 15032 (1994).
29. Louis Fisher, *Presidential War Power* (Lawrence: University Press of Kansas, 1995), 24–28.
30. 140 Cong. Rec. 15047, 15052 (1994).
31. 140 Cong. Rec. 19324 (1994).
32. 140 Cong. Rec. 19320 (1994).
33. Public Papers of the Presidents, 1994, II, 1559.
34. Public Papers of the Presidents, 1994, II, 1551.
35. Public Papers of the Presidents, 1994, II, 1549.
36. 140 Cong. Rec. H10972–73 (daily ed. 5 October 1994); 140 Cong. Rec. H11121–22 (daily ed. 6 October 1994); 108 Stat. 4358, sec. 1(b) (1994).
37. 140 Cong. Rec. 28236 (1994).
38. Public Papers of the Presidents, 1993, I, 594.
39. Public Papers of the Presidents, 1993, II, 1455.
40. Public Papers of the Presidents, 1993, II, 1781.
41. Public Papers of the Presidents, 1993, II, 1620.
42. 139 Cong. Rec. 22304–05 (1993).
43. Public Papers of the Presidents, 1993, II, 1763.
44. Public Papers of the Presidents, 1993, II, 1764.
45. Public Papers of the Presidents, 1993, II, 1770.
46. 139 Cong. Rec. 25479, 25485 (1993).
47. 139 Cong. Rec. 25483 (1993).
48. 139 Cong. Rec. 25483 (1993).
49. 107 Stat. 1474, sec. 8146 (1993).
50. Public Papers of the Presidents, 1994, I, 186.
51. Public Papers of the Presidents, 1994, I, 355.

52. Public Papers of the Presidents, 1994, I, 661.

53. "NATO Bombs Serbs in War's Biggest Air Raid," *Washington Post*, 30 August 1995: A1.

54. Public Papers of the Presidents, 1995, II, 1280.

55. Public Papers of the Presidents, 1995, II, 1280.

56. Public Papers of the Presidents, 1995, II, 1353.

57. 141 Cong. Rec. S14634 (daily ed. 29 September 1995).

58. 141 Cong. Rec. S14634 (daily ed. 29 September 1995).

59. 141 Cong. Rec. S14636 (daily ed. 29 September 1995).

60. 141 Cong. Rec. S14636 (daily ed. 29 September 1995).

61. 141 Cong. Rec. S14640 (daily ed. 29 September 1995).

62. "President Not 'Bound' by Hill on Deploying Troops, Christopher Says," *Washington Post*, 18 October 1995: A27.

63. Public Papers of the Presidents, 1995, II, 1630.

64. 141 Cong. Rec. H11398–422 (daily ed. 30 October 1995).

65. 141 Cong. Rec. H11403 (daily ed. 30 October 1995).

66. 141 Cong. Rec. H11404, H11407–08 (daily ed. 30 October 1995).

67. 141 Cong. Rec. H13248 (daily ed. 17 November 1995).

68. 141 Cong. Rec. H13224 (daily ed. 17 November 1995).

69. 141 Cong. Rec. H13229 (daily ed. 17 November 1995).

70. 141 Cong. Rec. H13239 (daily ed. 17 November 1995).

71. 141 Cong. Rec. S15394 (daily ed. 17 November 1995).

72. Public Papers of the Presidents, 1995, II, 1702.

73. 141 Cong. Rec. H13228 (daily ed. 17 November 1995).

74. Public Papers of the Presidents, 1995, II, 1784.

75. Public Papers of the Presidents, 1995, II, 1857.

76. 141 Cong. Rec. S17529 (daily ed. 27 November 1995).

77. "As Dole Equivocates on Troop Deployment, Most GOP Rivals Oppose Plan," *Washington Post*, 28 November 1995: A9.

78. 141 Cong. Rec. S17584 (daily ed. 28 November 1995).

79. 141 Cong. Rec. S17543 (daily ed. 28 November 1995).

80. 141 Cong. Rec. S18506–12 (daily ed. 13 December 1995), S18403–04 (daily ed. 12 December 1995), S18458–59 (daily ed. 13 December 1995), S18398–401 (daily ed. 12 December 1995), and S18465–66 (daily ed. 13 December 1995).

81. 141 Cong. Rec. S18512 (daily ed. 13 December 1995).

82. 141 Cong. Rec. S18470 (daily ed. 13 December 1995).

83. 141 Cong. Rec. S18552 (daily ed. 13 December 1995).

84. 141 Cong. Rec. S18549 (daily ed. 13 December 1995).

85. 141 Cong. Rec. S18550 (daily ed. 13 December 1995).

86. 141 Cong. Rec. S18550 (daily ed. 13 December 1995).

87. 141 Cong. Rec. H14796–872 (daily ed. 13 December 1995).

88. Public Papers of the Presidents, 1995, II, 1917.

89. Public Papers of the Presidents, 1996, II, 2221.

90. 34 Weekly Comp. Pres. Doc. 374 (3 March 1998).

91. "White House to Ask $1 Billion for Bosnia Troop Deployment," *Washington Post*, 28 September 1995: A24.

92. "Cost of U.S. Bosnia Force Put at $1.5 Billion," *Washington Post*, 11 November 1995: A21.

93. For details on this financing, see Fisher, *Congressional Abdication on War and Spending*, 99–100.

94. 34 Weekly Comp. Pres. Doc. 2008 (8 October 1998).

95. "Hill Signals Support for Airstrikes," *Washington Post*, 2 October 1998: A35.

96. "Italy's Center-Left Government Is Toppled by One Vote," *New York Times*, 10 October 1998: A3.

97. "Allies Grim, Milosevic Defiant amid Kosovo Uncertainty," *Washington Post*, 8 October 1998: A32.

98. 145 Cong. Rec. H1249–50 (daily ed. 11 March 1999).

99. 145 Cong. Rec. S3118 (daily ed. 23 March 1999).

100. 145 Cong. Rec. H2419 (daily ed. 28 April 1999).

101. 145 Cong. Rec. S4533–34 (daily ed. 3 May 1999).

102. 145 Cong. Rec. S4616 (daily ed. 4 May 1999). Most of the debate occurred on 3 May (see 145 Cong. Rec. S4514–70).

103. 145 Cong. Rec. S4553 (daily ed. 3 May 1999).

104. 145 Cong. Rec. S5809 (daily ed. 24 May 1999).

105. 145 Cong. Rec. S5920 (daily ed. 24 May 1999).

106. 145 Cong. Rec. S5939 (daily ed. 24 May 1999).

107. 145 Cong. Rec. S6034–40 (daily ed. 26 May 1999).

108. *Campbell v. Clinton*, 52 F.Supp.24, 43 (D.D.C. 1999).

109. *Campbell v. Clinton*, 203 F.3d 19 (D.C. Cir. 2000).

110. 34 Weekly Comp. Pres. Doc. 1643 (1998).

111. 34 Weekly Comp. Pres. Doc. 1644 (1998).

112. For further details and citations, see Fisher, *Congressional Abdication on War and Spending*, 104–05, 198.

113. Public Papers of the Presidents, 1996, II, 1469.

114. "Cleland Warns against Repeating Tonkin Gulf Mistake," *Congressional Quarterly Weekly Report*, 31 January 1998: 247; "Iraq Resolution Sends Chills through Some in Congress," *Washington Post*, 3 February 1998: A13.

115. 105 Stat. 3, sec. 2(a) (1991).

116. *Congressional Quarterly Weekly Report*, 1 December 1990: 4007.

117. 34 Weekly Comp. Pres. Doc. 2494–97 (16 December 1998).

118. 34 Weekly Comp. Pres. Doc. 2496 (16 December 1998).

119. "Jets Said to Avoid Poison Gas Sites," *New York Times*, 18 December 1998: A1.

120. 34 Weekly Comp. Pres. Doc. 2513 (18 December 1998).

121. 144 Cong. Rec. H11727 (daily ed. 17 December 1998).

122. "U.S. Warns Iraq of More Raids," *Washington Post*, 21 December 1998: Al.

123. "In Intense but Little-Noticed Fight, Allies Have Bombed Iraq All Year," *New York Times*, 13 August 1999: A1.

12

Conclusions about Congressional–Presidential Rivalries

James A. Thurber

As the fractious post–2000 election relationship between President George W. Bush and the 107th Congress reveals, relations between the president and Congress are still polarized and combative even though Bush campaigned on the promise of bringing more comity and bipartisanship to Washington. Bush promised to bring people together with pragmatism, to make government smaller and more efficient, and to "get it done" with pragmatism rather than ideology. In the campaign, Bush sought to put distance between his candidacy and the right-wing extremism of congressional Republicans. He sought to associate Gore and the Clinton administration with Congress as part of the "failures" in Washington. That campaign strategy, theme, and message reinforced rivalry and did not do well for building cross-party coalitions in Congress, as President Bush found out during his first few weeks in office.

The elections for the U.S. Congress were equally indecisive. For the first time since 1881, the U.S. Senate was tied between the two parties, and the U.S. House was split 221 to 212 in favor of the Republicans, effectively tied with the smallest majority in that body since 1953. The Democrats defeated five incumbent Republican senators, and it was the third consecutive election in which the Democrats gained seats in the House. Although President Bush had unified party government, the first time since 1954 for the Republicans, there were no presidential coattails, no presidential mandate, and no clear policy direction for Congress. The 2000 election created the perfect environment for conflict and deadlock between the president and Congress.

The studies in this book present original research that clearly shows that the rise in conflict between the president and Congress is not simply a matter of personalities. There are deep-seated constitutional, political, and structural sources for the recent increase in polarization between the executive and legislative branches.[1] These factors could not change simply because of President George W. Bush's "charm offensive" or his campaign promise to bring more comity to government. The relationship between the White House and Congress changes over time, alternating between reciprocal and combative, cordial and hostile, or even benign neglect.

The relationship between the Congress and the president is more partisan and polarized. This heightened partisanship started in the 1980s, as is shown by the steady increase in partisan congressional voting. The South is no longer the undisputed territory of Democrats. Like all recent presidents, Bush does not enjoy the ideological sympathies of members of the opposing party. James Pfiffner reminds us that political parties are more homogeneous—"Rockfeller Republicans" and "Boll-Weevils" are a thing of the past. The Jeffords defection, plus the marginalization of the Republican Party in the Northeast, reinforces this pattern. As a result, presidents and Bush in particular find it difficult to build and maintain the support of members from the opposing party for their legislative agendas. Filibusters have also increased, as have presidential threats to veto. These factors contribute to the contentious relationship between the president and Congress. The decline in civility in both chambers started in the 1970s and continues in the Bush–107th Congress. Bush is left with no natural congressional coalitional partners except on the far Right, and the very concept of coalition building based on political extremism may be inherently destabilizing. That is a difficult place to build bipartisan coalitions, which he promised to do in his 2000 campaign. President Bush, like other contemporary presidents, needs to coax members of Congress into coalitions but cannot count on his own party support or crossover support from members of the opposing party on most major issues. His historic opportunity to govern from the center after a disputed electoral college victory and a clear popular vote loss was substantially forfeited within days of his assumption of the presidency, as the newly inaugurated president invested his "honeymoon" political capital in reinforcing his ideological base and alienating moderates on both sides of the political aisle.

We are reminded that the constitutional design set by the Framers assigns the president little role in legislating. Stephen Wayne has provided a historical description of how and why presidents first began to enter the legislative arena. He argues that nineteenth-century presidents began to legislate through members. They also used their veto power, and threats of vetoes, to influence congressional activity. As the twentieth century progressed, presidents went even further. They developed a two-track agenda for influencing legislation. Major policy decisions received presidential attention, while the Office of Management and Budget (OMB) and executive agencies handled more minor legislative activity. Wayne also argues that the presidents since Ronald Reagan have most dramatically moved away from the Framers' intent. Chiefs of staff now focus almost exclusively on the legislative agenda, policy directors have Cabinet-level status, and the press is regularly used by presidents and their operatives to influence legislative activity. Presidents seek to sway public opinion and define legislative issues through sophisticated, permanent "public relation teams." These teams use polling, focus groups, and the press to strategically set priorities, cycle issues, and package proposals in ways most likely to ensure legislative success. This ongoing public relations campaign within the White House stands in contrast to the specified legislative role for the president. President George W. Bush has gone above the heads of Congress directly to the American public using grassroots techniques in support of his policy initiatives on a regular basis. His most specific targets were Democratic senators from states that he carried decisively in the November 2000 election. This confrontational approach has major ramifications for presidential and congressional relations.

The nature of party leadership within the House and the Senate has a direct impact on the rivalry between Congress and the president. Roger Davidson shows that within the House, strong party leadership developed as a result of the chaos and lack of responsiveness that characterized the House during the Gilded Age. Strong party leadership saw its zenith in the late nineteenth and early twentieth centuries, until structural and partisan factors led to its erosion in the 1970s. There has been a gradual reemergence of strong party leadership since the 1970s that has had a direct impact on presidential–congressional relations. This corresponds, not coincidentally, with increasing ideological cohesion in both major parties. On the Senate side, strong party leadership emerged roughly during the same period. The increased prominence and power of Senate party leaders, especially since the 1950s, can be traced directly to the need for Senate leaders who could confer with activist White Houses and help them manage their legislative agendas. The relative strength of party leaders in today's Congress is influenced by constitutional and partisan factors, despite the individualist tendencies of most members.

We are also reminded that the skills needed to campaign effectively for office are not the same skills that allow presidents to legislate effectively.[2] Richard Cohen argues that campaigns do have lasting effects for a president's legislative success. Candidate behavior and election results create the climate of expectations in Congress that governs the president's legislative possibilities. Inclusive candidates such as Lyndon Johnson and Reagan, who were big election winners, experience the most success with Congress. George W. Bush was not a big winner. He fell short in the national popular vote, trailing Al Gore by 540,000 votes or 0.5 percent of over 100 million total votes. Bush won in the electoral college by 271 to 267, the narrowest margin by only one election. He was the first minority president since 1888, and the outcome remained uncertain for over a month after the election. He did not have a mandate from the voters, and this had a major impact on his relationship with Congress. New presidents are best positioned to get their legislative agendas through when they enjoy clear mandates, something that obviously did not occur in the 2000 election. If there is no demonstration of inclusion and policy agreement with a substantial number of members of Congress throughout the campaign, then it is difficult to govern. When presidents with clear policy agendas and clear electoral mandates "hit the ground running" at the onset of their presidencies, Congress is most likely to respond favorably, which was not the case for Bush in his early months in office. The president's party is still likely to lose seats during midterm elections, but this loss is tempered by creating a lasting legislative package. Cohen argues that presidents who do not enjoy strong mandates—like George W. Bush, those who run against Congress, and those who do not articulate clear legislative agendas—are ill-advised to take proactive stances when it comes to forming the legislative agenda.

What is the best way to measure presidential influence over Congress? Most of the literature in political science on this topic has two dilemmas: (1) presidential influence often takes place "behind closed doors" and is inaccessible to scholars and (2) presidents often exert influence by doing nothing at all.[3] Measuring inaction by presidents when examining presidential influence over Congress is difficult but essential. Nathan Dietz's model of presidential–congressional relations predicts when policy changes will occur, what changes will be acceptable to moderate members, what policies will be in the "gridlock range," and the conditions under which presidents will veto policies. While his model of presidential influence over Congress has much predictive power, Dietz also takes into account how electoral conditions, divided government, constituents, party in government, and contextual factors affect the president's ability to influence Congress. Dietz also accounts for presidential reputation and prestige in his basic gridlock model of presidential influence.

Gary Andreas and Patrick Griffin, two former senior-level White House aides—one Republican and one Democrat—use their own experiences to critique existing conceptualizations of presidential "success" and "influence" and add to the Dietz explanatory model. They argue that most existing treatments fail to realize the importance of four factors. Presidents alone cannot drive the legislative agenda. Congress influences presidential behavior just as the president influences congressional behavior, presidents are both endogenous and exogenous forces in the legislative process, and contextual factors matter so much that the influence of a president is not constant. Institutional considerations such as the outcome of elections and our constitutional structure, which are outside the president's control, are important factors governing the relationship between Congress and a president.[4] Andres and Griffin argue that focusing simply on roll-call votes or whether a president can maintain and build legislative coalitions obscures the strategies that effective presidents can use to shape legislative outcomes. Presidential influence, winning and losing with Congress, is best evaluated using a broad tapestry of criteria across time and in different policy contexts.

Contemporary presidents use several mechanisms to facilitate communication, policy coordination, and coalition building across the branches, according to Lawrence Evans and Walter Oleszek. Over time a number of important and routinized meetings have developed for the transmission of information between the White House and congressional leaders, primarily within the president's own party. Both national political parties now develop organized message agendas, which feature policy proposals and symbols that party leaders and activists believe will resonate among voters. These message agendas help foster party unity within Congress and facilitate presidential coalition building—primarily within a president's own party. The most significant formal prerogative that presidents use to influence the Senate (and the House) is the veto.[5] Within the interbranch bargaining game, threatened vetoes probably are more important than actual vetoes, especially in divided party government. Formal presidential policy messages have become an important and institutionalized aspect of legislating in Congress, and they serve to enhance the role of the veto and the president in the interbranch bargaining process. Presidential coalition building in Congress is conditional and varies substantially from issue to issue. Thus, presidential success in Congress varies from issue to issue.

Presidential success in the congressional budget process is not absolute and is no exception to the rule that success varies from issue to issue. Leon Panetta uses his experiences and knowledge as former White House chief of staff, OMB director, and chairman of the House Budget Committee to analyze the role of the executive and legislative branches in budgeting, the time frame each uses to act on budgetary issues, and their considerable differences in style when it comes to fashioning, implementing, and agreeing on a budget. Presidents and the executive branch tend to offer detailed budgetary recommendations, and their actions are fairly predictable. There is little doubt that the president is the ultimate arbiter within the executive branch, but it is a different story within Congress. There is no central core of budgetary authority in Congress. Individualism is the norm. Members try to get their pet spending projects into the budget. As a result, congressional action in the budget process is less predictable. The budgetary politics in an era of surpluses has not changed the confrontation between the president and Congress, as has been shown by President George W. Bush's battle over the budget. The battle over budgets has become more contentious and bitter even as the surplus goes up and the debt goes down.

We are reminded by former member of Congress Lee Hamilton that presidents and presidents alone make foreign policy decisions. Presidents are still the chief actors when it comes to foreign policy making, but their dominance is no longer uncontested. Vietnam, Watergate, and the end of the Cold War changed the relationship between Congress and the president in foreign policy. Vietnam and Watergate made the public less trustful of presidents, especially, on matters of foreign policy. The end of the Cold War made foreign policy objectives less clear-cut, and this undermined the president's dominance of foreign policy. As the issues and international actors changed, members of Congress, interest groups, ethnic constituencies within the United States, and others have increasingly aimed to shape U.S. foreign policy objectives. Beyond these new actors, presidents are also forced to deal with more executive agencies that take an interest in foreign policy and an "Information Revolution" that has enabled ordinary citizens and political elites to have increased access to and understanding of foreign policy. The diversity and individualism of members of Congress have led to a more assertive Congress in the foreign policy arena. Hamilton argues for a relationship between the president and Congress that is based on consultation, not just satisfying constituents.

Louis Fisher considers the case of the first President Bush and President Clinton in detail to demonstrate the difference between presidents' formal war-making powers and their power in reality. He argues that the Framers feared concentrating war-making power in the hands of a single person and, as a result, gave Congress the authority to authorize military action. Today, Fisher argues, this constitutional design has been fundamentally transformed, and presidents now enjoy the monarchical power in war making that the Framers feared. While Congress issues nonbinding resolutions surrounding these actions, in practice, these resolutions do little to curtail the president. Using the actions in Panama, Somalia, Bosnia, Afghanistan, Yugoslavia, and Iraq to illustrate his point, Fisher argues that President Bush expanded the scope of presidential power, especially with the claim that he could go to war against Iraq without seeking authorization from Congress, and that President

Clinton built on this precedent. These examples suggest that international and regulatory organizations like the U.N. Security Council and NATO have become instruments for presidents to circumvent the constitutional role of Congress. Presidents go to them—not Congress—to authorize military action. Members of Congress have facilitated this shift in institutional power by only being willing to rally behind nonbinding resolutions for military actions.

CONCLUDING OBSERVATIONS ABOUT PRESIDENT GEORGE W. BUSH AND CONGRESS

No single issue dominated the 2000 election campaign. Both Gore and Bush talked about education, taxes, defense, Medicare, Social Security, and health care, with Bush being more thematic and Gore being more program specific. With the exception of normative intangibles like "character and leadership," the American people, as measured in exit-polling interviews, seemed to be closer to Gore's position than to Bush's and were certainly closer to the Democratic Party than to the Republican Party on issues ranging from environmental policy to a patients' bill of rights. Early Bush policy decisions reinforced a perception by the American people that he was more closely identified with business interests than with the day-to-day problems of the people. This was particularly true on issues relating to the environment and energy policy and may have precipitated or accelerated the Jeffords defection and the Republicans' loss of Senate control. Bush's concern with the reinforcement of his political base and appeasing his party's most conservative wing (especially from the South) may have contributed in large measure to the policy and public relations trap that he may have spun for himself on the issue of federal funding of stem cell research just six months into his administration. A similar pattern also emerged in Bush's early public statement that he would veto the Senate-passed Patients' Bill of Rights, despite the fact that it had strong support from his party's moderate wing and enjoyed strong support from the American people. Six months into the Bush presidency revealed growing public disenchantment with the pro-business policies of the new president, as measured by falling approval ratings and serious concerns about the direction in which he was leading the country on key issues. President Bush spent much of his time out of Washington (see the number of states he visited in table 12.1) using a grassroots strategy to build support for his tax reform package. He had fewer public laws passed, just nineteen, in the first six months than any president since Richard Nixon.

The early difficulties in the George W. Bush presidency may stem directly

Table 12.1 Presidential Six-Month Benchmarks

	George W. Bush	*Bill Clinton*	*George H. W. Bush*	*Ronald Reagan*	*Jimmy Carter*
Executive Orders	23	22	15	27	36
Public Laws	19	52	56	23	67
News Conferences	11	23	18	3	11
Countries Visited	8	3	13	1	2
States Visited	33	21	25	7	8

Source: "Comparing Six-Month Benchmarks," *The Washington Post,* 20 July 2001: A29.

from initial decisions about governing. Bush acted as if he enjoyed a strong popular mandate, a unidimensional focus on reinforcing his political base, but simultaneously jeopardized his ability to compete for persuadable moderate voters. President Bush's self-administered confrontational policy debates on the faith-based initiative, the environment, energy policy, partial private funding of Social Security, and expanded funding for missile defense made it difficult going with Congress (especially the Democrats) early in his administration.

The early days of George W. Bush's administration revealed that the type of policy pursued by the White House has an impact on the president's success.[6] President Bush successfully passed his tax cut policy and an education reform initiative with broad bipartisan support. He found it tough going in many other policy arenas such as environmental policy, defense policy, and health care policy. Clinton and Bush had a strong similarity in their approaches to policy making: "The signature of Clinton's White House—and a key to his survival during impeachment and a host of other crises—was the way policy and politics were routinely interwoven in his decision-making process. Clinton's top political and policy aides met weekly to pore over polling and to plot strategy. Senior Bush aides acknowledge they convene weekly to do precisely the same thing."[7]

Initially, the type of policy pursued affects the lobbying strategy by a president or by members of Congress and consequently the success of these two institutions, as shown with President Bush's grassroots strategy on his tax reform initiative and the congressional Democrats' interest group coalition building and issue advertisements against the president on the Patients' Bill of Rights.[8] Presidential–congressional policy making takes place in a wide variety of policy-making settings ranging from fairly open and public systems involving a large number of White House and congressional actors to relatively closed systems with few participants. The location of decision making in the White House or Capitol Hill, the scope of the issue, the nature of a policy, and the number of participants involved in a decision all have an impact on the characteristics of the presidential–congressional policy-making system. The type of policy being considered affects the politics of the decision-making system handling it. New policy initiatives by the president create new politics on the Hill. Circumstances may develop that are beyond the immediate control of presidents and members of Congress. The Organization of Petroleum Exporting Countries oil embargo in 1973, the decline of communism and breakup of the former Soviet Union, droughts and floods in the United States, the Exxon *Valdez* oil spill, the Three Mile Island nuclear power plant accident, the collapse of the Soviet Union, and the invasion of Kuwait all changed the type of presidential–congressional policy-making system that routinely handles these energy, foreign policy, and environmental policies. President Bush's strategies for education, taxes, faith-based initiatives, missile defense, Medicare, and Social Security all had different politics and the need to develop "situational coalition building" (each policy and program created the need to build a slightly different coalition).

Presidential–congressional decision-making systems operate within constitutional, electoral, and political party structures of the wider U.S. political system and in effect make them work. Interested individuals, businesses, and groups cluster naturally around the White House, congressional committees, and executive branch agencies whose decisions affect them either positively or negatively. An explanation of the organization and behavior of these decision makers is essential to an understanding of presidential–congressional relations.

It is a useful analytic tool to think of White House–Capitol Hill policy-making processes as falling into specific kinds of systems.[9] One way to think of them is as a continuum ranging from *macropolicy systems*, or "high politics" (general policy decisions with major electoral/political effects involving the president and broad public interests, visibility, divisiveness, extensive media coverage, and many participants), to *policy systems* (with minimal presidential involvement in highly technical issues), to *micropolicy systems* (narrowly focused decision making involving a very small and often closed group of decision makers). Policy issues may move up or down the decision-making continuum from micropolitics, to subsystems, to macropolicy-making systems. Each level of policy making has varying degrees of White House involvement as revealed in the Clinton and George W. Bush presidencies.

Foreign policy initiatives are excellent examples of macropolitical decision making.[10] Foreign policy initiatives are normally pursued using bipartisan strategies, though the missile defense initiative by Bush was not pursued this way. When a president proposes a set of major foreign policy initiatives, like President George H. W. Bush did during the congressional vote to authorize the use of force in the Persian Gulf, the administration realizes that the proposals will gain maximum support if they appear "above politics." In selling his proposal to Congress, Bush articulated his position above the leaders in Congress directly to the American people using high moral and national interest rhetoric. "The liberation of Kuwait and the defense of Saudi Arabia" appealed to the American public on the level of moral correctness and national self-interest, not partisan politics. Many foreign policy initiatives such as Clinton's battle for the North American Free Trade Agreement and the permanent normalization of trade relations with China adopt a nonpartisan flavor, which fundamentally affects the way the White House lobbies Congress.

Policies more technical in nature or "subsystem politics," such as the 1990 Clean Air Act and legislation to recapitalize the depository insurance funds for banks and savings and loans during the Clinton administration or the education reforms of Bush in 2001, usually will also require bipartisan approaches. This type of policy, however, relies on the technical expertise of lobbyists and congressional committee members and staff with jurisdiction over the issue (the technical network—or subsystem). On issues like this, lobbying by the White House takes on several other characteristics. First, the technical nature of the issues requires a division of labor, that is, the involvement of other administration personnel and interest groups with appropriate expertise. Expanding the number of those involved also requires added coordination by the White House staff. Second, issues that are more technical in nature require early White House involvement by technically competent stakeholders.

Subsystems that control distributive policies also produce their own unique lobbying strategies by the White House, as seen by the energy deregulation debate in 2001.[11] Congress and regulatory agencies, not the president, do much of the formulation of distributive policies. The White House will then join the "dance" later in the process, adding its blessing to the legislation or signaling its unhappiness with some regulatory agency action. Normally a president's concern deals with some broader policy proposal attached to the distributive bill. For example, over the past ten years two distributive highway bills led presidents to wage policy battles on issues such as the federal speed limits and drinking ages but not on the details of the distribution of highway funds. Both broad-based policy issues were eventually resolved with presidential involvement. The micropolicy of distribution of funds was handled by a small group of expert participants on the Hill, in agencies, among interest groups, and in the White House.

Unified party government helps smooth the way for solid legislative accomplishments, as shown in the first five months of the Bush administration in 2001 and the first two years of the Clinton administration. Success changed rapidly for President Bush when Jeffords changed the power structure in the Senate, giving majority status to the Democrats. President Clinton had this luxury during the first two years of his administration (1993–94) and was able to push through some of his campaign promises, such as a major down payment on reducing the deficit, which passed by one vote and was supported by all the Democrats; the Goals 2000 and other educational reform measures; significant installments on the vice president's initiatives on reinventing government; family medical leave; and motor voter legislation, among others.

The relationships between the president and Congress are dynamic not static, just as the policy process is dynamic not static. Presidential–congressional rivalry must be viewed as an active set of relationships and policy cues that ebb and flow throughout the course of an administration.[12] Sometimes the relationship is strong and lends itself to cooperation, reciprocity, compromise, and legislative accomplishment. At other times, because of a host of political circumstances, relationships can sour, creating an environment of hostility and mistrust. There is always built-in institutional rivalry whether there is unified or divided party government.

A constant struggle for President Bush and his team was the trade-off between forging majority coalitions (comity and bipartisanship) and party building/winning elections (the permanent campaign). Throughout his administration, legislation such as the tax bill, education reform, and the Patients' Bill of Rights have required bipartisan support from Senate Democratic Party committee chairs and rank-and-file members to generate enough majority support for his policies. Discussions with the Democratic Party leadership were often met with apprehension and suspicion by George W. Bush's own party members in the House (as was the case with his father's administration on a variety of issues). The White House's task during these exercises was to balance the needs of the president's party members for consultation and attention with the demands of the majority in order to compromise and move legislation forward. Although President Bush could have negotiated with Senate Democratic Party members in furthering his legislative agenda, the need to build and promote his own party's particular policies and preferences was a limiting factor. President Clinton faced similar trade-offs during the last six years of his administration, confronting a Republican majority in Congress.

Trade-off problems for a president are not isolated to his own party, however. The trade-off issue faced the Bush administration when Bush advocated legislation that was more ideologically conservative. His attempt to build coalitions with the more moderate Republicans and conservative Southern

Democrats caused northern moderate Republicans to bolt from the party permanently, like Senator Jeffords, or temporarily, like other members of Congress, on key votes.

The White House must face the trade-offs inherent in building coalitions with an ideologically diverse set of lawmakers—whether they are from the conservative or liberal wings of a president's party or they are from the opposition, as shown with all presidents since Jimmy Carter. Regional political trade-offs also challenge a president's relationship with Congress. During and immediately after the oil embargo, Presidents Carter and Reagan often faced difficult trade-offs between the interests of energy-producing states and the demands of more consumer-oriented midwestern or northeastern states. President George W. Bush faced the same trade-offs in 2001 over energy and environmental policy. For representatives and senators, how to vote for their constituents' best interests was clear, especially if their constituents had been facing an energy crisis in California in 2001. For a president, trying to build national coalitions as well as satisfy the local demands of numerous lawmakers is one of the most difficult political problems facing the White House.

The constraint of "time" is another trade-off that the White House must manage. Members of Congress regularly criticize the White House for only being able to focus on one single issue at a time, a trait common to the White House legislative office that routinely works this way during major legislative battles, focusing its attention on winning a key vote on the House or Senate floor, going over the heads of Congress directly to the American public, or disposing of an issue before moving on to another project.[13] Presidents must trade off time in Washington or in states or other countries to pursue their policy agendas (see table 12.1 for comparisons of presidential foreign and domestic travel). Whether they use press conferences or not to highlight their agendas again depends on each policy area and on their strategies and tactics (see table 12.1 for comparisons of the number of news conferences used by the last five presidents). They must trade off different strategies for policy change such as using executive orders versus pushing new public laws (see table 12.1 for a comparison of George W. Bush to all presidents since Nixon).

Congress, with its diverse committee system and decentralized power structure, processes a variety of issues simultaneously. Given all the issues that Congress can present to the president and the limited number of hours in a day or week, how the White House prioritizes is critical. The White House must decide which issues to get involved with and how (executive order versus public law) and which to ignore or delegate to others within the administration.[14] The resolution of these choices and the trade-offs ultimately shape the White House–congressional agenda.

Presidents know they can only ask for support from Congress on tough votes. White House staff must advise the president and seek support from the congressional leadership to sequence votes in such a way that the president does not wear out his welcome on Capitol Hill.[15] Calculating when, when not, and how often to request favors and support is fundamental to the strategic relationship between the president and lawmakers. How this aspect of White House–congressional affairs is handled has major consequences for the quality and degree of separation of powers during any given stage of a presidency.

The research reported in this volume supports the conclusion that institutional variables (e.g., divided versus unified government and bicameral rules) are among the most important factors in understanding outcomes.[16] Moreover, depending on the exact configuration of institutional variables, presidents need to adopt vastly different approaches to dealing with Congress, as shown with the unified and divided party governments of the Clinton and Bush administrations. President Clinton knew he had a rare opportunity with unified party government in the first two years of his presidency and actively sought out his party's majority to enact as much legislation as he possibly could. President Bush had unified party government for six months and tried the same approach with his appointments, tax reform, education policy, and faith-based initiative. Both Clinton and Bush witnessed the difficulty of moving comprehensive legislation through the Congress because of divided party government and the supermajority rules in the Senate. The research reported in this book concludes that the analysis of presidential influence in Congress deserves more attention to bicameral issues and divided versus unified party government—as we are reminded in the Bush administration.

A major final conclusion about the rivalry between the president and Congress is that we should not be too hasty in judging the success and quality of a particular president's relations with Congress or his success or influence in passing programs. As shown with Bush and Clinton, presidents may have good relationships during certain periods of time, then their relationships may deteriorate for some time, and then they may regain a friendlier environment again, all during one congressional session. These dynamics change dramatically over the course of a president's tenure: just observe the successes and failures of President Clinton and of George W. Bush's administration.

Most presidents, unless they are blessed with extraordinary electoral mandates and political and institutional circumstances and they possess incredible leadership skills, will give up a lot to Congress.[17] Sacrificing much to Congress, getting less than one hopes for, and moving an agenda more slowly than expected are the realities of the modern rivalry between the president and Congress—as President George W. Bush has discovered.

NOTES

1. Edward S. Corwin, *The President: Office and Powers*, 4th edition (New York: New York University Press, 1957); Thomas E. Cronin, *The State of the Presidency*, 2d edition (Boston: Little, Brown, 1980); George Edwards, *At the Margins: Presidential Leadership of Congress* (New Haven: Yale University Press, 1990); Michael Foley and John E. Owens, *Congress and the Presidency: Institutional Politics in a Separated System* (New York: Manchester University Press, 1996); James A. Thurber, *Divided Democracy: Cooperation and Conflict between the President and Congress* (Washington, D.C.: CQ Press, 1991); and Stephen J. Wayne, *The Legislative Presidency* (New York: Harper and Row, 1978).

2. Fred I. Greenstein, *The Presidential Difference: Leadership Style from FDR to Clinton* (New York: Free Press, 2000).

3. Jon R. Bond and Richard Fleisher, "Assessing Presidential Support in the House II: Lessons from George Bush," *American Journal of Political Science* 36 (1992): 525–41; Jon R. Bond, Richard Fleisher, and Glenn S. Kurtz, "An Overview of the Empirical Findings on Presidential–Congressional Relations," in *Rivals for Power: Presidential–Congressional Relations*, ed. James A. Thurber (Washington, D.C.: CQ Press, 1996); Richard Fleisher and Jon R. Bond, "Partisanship and the President's Quest for Votes on the Floor of Congress," in *Polarized Politics: Congress and the President in a Partisan Era*, Jon R. Bond and Richard Fleisher, eds. (Washington, D.C.: CQ Press, 2000); Mark A. Peterson, *Legislating Together: The White House and Capitol Hill from Eisenhower to Reagan* (Cambridge, Mass.: Harvard University Press, 1990); David W. Rohde and Dennis M. Simon, "Presidential Vetoes and Congressional Response: A Case Study of Institutional Conflict," *American Journal of Political Science* 29 (1985): 393–427; and Barbara Sinclair, "Hostile Partners: The President, Congress, and Lawmaking in the Partisan 1990s," in *Polarized Politics: Congress and the President in a Partisan Era*, Jon R. Bond and Richard Fleisher, eds. (Washington, D.C.: CQ Press, 2000).

4. Kenneth E. Collier, *Between the Branches: The White House Office of Legislative Affairs* (Pittsburgh: University of Pittsburgh Press, 1997).

5. Laura W. Arnold and Rebecca Deen, "Presidential–Congressional Relations: Veto Threats and Policy Outcomes," paper presented at the Annual Meeting of the American Political Science Association, Atlanta, 1991; Charles Cameron, *Veto Bargaining: Presidents and the Politics of Negative Power* (New York: Cambridge University Press, 2000); and Richard S. Conley, "Presidential Influence and White House Lobbying on Veto Overrides: New Evidence from the Ford Presidency," *American Politics Research*, forthcoming.

6. James A. Thurber, "Political Power and Policy Subsystems in American Politics," in *Agenda for Excellence: Administering the State*, ed. B. Guy Peters and Bert A. Rockman (Chatham, N.J.: Chatham House, 1996), 76–104.

7. John F. Harris, "Clintonesque Balancing of Issues, Polls: Role of Politics Evident in Bush's White House," *The Washington Post*, 24 June 2001: A1.

8. Harris, "Clintonesque Balancing of Issues, Polls," A1.

9. Harris, "Clintonesque Balancing of Issues, Polls," A1.

10. James A. Thurber, ed., *Rivals for Power: Presidential–Congressional Relations* (Washington, D.C.: CQ Press, 1996).
11. Thurber, *Rivals for Power*.
12. Thurber, *Rivals for Power*.
13. Collier, *Between the Branches*.
14. James P. Pfiffner, *The Strategic Presidency: Hitting the Ground Running*, 2d edition (Lawrence: University Press of Kansas, 1996).
15. Collier, *Between the Branches*.
16. James A. Thurber, "The Constitutional Structure of National Government in the United States: Is It in a State of Crisis?" *The Administrative Law Journal* 9, no. 1 (spring 1995): 1–42.
17. Richard E. Neustadt, *Presidential Power: The Politics of Leadership from FDR to Carter* (New York: Macmillan, 1980).

Index

About the Contributors

Gary Andres is currently senior managing partner of the Dutko Group Companies, a political consulting firm in Washington, D.C. He served as deputy assistant to the president for legislative affairs in the administration of George H. W. Bush.

Richard E. Cohen has been a congressional reporter for *National Journal* since 1977. In that position, he writes about both legislative and electoral politics and deals regularly with a broad cross section of members of Congress. In 1990, he was the winner of the Everett McKinley Dirksen Award for distinguished reporting of Congress. In addition to his magazine work, Cohen is author of several books about Congress and a frequent contributor to national publications on matters concerning presidential–congressional relations.

Roger H. Davidson is a professor of government and politics emeritus at the University of Maryland and a visiting professor of political science at the University of California, Santa Barbara. He is the coeditor of the four-volume *Encyclopedia of the United States Congress* (1995) and coauthor of *Congress and Its Members* (8th ed., 2001).

Nathan Dietz is an assistant professor of government at American University and a senior research fellow at the Center for Congressional and Presidential Studies. He is a graduate of the University of Rochester, and his book on presidential influence in the House of Representatives is forthcoming from Texas A&M University Press.

C. Lawrence Evans is a professor of government at the College of William and Mary. A former Brookings Institution Fellow and American Political

Science Association Congressional Fellow, he is the author of *Leadership in Committee* (University of Michigan Press, 1991), coauthor of *Congress under Fire* (Houghton Mifflin, 1997), and author of numerous articles about congressional organization.

Louis Fisher is a senior specialist in the separation of powers at the Congressional Research Service, the Library of Congress. He testifies frequently before congressional committees on executive–legislative disputes. His books include *Presidential War Power* (University Press of Kansas, 1995) and *American Constitutional Law* (4th ed., Carolina Academic Press, 2001).

Patrick J. Griffin is a scholar in residence in the Department of Government and the Center for Congressional and Presidential Studies (CCPS) at American University, where he teaches a graduate seminar on the legislative process and is the academic director of the Lobbying Institute for CCPS. In addition to his service in the Clinton administration, his private sector experience includes founding the Washington, D.C., government relations firm Griffin, Johnson, Dover and Stewart, where he continues to serve as president. In the U.S. Senate he held the position of secretary for the Democrats and the position of professional staff member on both the Senate Democratic Policy Committee and the Senate Budget Committee.

The Honorable Lee H. Hamilton is the director of the Woodrow Wilson International Center for Scholars and the director of the Center on Congress at Indiana University. He served as U.S. Representative from Indiana from 1965 to 1999 and as chairman of the House Foreign Affairs Committee from 1993 to 1995.

Walter J. Oleszek is a senior specialist in U.S. national government at the Congressional Research Service. He is an adjunct professor of political science at American University and a frequent lecturer on political affairs. Oleszek is the author of several books, including *Congressional Procedures and the Policy Process* (5th ed., CQ Press, 2001), and is coauthor with Roger H. Davidson of *Congress and Its Members* (8th ed., CQ Press, forthcoming) and with C. Lawrence Evans of *Congress under Fire: Reform Politics and the Republican Majority* (Houghton Mifflin, 1997).

The Honorable Leon E. Panetta is currently the director of the Leon and Sylvia Panetta Institute for Public Policy, which is located at California State University at Monterey Bay. He is a former chief of staff to President Clinton, director of the Office of Management and Budget, and chairman of the House Budget Committee. He served as U.S. Representative from California from 1976 to 1993.

James P. Pfiffner is a professor of governance and public policy at the School of Public Policy at George Mason University. He is the author or editor of ten books on the presidency and U.S. government, including *The Strategic Presidency: Hitting the Ground Running* (University Press of Kansas, 1996) and *Character and the Modern Presidency* (forthcoming).

James A. Thurber is a professor of government and the director of the Center for Congressional and Presidential Studies at American University. He is the author of more than sixty articles and chapters and the editor or coeditor of books on Congress, the presidency, U.S. elections, and American politics generally, including *Battle for Congress: Consultants, Candidates and Voters* (Brookings Institution Press, 2001), *Campaign Warriors: Political Consultants in Elections* (Brookings Institution Press, 2000), *Campaigns and Elections American Style* (Westview, 2001), and *Congress and the Internet* (forthcoming). Thurber is the principal investigator of a six-year Pew Charitable Trusts Improving Campaign Conduct Project.

Stephen J. Wayne is a professor of government at Georgetown University. An expert on the presidency, he has written *The Legislative Presidency* (Harper and Row, 1978), *The Road to the White House* (Bedford/St. Martin's, 2000), and (with George Edwards) *Presidential Leadership* (St. Martin's, 1999).